Advance Praise for
JOHN CLARKE: Explorer of the Coast M

"John Clarke floated across the landscape in a kind of dream state, completing more epic wilderness journeys in British Columbia than anyone ever has, or probably ever will. This book captures the brief, bright, shining life of a man who was like the Jack Kerouac of mountaineering. He followed his own path—and left those who knew what he'd accomplished, breathless and in awe."

> —Mark Hume, national correspondent for *The Globe and Mail*

"John Clarke slogged through bush and bugs, tramped along icy ridges and climbed hundreds of remote peaks in BC's Coastal Mountains—usually alone, fuelled by oatmeal and lentils. Lisa Baile skilfully and gracefully traces Clarke's singular drive, and tells us how he inspired others to explore and protect these spectacular wild spaces that have been sculpted by time. It's no surprise the Squamish people named him *Xwexwselken*, or Mountain Goat."

> —Mark Forsythe, host of CBC Radio's *B.C. Almanac*

"Wandering from range to range through the Coast Mountains of British Columbia, John Clarke embodied a new style of mountaineering—in tune with the landscape and one's inner self. In his environmental work he displayed a passion that motivated thousands and ultimately made a real difference. Read this book and explore John's world of soaring peaks, ancient forests and cascading glaciers, and discover his passionate love for all things wild. You will not be disappointed."

> —Chic Scott, author of *Pushing the Limits:*
> *the Story of Canadian Mountaineering*

"As a newcomer to BC, I am just beginning to explore the jaw dropping scenery of the West Coast by water. At the top of Bute Inlet, snow capped Mount Waddington towers above the surrounding peaks. Never before have I looked up at glaciers from the deck of my own boat. Lisa Baile has taken me to the top of those same peaks to look down through the incredible adventures of John Clarke, complete with the severe weather, bears, emergency landings, equipment failure and even death that came with his remarkable explorations. This well-written and captivating book is a view from the top of our glorious Coast Mountains as no one else has seen them."

> —Bob McDonald, host of CBC Radio's *Quirks and Quarks*

JOHN CLARKE

EXPLORER OF THE COAST MOUNTAINS

Lisa Baile

with a foreword by Wade Davis

HARBOUR PUBLISHING

1 2 3 4 5 — 16 15 14 13 12

Harbour Publishing Co. Ltd.
P.O. Box 219, Madeira Park, BC, V0N 2H0
www.harbourpublishing.com

Edited by Betty Keller
Maps by Tim Wilson and Lisa Baile
Data sources for maps:
John Clarke first ascents: Compiled by Lisa Baile and John Baldwin. Some data sourced from www.bivouac.com.
1:10M shoreline, glaciers, lakes, rivers, streams: Province of British Columbia under the Open Government License for Government of BC Information v.BC1.0"
www.naturalearthdata.com/about/terms-of-use.

Front Cover: John Clarke on the eastern cliffside of the Tahumming River, 1986. Photo by John Baldwin
Front Flap: Coast Mountains reflected in tarn, 1993. Photo by John Clarke, courtesy Annette Clarke
Back Cover: John Clarke in 1998 approaching Sun Peak, later renamed Mount John Clarke. Photo by Greg Maurer
Back Flap: Photo of Lisa Baile by Peter D. Paré.
Cover design by Teresa Karbashewski
Text design by Mary White
Printed on Forest Stewardship Council certified paper using vegetable-based inks.
Printed and bound in Canada

Harbour Publishing acknowledges financial support from the Government of Canada through the Canada Book Fund and the Canada Council for the Arts, and from the Province of British Columbia through the BC Arts Council and the Book Publishing Tax Credit.

Library and Archives Canada Cataloguing in Publication

Baile, Lisa
    John Clarke : explorer of the Coast Mountains / Lisa Baile.

Includes bibliographical references and index.
ISBN 978-1-55017-583-7

    1. Clarke, John, 1945–2003. 2. Mountaineers—British Columbia—Biography. I. Title.

GV199.92.C525B35 2012   796.522092   C2012-904300-1

For Nicholas Clarke

Contents

Coast Mountains showing the general locations of areas explored by John Clarke.

Foreword

A celebrity is known for being known. A hero is known for what he or she has done. This is a story of a true hero, which may explain why so many of us do not know his name, John Clarke. Until now, that is, with the publication of this heartbreaking book, which is surely destined to elevate this legendary climber into the realm of the Titans, a place he never sought to be, but where surely his soul now resides.

I confess that I too did not know of John Clarke's extraordinary life and impossible achievements as a mountaineer until I was sent the manuscript of this marvelous book. My immediate thought upon reading but a few chapters was that I had found Canada's John Muir. The parallels between the lives of these two men, one an obscure Canadian, the other the legendary founder of the Sierra Club and prophet of the modern environmental movement, are uncanny. Both were immigrants: Muir from the austere Presbyterian air of Scotland, Clarke from the wilder spirit of Ireland, the dark streets of Dublin. Muir came into the world with a "restless spirit." John Clarke was born, his mother recalled, "with his crampons on." He had from childhood, "a passion for mountains. He loved climbing and going to new places." So surely did John Muir.

Arriving in San Francisco in 1868 Muir left immediately for Yosemite, where he found his muse. Scrambling down cliff faces, scaling mountain walls, yelling and hollering at the incomparable vistas, he found his every nerve quivering, as the spirit of the place filled every pore and cell of his body. John Clarke found his spiritual home in the formidable Coast Mountains of British Columbia, a land so wild and vast that you could throw Yosemite to any corner and the Americans would never find it.

John Muir famously spent months at a time in the mountains, travelling alone, with only a "tin cup, a handful of tea, a loaf of bread and a copy of Emerson." So did John Clarke, only his grub of choice was granola. He would spend his winters in the city, cobbling together a bit of cash, making plans, staring always to the north and the snow clad summits of the mountains that rose above Vancouver and ran away a thousand miles to the Yukon. Like Muir he slept wherever he hung his hat, living as a nomad even in the heart of the city. He was no recluse, just a man whose heart never left the mountains. With maps and aerial photographs, he charted new routes by day, while by night he trained, adding bricks to his backpack and running some thirty-five kilometers from downtown across the Lion's Gate, east to the Second Narrows, and then back to home on Point Grey Road.

Like Muir, John, though a fine mountaineer, was less a climber than a wanderer who frequently found himself on the summits of mountains. He had no interest in first ascents for the sake of them, though in a forty-year career he would establish more firsts than anyone in the history of Coast Mountain exploration. In 1972, his most productive season, he spent nine months alone in the wilderness, climbing some fifty mountains, all for the first time. The year before he had set out to explore the Misty Icefields in the eastern reaches of Garibaldi Park. It was a typical outing for him. He took a boat the length of Pitt Lake, walked twenty miles to the end of a logging road and by nightfall had trudged through the tangle of coastal forest to the alpine. Travelling light he slept under the stars, using his only food, a bag of granola, for a pillow. In five days, walking sixteen hours a day, he covered 525 square kilometers of wild country, reaching the summits of twelve previously unclimbed peaks. "The clearest way into the Universe," wrote John Muir, "is through a forest wilderness." This surely could be inscribed as the epitaph of John Clarke's life.

Like Muir, John Clarke turned in time inevitably to conservation.

"When we try to pick out anything by itself," Muir said, "we find it hitched to everything else in the universe." This was something John Clarke knew to be true in the very fibre of his being. His love of the heights was matched in its intensity by his concern for what was unfolding on the lower flanks of the mountains, in the coastal valleys where the richest temperate rainforests on earth were increasingly under siege by industrial forces, the timber giants who in mere decades had ravaged the homelands of the Kwakwaka'wakw and the Haida, the Nuchatlaht, the Tsimshian and the Squamish.

Even as he fought for conservation, John increasingly recognized that his greatest gift lay in his ability to inspire the youth of every nation, bringing together rich and poor, Native and non-Native, in a common celebration of awe, inspired by the mountains he knew and loved better than any man alive. Wilderness training and outdoor education became yet another of his many passions.

Before he died John Muir had a mountain named in his honour, a secondary peak a mile south of Mount Whitney in the High Sierra of California. So too would John Clarke be recognized on August 28, 2010, in a moving ceremony that opens this book. As the Squamish chiefs do honour to his memory, John Clarke's only son, a lad of eight named Nicholas, is present for his father.

In 2002 John Clarke was diagnosed with a malignant brain tumour. In the spring, Nicholas was born. That summer, in recognition of his pioneering work as a mountaineer and explorer, John was awarded the Order of Canada. He died January 23, 2003, a month shy of his fifty-eighth birthday.

This book does much to honour his memory and the author deserves our gratitude. As for the rest of us perhaps the best thing we can do to acknowledge the legacy of this great Canadian is to heed and act upon the advice of his spiritual predecessor:

"The mountains are calling and I must go," wrote John Muir. "Keep close to nature's heart ... and break clear away, once in awhile, and climb a mountain or spend a week in the woods. Wash your spirit clean."

—WADE DAVIS

Introduction

In the morning, we moved up through snow and slabs to the 6000 ft col, our base-camp for all the peaks in this range. After anchoring the tent and building a rock kitchen nearby, we burrowed deep into the bags since there was no view. In the morning, it was clear! We crawled out and gaped at the fabulous scene, made wilder by the cold and wind. We walked around bundled up in all our clothes and looked down at the lake 5800 ft below.

Despite many days cocooned in the bags, we managed to wriggle up every peak in the range ... We walked ridges in cloud, threaded through crevasses, read our books and fiddled away happy hours on peaks that were gardens of mosses and lichens. On some mornings it seemed like someone was hosing the tent with jets of water, and I don't think I've ever seen it colder in mid-July. Lisa did the heroics with porridge and tea on the filthiest mornings.

—John Clarke (*Canadian Alpine Journal*, 1999)

The Lisa referred to in the above excerpt is me, and although this book is about John Clarke, a brief account of why I was making the porridge and tea and how I came to write this book is warranted.

When you spend your formative years in the flatlands of Lincolnshire as I did, there is little in your life to suggest that one day your favorite pastime will be exploring the Coast Mountains of

British Columbia. However, when I came to live in Vancouver decades later, whenever I wasn't out in the wilds of the Coast Mountains I would be scanning through a pile of *Canadian Alpine Journals*, reading about who'd done what and when in those same mountains. It was impossible to miss the name "John Clarke." I read with incredulity about his many long solo traverses and the scores of peaks he had climbed. I learned that Clarke had made more first recorded ascents than anyone in the history of Coast Mountain exploration—possibly more than anyone in the world.

I joined the Alpine Club of Canada (ACC) in 1974, and when I moved to British Columbia three years later I became a member of the Vancouver section of the ACC, as well as the BC Mountaineering Club (BCMC). It was around this time that I had the opportunity to attend one of Clarke's very popular slide presentations on his exploits in the mountains. I'd expected him to be some kind of antisocial recluse—but not a bit of it. He was gregarious, full of fun (in fact, downright hilarious) and a gifted speaker. He had his audience in the palm of his hand.

For years after that presentation I fantasized about doing a trip with John Clarke but felt too inexperienced and far too shy to ask if I could come along on one. As a result it wasn't until the mid-nineties that I had my first real conversation with him. It was by phone. My husband Peter Paré, two friends and I were planning to do the extended traverse across the high peaks from Princess Louisa Inlet at the head of Jervis Inlet to Meager Creek near the end of the Pemberton Valley (now popularly known as the Stoltmann Wilderness Area). Clarke was the obvious person to ask for advice, which he provided with enthusiasm and in detail.

That two-week traverse was a life-changer. The beauty and diversity of the wild, rugged terrain blew me away. Soon after I returned in the fall of 1995, I committed to doing conservation work, and as it happened John Clarke had also joined the conservation movement by that time and was similarly dedicated to preserving the wilderness of the Coast Mountains. During the following year we became better acquainted. I had many opportunities to observe him in his new role as a conservationist and wilderness educator as he journeyed around the Lower Mainland of BC giving informative talks and showing slide presentations to the public.

In 1996 John and I founded the school-based Wilderness Education Program. I ran the program and John worked at the forefront as the wilderness educator. From that time on he was one of the family to Peter and me, and shared our Vancouver home—the base for our educational and conservation work. He connected thousands of youth with nature and introduced them to BC's wild spaces, and then—along with Bill Williams, hereditary chief of the Squamish First Nation, and photographer Nancy Bleck—he founded the Witness Project, a peaceful model of conservation bringing Native people and non-Native urbanites together to raise cross-cultural awareness.

Over the years John Clarke shared some of his most coveted destinations with me, and we did several mountaineering trips together, including a month-long trip in the remote Kitimat Range, thirty miles (fifty kilometres) west of Terrace, BC. And in 2002, after he was diagnosed with a malignant brain tumour, John sent me on a mission to complete some unfinished business in Middle Ground, so named by BC's famous mountaineering couple Don and Phyllis Munday because it lies between the Klinaklini Glacier and the Klinaklini River. John had climbed throughout the range in 1986 but missed some peaks when he was forced to retreat because his second food cache had been consumed by wolverines:

> A loaf of bread sat on the snow, its underneath like a waterlogged sponge, its top as hard as a rock from the sun. The whole of it was covered with teeth marks and wolverine slobber that looked like dried slug trails. The lack of food and the constant rain made the [four-day] walkout to Knight Inlet a very hungry affair. So, if you're looking for a howling wilderness with real gripping remoteness and incredible beauty around every corner, the Klinaklini is for you.

So that year I made a traverse of the area with Peter and our friend Jack Bryceland. We followed in John's footsteps, marvelled at the rugged peaks he had climbed alone, camped on the spot where his food cache had been ravaged by wolverines and climbed all but a few of the virgin peaks.

After John died in 2003, I assumed someone would write his story, and only slowly did I come to realize that it could be me. When I approached Howard White of Harbour Publishing with the idea, he was receptive. He had always wanted John to write a book and even encouraged him to do so; in a book that he once gave to John, he wrote: "This book's for you in the hopes you will do one like it some day."

John Clarke had a profound influence on my life, and since his death he has never been far from mind. I hope to inspire others by bringing his remarkable life, his special relationship with the geography of British Columbia and his innovative approach to wilderness education and conservation to the page.

The quintessential John Clarke at home in the Coast Mountains. PHOTO BY JOHN CLARKE, COURTESY OF ANNETTE CLARKE

The Naming of a Mountain: August 28, 2010

The mountains have called and I must go.

—John Muir

You don't think about whether you're going into the mountains. You just try and figure out where. You pack your bag and you go.

—John Clarke

A single drumbeat spirals up the steep banks of Sims Creek in the heart of the Squamish Nation's land, though the sound is muffled by the lichens drooping from the branches of the ancient trees. These waters have journeyed from the glaciers of Mount Tinniswood and curved through the sacred valley *Nexwayántsu* (the place of transformation) to hurtle and tumble down the nearby falls—all power, light and sound. It is here Sims Creek broadens, spreads out and changes course.

A raven peers down curiously from the branches of a cedar tree at the assortment of people below: old folk, young folk and a smattering of kids, some Native and some non-Native. They are teachers, academics, handypeople, writers, artists, engineers, some with well-honed bodies and others with more traditional builds. Silent and respectful, they form a circle around the drummer as the ceremony for the naming of the mountain begins. The drummer is dressed in the

Aaron Nelson Moody of the Squamish First Nation conducts the ceremony for the naming of Mount John Clarke on the banks of Sims Creek, August 28, 2010. PHOTO BY LISA BAILE

Squamish Nation's traditional fashion: a woven blanket folded and draped diagonally over one shoulder, the two ends pinned together; a small woven purse and a cluster of twenty-dollar bills are fastened at the upper corner. A bandana circles the man's broad forehead.

As the celebrants are called to speak, to witness the occasion according to the Squamish Nation's custom, their words provide glimpses into the life of the man they are honouring today. He was father, son, brother, friend, lover, adventurer, explorer, mountaineer, educator, conservationist, entertainer and humanist. He won awards and accolades, yet he was a humble man, a minimalist. The Coast Mountains of British Columbia were his home, and for forty years he travelled them and cherished them with a passion few can comprehend. Yet he was no recluse. He loved people and touched the hearts of all he met—made their spirits soar, made them laugh—and left indelible marks on all of their lives.

A small curly-haired boy breaks from the circle to scramble up an alder sapling. His name is Nicholas and it is his father who is being honoured today. He doesn't remember him, though he has heard the stories and seen the photos.

Now the blanketed, deep-voiced drummer speaks:

It is an important thing to change the names on maps—it changes the way we look at the world and maybe people will hear that. They will hear that new name and they will wonder why and maybe they will start to look into the kind of man that he was ... The name of this mountain will be Mount John Clarke.

One by one the people in the circle are called forward to speak of the man they are honouring. When the speeches are over, I am one of the fifteen climbers who leave the sacred circle to prepare for the pilgrimage to the top of Mount John Clarke. Silently we step off the logging road into the enveloping green and quiet of the forest, our heavy packs enforcing a measured pace up the steep trail to the alpine meadows above, where there will be ample time to reflect on John's life.

The boy and his mother remain behind to camp on the sandbar. The boy looks for wild animal tracks and plays in the quicksand he's already discovered. Clutched in his hand is a letter he's just been given. It's from his father and it is dated 2002, the year he was born.

A note to my beautiful son Nicholas—from your father.

Nicholas, right now you are 8 weeks old and you are wearing a pair of socks that are way too big for you and you look really cute in them! I'm in the hospital today to get an operation tomorrow and I just want to say that at this time in my life I'm thinking about you a lot. I love you very much and hope that you will be happy for your whole life. I love

The view from Mount Wilson of Mount John Clarke (upper right). The route from the Sims Creek valley to the summit of Mount John Clarke follows the upper skyline ridge. PHOTO BY DWAYNE HIMMELSBACH

you and your mother very much and we are both very lucky to have her in our lives! She takes very good care of you all the time, day and night. Everything that you do in your life—do it as best you can and take pride in everything you do. Even though you are only 8 weeks old now, I can see you have an enormous amount of energy. I know you will find something that you love to do more than anything else and you will have a chance to direct that energy. That's what I did with my mountain travels and the mountains made me very happy. Maybe you will find something different than the mountains but I know you will succeed. Always remember that I love you and always will.

Your father, John

Gestation

The wind blows where it pleases. You hear its sound, but you do not know where it comes from or where it goes. This is how it is with all who are born of the spirit.
—The Gospel According to St. John, chapter 3, verse 8

I f there is a gene for exploration, then John Clarke inherited it. His destiny was shaped by the land, but the seeds of that destiny were sown in Ireland, where he was born on February 25, 1945. When I asked his mother, Brigid, whether his birth was difficult, she laughingly replied, "Oh, yes! He had crampons on." And John's father, Kevin, nodding, added, "I think he was born with a passion for the mountains. He loved climbing and going to new places."

Occasionally John would talk about his early childhood. He spoke of the little row house on Jamestown Road in Inchicore, only a fifteen-minute drive from downtown Dublin, where he lived with his parents, younger sister Cathaleen and younger brother Kevin. The number 76 beside the door and the arched window were the only features distinguishing it from all the other houses in that row, all of them built by John's maternal grandfather, J.J. Conway. John shared a bedroom with his brother while Cathaleen slept in the box room (traditionally a small room used for storing boxes, trunks and portmanteaux) until their dad took up photography and she had to move in with the boys.

There were no toys in those days—kids were sent outside to play. John would ramble around the hills of Dublin with his friend John

Philips, camp with the Boy Scouts, build fortresses in Dunn's field a stone's throw away from their modest row house or go on outings to the surrounding countryside. Every Saturday, regardless of the weather, the family would squish into their little blue Ford Anglia and head out of town, taking along as many other neighbourhood kids as they could fit in. John remembered the time a neighbour across the way called out to his Mom, "Where're you off to? It's raining!" They all stared at her. What did she mean?

Mostly they'd go up Sugar Loaf Mountain or to Brittas Bay, with its long, sandy, sheltered beach, but their most cherished outings were summertime visits to the strawberry fields, where they picked their own and the kids crammed the juicy red berries into their mouths. And John loved the endless summer holidays at Greystones (Na Clocha Liatha), a tiny seaside town backed by the Wicklow Mountains on Ireland's east coast.

Uncle Paddy, his Mom's brother, and Aunt Maureen lived next door. The house next to them belonged to J.J. (John Joseph) Conway, John's authoritarian grandfather and namesake. "The Governor," as he was known, was president of his own foundry, Conway Engineering, and had been president of the Irish Manufacturers' Association. In those days boys who were named after their grandfathers were supposed to inherit their merits, but John was quite the opposite—a big-hearted dreamer. John told me he didn't remember a whole lot about his step-grandmother, "The Missus," who from his child's perspective had a heart as cold as the steel in his grandfather's foundry. He never did get a hug from her in all the years he lived in Ireland.

According to his mother,

The Clarke children, (L-R:) Kevin Jr., Cathaleen and John, enoy a "ride" on their mother, Brigid, on an outing at the beach at Brittas Bay near Dublin, Ireland, circa 1955.
PHOTO COURTESY OF CATHALEEN CLARKE

John "was always different" as a kid. She recalled for me the time they went to bring eight-year-old John home from St. Kevin's hospital after he had his tonsils out. "The little nun comes trotting across the floor," said Brigid. "'Oh, Mrs. Clarke,' said Sister Josephine, 'Please, is there any chance that we could keep John for another couple of days?' 'Oh, what's happened to him?' I asked. 'Oh, nothing's happened. But we have a little boy over there in the corner and his parents are too poor to come in and visit him very often. John goes over and talks to him and there's just a remarkable change. He's getting better,' Sister Josephine said. 'I wonder if you could leave John for a couple of days to help?'"

John's sister, Cathaleen, recalled how John adored his Dad—a gentle, soft-spoken man with a quick Irish wit and an angel of a voice; some said he could have been a professional musician. Kevin Clarke played his diminutive mouth organ like an accordion, and when he sang "Danny Boy," it would bring tears to the eyes of his listeners. A butcher by trade, he worked in one of the three thriving butcher shops owned by his father, Christopher Clarke—one on busy Pearse Street in the heart of Dublin, another in Cabra, north of the city, and one in Summerhill, another district. The elder Clarke also owned a slaughterhouse in the Bluebell district.

Brigid was her husband's opposite—all business. Loving yes, but strict, with no time for silly nonsense. She'd get her husband to "do things" when he returned home from work, and he would line up the three kids on the kitchen table to wash their faces and hands before bed. First he'd gently wring out the cloth in warm water and then carefully, lingeringly, wash their faces. Brigid, impatient to get the kids to bed, would snatch the cloth from his large hands and go *swish-swish-swish*, and it would be over in a flash. "That just about summed up their divergent personalities," Cathaleen said. "The joke between us kids was that, in times when discipline was necessary, we'd overhear Mom and Dad protesting, 'They're *your* children!' 'No! They're *your* children.'"

Each day, rain or shine, John and his brother walked the mile (two kilometres) to and from the school owned and run by the Oblate Fathers in the parish of Mary Immaculate. It was an intriguing blend of educational institution, church and monastery, and behind its grey

John Clarke wears his "Sunday best" for his confirmation day in Dublin, Ireland, circa 1953. PHOTO COURTESY OF CATHALEEN CLARKE

stone–walled buildings a spacious garden overflowed with vegetables, flowers and espaliered fruit trees. Many of the schoolkids, John included, were altar boys and would serve Mass wearing white surplices over long black cassocks. For John, lessons and school work were the least memorable aspect of his school days; instead, his strongest memories were from the rituals that permeated his life: the sweet, resinous scent of incense, the hypnotic chanting of the monks and processions weaving through the blossom-filled garden to the shrine of Mary, the mother of God.

The Clarke family's move to Canada was part of the wave of immigration encouraged by the Canadian government in the postwar years because the homegrown manpower supply could not fill the needs of the country's booming economy. In 1957 Canada admitted a record number of immigrants and over 100,000 of them came from the British Isles. Among them was Kevin Clarke Sr., who had secured a job as a butcher in Vancouver. The family joined him one long, lonely year later.

The decision to emigrate had come mostly from Brigid, as she felt there would be more opportunities in Canada, especially for her. In those days, women in Great Britain were not encouraged or expected to be part of the workforce or to obtain more than a rudimentary education; they were expected to marry and become their husbands' responsibility. As a result, Brigid would inherit nothing from her father; it was a given that he would leave the foundry to his sons, Paddy, Sean, Liam and Mossy, who were already working in the business.

In Vancouver Kevin Sr. worked long hours as a butcher at the

Burns meat packing plant, though during that lonely year away from his family he always found time to write letters to Brigid, "my little woman," and the kids. Then in May 1958 the Clarke family was reunited. They all stayed with the plant manager, Thurstein Isackson, and his family for a couple of weeks before moving into the little house that Kevin had bought for $3,000 at 550 Rupert Street, where they would live for the next ten years. In many respects their new home was similar to the little row house they had left behind in Ireland—a modest two-bedroom bungalow, grey with green trim and a plain wooden front door—but from the street and the roomy backyard there were views of the North Shore mountains.

The Clarkes soon knew the region's beauty spots better than any of their neighbours. "Where are you off to?" would be the weekly refrain, as Kevin, Brigid and the three kids piled into the car and headed for Squamish, Lynn Canyon or Harrison Hot Springs—places the neighbours had never been to and hardly knew existed. On several occasions the family was included in salmon bakes held by First Nations people in North Vancouver. To young John the Native people were an impressive sight in their traditional clothing, chanting

Christmas at 550 Rupert St, Vancouver. *Clockwise from left:* Kevin Jr., Kevin Sr., Brigid, Cathaleen and John, circa 1959. PHOTO COURTESY OF CATHALEEN CLARKE

and drumming. One day he turned to one of the men and asked, "Are you a *real* Indian?" He responded with a smile, "Yes, I certainly am."

Of all the places the Clarkes visited, Cultus Lake was their favourite. Nestled within the folds of the Cascade Mountain Range, this lake is about fifty miles east of Vancouver. On summer weekends the family would camp in a big high-walled canvas tent, take a boat out onto the lake and fish and swim in the warm waters. John, who missed his childhood friends back in Ireland, would often wander off up the logging roads along Liumchen Creek while his siblings hung out at the lake. He found real solace in those long rambles on the fringes of the wilderness.

The freedom of these summers seemed limitless, especially in the later years when Brigid and Kevin would leave the three kids at the lake with enough food for a week or more and return to town. John was fourteen or fifteen by this time and, as the eldest, was expected to look after his younger siblings. "We had the whole week to fool around in the boat and have a good time," he recalled. "One day we were out in the boat and the outboard motor slipped off the back of the boat. There it was, noisy one minute and totally silent the next, and all of us peering down into the water. Of course, the first thing that comes to your mind is: 'What are we going to say when Mom and Dad show up on Friday night?'" When their parents did return, they hired a scuba diver to search for the motor, but they never did find it.

In the fall of 1958 John began attending Notre Dame High School, where he made friends with Ted McCaffey. "Like most kids that age we'd go fishing every day during those long hot summers that seemed to go on forever," John recalled years later in an interview with Greg Maurer. "We fished and fished and fished. That gradually evolved into

John Clarke rides the Grouse Mountain Chair lift, circa 1959. PHOTO COURTESY OF CATHALEEN CLARKE

hiking into semi-remote lakes to fish—and that's where Ted started losing interest a little bit because eventually I decided I'd like to hike into higher alpine lakes whether they had fish or not. That developed into hiking into alpine destinations whether they had lakes or not and ultimately getting to the tops of peaks. Once I got hooked on climbing peaks of course, that went on forever."

John Clarke (left) with his best friend Ted McCaffey scheming inside their "fort." Vancouver, circa 1959. PHOTO COURTESY OF CATHALEEN CLARKE

Back in those days Cathaleen would often return home from school with her best friend, Diane Lavoie, and John soon became good friends with Diane's three brothers, and all the kids would be in and out of each other's houses. In summer they would spend whole days at New Brighton Park, north of Hastings Street, where a spacious outdoor swimming pool kept them entertained. Recently Diane recalled that John "was always smiling, always on the move. He was always kind to everybody . . . never nasty to anybody."

The Clarke family home was located close to Empire Stadium in Hastings Park, and with an entrepreneurial spirit that their grandfather, John Joseph, would have been proud of, John, Cathaleen and Kevin used to lure people heading to the football games into their spacious backyard and charge fifty cents a car. John would stand out in the street yelling "Parking fifty cents, parking fifty cents!" while Kevin and Cathaleen marshalled the cars into the yard. Late at night when the owners returned to retrieve their vehicles from the often soggy yard, the Clarkes would awaken to the sound of spinning wheels and cursing.

For grades eleven and twelve John chose to attend Christ the King Seminary School at Westminster Abbey, above the town of Mission in the Fraser Valley. The abbey is tucked up against the foothills of the

Coast Mountains, and despite its relatively low elevation—just 600 feet (180 metres)—it sits above the surrounding terrain and provides sweeping views across the valley: east to the mountains known as the Lucky Four Group, south to Abbotsford and west toward Vancouver. To the north the Coast Mountains stretch for 1,000 miles (1,600 kilometres), eventually reaching the Alaska–Yukon border. The abbey is home to the Benedictine monks, who have created a self-sufficient, pastoral lifestyle for themselves and produce much of their own food—including chickens, cows, pigs, fruit and vegetables—on their 200-acre farm. Its eye-catching bell tower is Mission's best-known landmark, and the clear tones of the bells announce each day, their sound reaching clear across the valley.

There is little doubt that John's two years at the seminary played a fundamental role in his decision to embark on a life of exploration, but it's likely that he never knew exactly why he decided to go there. He was only fifteen at the time, a lonely Irish boy who had yet to find his way. As with many things that were close to his heart, he never talked about his decision in later years—did not even divulge the reasons for it to his closest friends—but the church with all its rituals had been an integral part of his life up to that time. His parents claimed they had no influence on his decision, though it was a tradition at that time in Ireland for the eldest son to take up the priesthood. Besides, John was a compassionate person, and compassion was an essential ingredient for those aspiring to the priesthood. On the other hand, it is possible that he simply wanted to spread his wings, get away from home and be even closer to the mountains.

In the early 1960s, when John Clarke attended the seminary, the rector of the abbey was Father Placidus. Today he is a man of eighty-odd years but appears far younger, as he is completely at one with his world, relaxed, engaging and bubbling with humour. "The idea of going to a seminary school is to discover whether you have a calling for the priesthood," Father Placidus explained. "It's a chance to try it out before making a commitment. It's really a unique experience because newcomers are thrown in with a group of youngsters with the same thing in mind, all going in the same direction. And they get to know one another as in no other kind of school."

John Clarke met his lifelong friend Mark Ruelle at the seminary.

Although he was almost the same age as John, Mark had already been there for a couple of years and knew the ropes. "We just seemed to hit it off," Mark recalled, "and I think his interest in the outdoors reflected my interests, too." However, certain aspects of life at the seminary irked John. He had not counted on the discipline or the predictability of each day. Prayers punctuated the day with metronomic regularity: Mass at 6:30 a.m., prayers before lunch, vespers at 5:30 p.m. and vigils at 7:15 p.m. The boys rose at 5:30 a.m. Meals were eaten in the refectory, with breakfast the only chance for the boys to chat after twelve hours of "major silence." Chores were allotted after breakfast and then classes began. Sports followed the noon meal: volleyball and touch football in the fall and spring, soccer during the soggy winters. Classes then resumed and went until 4:30 p.m., when there was an hour's break before vespers. Mark and John would often take this opportunity to go for a run together and escape the confines of the classroom. "The seminary was like boarding school," Mark recalled. "A bit like Harry Potter on steroids—lots of camaraderie, lots of sports, very disciplined. No specific uniform—just shirt and tie."

The evening meal, taken at 5:55 p.m., was eaten in silence, the boys seated at the long refectory tables. The sound of the stuffing of

John Clarke (centre, front) in class at the Seminary of Christ the King, Mission, BC—1962.
PHOTO BY MARK RUELLE

sixty hungry mouths was muffled by the resonant tones of the monk who read the book of the day from the pulpit. One such book was *The Silent World: A Story of Undersea Discovery and Adventure* (1953), co-authored by Jacques Cousteau. "I'd like to be like that guy," John whispered in Mark's ear.

Like many deeply spiritual people, the Benedictine monks at Westminster Abbey shared a deep love of nature, and several of them, particularly Irish-born Father Damasus Payne, were well known in the BC mountaineering community. Payne never passed up an opportunity to climb, and once on the summit of his chosen peak, he would celebrate Mass. He was also an excellent photographer and would share his expertise with the young seminarians. "Father Damasus loved nature," said Father Placidus, "but ... for him a mountain was a challenge, just an automatic challenge."

John was a diligent though dreamy student. When he was confined to the classroom, his gaze would inevitably be drawn out the windows to the spectacular views of the snow-capped mountains. As a result, Father Damasus's enthusiasm and broad knowledge of mountaineering weren't lost on him. According to Father Placidus,

> Damasus had a character much like John's—quiet, unassuming, genuine as sterling silver. They didn't put themselves forward. The two of them [were] so much alike in their quiet, Irish sense of humour. Very genuine, playful—you can see it more in their eyes and their mouths than you can anywhere else, but also that aesthetic sense, that sense of wonder and beauty. And then the sense of a challenge, and a certain loner aspect to the two of them. They are not afraid to be out on their own and ... not frightened by being out in the wilds. They are just enjoying God's creation.

Father Damasus introduced John to the observation deck on the top of the bell tower, which was definitely *the* place to enjoy a panorama of the surrounding peaks. The deck was accessible via a staircase that led to a platform about twenty feet up, where the bell-ringers stood to peal the bells. From that point a spiral staircase wound upward within the tower for another hundred feet to the observation deck, which was surrounded by a narrow parapet. One day after classes, Mark and John leaned on this parapet while Father Damasus pointed out the peaks one by one as if they were his friends: Cheam, Lady, Knight, Foley, Baby Mundy, Judge Howay. He had even put markers on the parapet to aid in the identification of each peak. Another time Damasus climbed on the parapet to take a photograph of a group of boys, completely at ease in that high, exposed spot.

Each year the monks of the abbey would spend a couple of weeks at a little summer residence just outside the town of Lillooet on Seton Lake, relaxing, hiking and climbing after a busy year of teaching the seminarians. After climbing in the Lillooet Range, Father Damasus named two peaks after two venerable nonagenarians: Mount Rohr, eleven miles (eighteen kilometres) southeast of Birken, after Father Victor Rohr, an Oblate missionary to the Mount Currie First Nation from 1935 to 1940, and Mount Duke, a prominent peak fifteen miles (twenty-four kilometres) east of Mount Currie at the south end of the Caspar Creek valley, after William Mark Duke, who founded the seminary and was the longest serving archbishop of Vancouver (1931–64).

Father Damasus fell to his death in October 1978 from a point near the summit of Edge Mountain in Golden Ears Provincial Park. As usual, he had planned to celebrate the Eucharist when he reached the summit; as Father Placidus told me, "the mountains were his church." Intent on photographing the scene, he turned to the two

---

The Act of Father Damasus

Shrewd, he was full of shit and vinegar,
Squint-eyed Benedictine swinger, and singer
of his god's praise.
In finger holds on alpine walls,
At afterglow, he never felt the pinch
Of death scrupulously collecting tolls,
Spying on his sacraments. Janus-like,
Leth's fiery glint, half-formed, reflects
Magnificence: Mountains neither gothic nor Romanesque
Limned by orphic air echoing calls.
For some they are bucolic sepulchers, alpestrine air
Inducing delirium.
Below dark dogs silently swim
The rivers,
fell
Arms raised in ritual awe,
Songs still shaped in praise.
Lithe, spare, he slipped on ice
Invisible as air where
None could rescue him
Or catch his final measured hymn,
Wine vaporous, prayers hushed,
Bread crimson: the clarity
Of his falling act.

—Claora Styron
(*Canadian Alpine Journal*, 1979)

seminarians who accompanied him and said, "I'll be with you in just a bit. Hasn't the Lord sent us a beautiful day?" Those were his last words.

Today Father Damasus has his own mountain: Mount Payne rises more than 8,000 feet (2,400 metres) in the rugged Hope–Silvertip sub-range south of Sunshine Valley, southeast of Hope. But Damasus's love for the mountains had also extended to conservation. A year before his death he wrote a much-quoted treatise on the need to preserve the Stein Valley, a spiritual heartland for the Nlaka'pamux people, who have lived in the area for thousands of years. Although he knew he might not live long enough to see its preservation, he acknowledged that future generations "would find to their joy one needful resource of our province that cannot be renewed or restored—the beauty of this land as it came from the hand of God." Nearly twenty years later, in 1995, 435 square miles (1,125 square kilometres) of the Stein Valley was pronounced a provincial park. Named Nlaka'pamux Heritage Provincial Park, it is co-managed by the Lytton First Nation and BC Parks. Just as Father Damasus had envisaged, the Stein is a living museum of cultural and natural history.

Brother Luke, or Frank Smith as he was known before he joined Westminster Abbey, also had a profound influence on John Clarke's life during his seminary years. He and his wife, Loretto, had been charter members of the BC Mountaineering Club and were close friends of mountaineering legends Phyllis and Don Munday. Together they had climbed in the Cheam Range, the dominant peaks to the east of the abbey. After Don Munday's death in 1950, Phyllis used to make regular spiritual retreats to the abbey, and when Loretto died in 1958, Frank joined the abbey as a lay brother and looked after the abbey library. His set of mountaineering journals still graces the library shelves.

Brother Luke's influence on John began one evening during the free time after supper, the time of day John cherished the most. He would spread out his vast collection of topographical maps on the floor of the recreation hall and pencil in routes and potential journeys through the wilderness of British Columbia. "Amazingly," he recalled years later, "I had this big collection of maps but not a very clear idea how to do anything in the mountains or the bush. [And] I had all these pencil lines drawn on the maps keeping away from glaciers because I had this notion that I couldn't walk on one. It would swallow you up or something terrible would happen to you. So my pencil lines for trips I'd planned all around Garibaldi Park avoided these really nice easy routes and had the pencil line on a ridge crest with massive gaps and spiky peaks." One evening when he was engrossed in this project, Brother Luke peered over his shoulder and pointed to the map.

"John," he said, "you know you can just walk right up the glacier there."

"How do you know that?" John asked.

"Well, I was there in 1911 when we climbed Mamquam," Brother Luke told him.

He began teaching John how to interpret topographical maps and how to choose logical routes. As he was also the one to select the guest speakers at the abbey, he often invited mountaineers to give talks on their exploits. "There was a kind of love for the mountains in the atmosphere [here]," said Father Placidus, who climbed well into his sixties. "John grew up with that. He went for it like a duck hitting water, and then this seed finally grew and blossomed."

It was soon evident that for John Clarke his time as a seminarian was not really about the monastery. It was all about the mountains. But it was the quiet and solitude of abbey life that allowed him to connect with his inner self and provided opportunities to reach out and appreciate the beauty of the natural world around him. It taught him resilience, humility and frugality and showed him that people can get along under tough conditions, slogging it out while still remaining respectful, compassionate and kind. These qualities would be expressed throughout his life, especially in the mountains. Father Placidus sees no contradiction in John's life journey: "Through all of his meanderings there was a love for seeking God. It wasn't just the mountains, it went beyond the mountains. Regardless of where he found what he thought was beautiful, it was the beautiful that actually drew him."

Mark Ruelle recalled their final weeks at the seminary in the late spring of 1962. He and John relieved the tedium of cramming for final exams by climbing the abbey's bell tower, seeing the Fraser

Valley spread out beneath them and the Cheam Range that rose to the east. One day John turned to Mark and pointed at Mount Cheam. "We're going to climb that," he announced. Cheam's pyramidal form rises above Bridal Falls in the eastern Fraser Valley. Its north face, unclimbed till 1981, plunges 6,562 feet (2,000 metres) to the valley floor. The Halkomelem First Nation named it *Theeth-uhl-kay*, which means the source or the place from which the waters spring.

The two boys graduated together from the seminary that spring; John returned to Vancouver, but Mark stayed on for another year. One day shortly after school was out in 1962, John phoned Mark to announce that the time had come to climb Cheam. At dawn on the Saturday of the Dominion Day weekend, the two boys staggered from the Clarke family home at 550 Rupert Street and headed east on the recently constructed freeway. Their Trapper Nelson frame packs—a pack design introduced by Lloyd Nelson in 1920 based on a North American Native backpack of sealskin stretched over willow sticks—bulged with all the supplies that young inexperienced wannabe mountaineers think they should take on such a venture. "We pretty much had every comic book notion about mountain climbing that a kid would have at the time," said John years later. "We filled our packs up with everything we weren't going to need and omitted all the things that we were going to need. The two of us with stars in our eyes, heading off on a trip that we knew nothing about."

They hitched a ride to Bridal Falls and began marching up a deserted logging road. Full of optimism, they had little idea what they were doing but just knew there was a mountain up there—somewhere. "The best thing we had on our side was an ardent desire to get to the top," said John. "Equipment and technique were nonexistent."

That evening they kicked a platform on a snowy ridge, laid down a piece of plastic and wriggled into their old sleeping bags. They froze! In the morning, numb from cold and lack of sleep, they crested the next bump and saw a perfectly flat spot under the trees, cushioned with a big bed of pine needles. "We could have slept like princes up there," Mark said, laughing.

They continued upward, and John's spirits soared as he gained the final ridge and burst into the alpine. "Wow! Ruelle, I love this!" he yelled. "I *love* this!"

Forty-six years later Mark recalled the final moments of this first ascent as if it were yesterday: "We got up to the peak, of course, and there was some exposure as you go up the last shoulder on the peak of Cheam. I remember John went puzzling around. We had an old rope and he tied it around me, then he went first because he didn't want me to be too nervous. We got up to the summit and to the cairn. We found an old tobacco tin with two or three hundred names in there and we added our names and put it back in the cairn. It was just a wonderful trip."

"That was the first high peak I climbed and I really liked it," John recalled years later. "It took us three days. We made every mistake in the book."

The ascent of Mount Cheam whetted John's appetite for climbing, and that summer he and Mark headed out to explore more of the local mountains. A black and white photo of the two boys just back from a climb captures the essence of those early climbing days. "They looked like nobody owned them," recalled the mother of his friend Diane Lavoie. "Scruffy, dirty, baggy pants and totally trashed, leaning on their ice axes with big grins on their faces."

Looking back to that memorable summer, Mark said: "I think that [first ascent] was the beginning of John's love affair. His capacity for enjoying that beauty was endless. He never got tired of it or bored with it. It was probably the same enjoyment twenty or thirty years later as the very first time he went up."

John also started making trips with the BC Mountaineering Club (BCMC). His very first club trip to the Needles, the isolated, scruffy, ridge-top peaklets above Lynn Creek in North Vancouver, turned into an epic adventure. When the group wound up

John Clarke and Mark Ruelle just returned from a successful climbing trip, Vancouver, circa 1962. PHOTO COURTESY OF CATHALEEN CLARKE

descending through steep bluffs at dusk, John, the only youngster among the group of old-timers, sped ahead to the cars and returned to the rescue with flashlight in hand. He recalled, "We had this kind of death march getting back to the cars. And I remember Laurence [the trip leader] telling me, 'Gee, you know, it's not always like this. I hope this doesn't put you off mountain climbing.'"

It was taken for granted that the three Clarke children would go to university after high school, so in the fall of 1962 John enrolled at City College, King Edward Centre, to take grade thirteen. Though he lived at home for that year, he made frequent visits to the apartment that his sister Cathaleen shared with Diane Lavoie and would sometimes stay there for supper. After one of these visits Diane told Cathaleen that she'd always wanted an older brother. "It's just so nice to have a brother who comes to visit you like that," she told Cathaleen, who stared at her and said, "Boy, are you stupid!"

John and Diane started dating just two months before she and Cathaleen left for Europe, and when Diane returned the better part of a year later, John introduced her to hiking. One day, confident that she had acquired the necessary skills, he took her up Mount Brunswick, a rugged mountain on the North Shore. (This trip became *de rigueur* for all his subsequent girlfriends.) "He was a very good teacher and he made sure you knew exactly how to grasp the ice axe and what it did and why you were doing it that way," said Diane. "You never felt talked down to or lectured." But although she enjoyed hiking, she never did take to mountaineering. "John called me a rambler."

They continued dating until it came to the point when they either got married or split up. Looking back, Diane commented, "Being attracted to somebody, enjoying their company and even being madly in love with them is not enough ... We didn't share enough of the same things." She wanted a conventional life, but settling down wasn't even on John's radar at age twenty-two. "John was the kind of man who belonged to everybody, and even if you were married to him, you might not get a lot of his time. He would be off in the mountains, which would be fine if that was something that you shared." Several years later, when Diane told John she was engaged to be married, he said, "What! You're getting married and I'm not going to be the groom?" She told him, "You never wanted to be." He couldn't answer that.

John was never a stellar student—he had too many distractions—but he did well enough at King Edward to be accepted by the University of British Columbia (UBC) in the fall of 1963. He had decided to become a geologist; it was a profession that would allow him to work outdoors. He didn't want to be cooped up in an office tower and have a steady job, a mortgage and two kids. However, after one winter of mathematics, chemistry, physics, geography and geology, he withdrew from university.

Part of his decision to quit can be blamed on a map. During the school year an uneasy truce had existed between his passion for the mountains and his studies, but his studies came completely unhinged one fateful day when he wandered into the club room of the Varsity Outdoor Club (VOC). There, sprawled across the wall in front of him, was a topographical map of the Coast Mountains. Two young geologists and avid mountaineers, Dick Culbert and Glenn Woodsworth, had put all the information they had gathered on a single map. "They had this massive map on the wall from the Nass down to Pemberton," said John years later. "It had every piece of information they could find on it—from the archives in Victoria, all the *Canadian Alpine Journal* issues back to 1908, with the first ascent of Garibaldi. They even hitchhiked up to Prince Rupert and talked to every mad trapper they could find. So there were pins all over the map ... But there were still seven-hundred-square-mile gaps [between] the pins all over the range." In an instant he grasped the fact that vast areas of untracked wilderness remained unexplored and hundreds of peaks had not been climbed, and he resolved to fill in the gaps on the map. "I'm sure I would have done better at UBC had that map not been on the wall. I spent so much time staring at it. But again, I was just dreaming. I had no abilities of any kind."

In 1967, a decade after moving to Canada, the Clarkes sold their little row house back in Dublin to help finance a move to 2474 Point Grey Road, into a magnificent Craftsman-style house close to the small yacht club in Kitsilano. The house lent itself to parties, and Cathaleen would turn the living and dining rooms into a ballroom for this purpose. "Fabulous parties. Huge parties," she recalled, laughing.

"I had a party when Armstrong landed on the moon. And the music! You could hear it three blocks away. Point Grey Road was *the* house."

But if Cathaleen was the family's party girl, John was the family jester. "Nobody ever made my dad laugh the way John did," she recalled. "My dad would be just bowled over, laughing to the point when he could hardly breathe … [but] it's interesting how John was so serious *and* so funny." One Halloween Cathaleen invited Diane Lavoie to a party and introduced her to her new friend, Joanne. As Diane remembered it:

> [We were] chatting away and I thought she was really nice. Then after about ten minutes Joanne says, "You don't know me, do you?" "Well no," I confessed. "Have we met before?" And in a deep voice Joanne says, "It's me, John!" And he explodes into laughter. I didn't recognize him, didn't have a clue! There's John in this slinky dress and sling-back shoes. "It's hard to keep a good man down," he says, a huge grin spread across his face.

In the new house John and his brother Kevin shared a bedroom in the basement, where John slept under the table on which he kept his precious maps. On the wall beside his bed he pinned a huge map of Garibaldi Park, because many of that park's rugged peaks remained unclimbed and were never far from mind.

John's dreams had escaped the confines of the abbey and his home, and in his heart he knew his life was changed forever. With the map on the wall of the VOC club room imprinted on his mind, he resolved to climb the virgin peaks of the Coast Ranges and explore the surrounding wilderness as well. He had little idea where his journey would take him—he just knew that he had to go.

Vocation

I had to know what was beyond the next horizon.

—John Clarke

Within the climbing community there is a wide range of motivations and styles. At one end of the spectrum is the "peak bagger," whose goal is to climb the highest and most technically demanding mountains; once they have conquered them, they have little interest in the lesser peaks in the area. At the other end of the spectrum is the exploratory mountaineer whose motivation is mainly to be "out there," to travel remote territory and be rewarded by the thrill of discovering unknown landscapes. John Clarke was to become a complex combination of these—he wanted to climb peaks and be the first to do it, but it was not the highest, most spectacular mountains that drew him. Rather, the utter remoteness of the area was the magnet. And for him, doing it "right" would be as important as getting to the top.

Climbing mountains for recreational purposes is a relatively recent human endeavour. Europeans started to climb for the challenge and fun of it in the late eighteenth century, and when they had climbed the grandest peaks in the Alps, they would seek new and more demanding routes to attain the same summits. In the late 1880s Swiss mountain guides sought new challenges in Canada's Rocky Mountains, which had just become accessible with the construction of the Canadian Pacific Railway.

Recreational climbing in the Coast Mountains only started

Grades of Difficulty for Hiking and Climbing:

Class 1: Hiking
Class 2: Scrambling
Class 3: Easy climbing
Class 4: Use of rope and continual belaying
Class 5: Rope and climbing hardware required
for protection (Class 5 is subdivided into
5.1, 5.2, etc. as difficulty increases.)

in earnest near the beginning of the twentieth century, and members of the Vancouver Mountaineering Club, founded in 1907 and soon to become the BC Mountaineering Club, made the first recorded ascents of some of the highest mountains on the North Shore. By the early 1930s climbers in Europe and in other ranges in North America had progressed to finding technically difficult routes on previously climbed mountains. The remoteness of the Coast Mountains and the relative isolation of the climbing community here meant that only the highest mountains had been climbed by that time, and all of them by the easiest routes.

Don and Phyllis Munday were the renowned pioneers of Coast Mountains exploration. In 1924 Phyllis Munday and Annette Buck became the first women to reach the summit of Mount Robson, the highest mountain in the Rockies. In June of the following year, while on a climb of Mount Arrowsmith on Vancouver Island, the Mundays were inspired by the view of an unusually high mountain on the mainland and resolved to find it. That fall they travelled up the coast to the head of Bute Inlet to investigate their "Mount Massive," only to discover there was an even higher mountain beyond it in the Homathko Valley. "It was one of those supreme moments sometimes vouchsafed to mountaineers," wrote Don Munday in the *Canadian Alpine Journal*, "and one has little quarrel with fate if he has been granted such a sight." Their mystery mountain was later named Mount Waddington. At 13,260 feet (4,019 metres), it is the highest peak in British Columbia, and the most challenging.

The Mundays made nine expeditions to the Waddington Range and spent every climbing season in search of a route up their mystery mountain. As there were no roads, they gained access by boat and then by cutting trails through the dense bush and relaying their supplies up the valley. River crossings were treacherous and encounters with grizzly bears not infrequent. But Phyllis's strength and good nature were legendary: as two fellow mountaineers wrote in her 1990 obituary, "Phyllis was a strong woman capable of carrying a pack and taller than Don by a bit. There was never any question that she was the driving force that took them anywhere."

After twice gaining the secondary peak of Mount Waddington (1928 and 1934), the Mundays abandoned their attempts to attain the main summit. (The first ascent of the main peak of Mount Waddington was made in 1936 by Fritz Weissner and William House.) Instead the husband and wife team focussed their prodigious energies on exploring the area around the massive Klinaklini Glacier, a vast river of ice where, as the snow accumulates, it compresses the snow underneath, turning it to ice. The weight of the snowfalls on Klinaklini are so great that the glacier flows downhill at the rate of 330 feet (100 metres) per year, descending to a point just 980 feet (300 metres) above sea level. The upper, less compressed layers of the glacier are more brittle and

often fracture to form crevasses or fissures that can be up to 100 feet (30 metres) deep; when these are covered by fresh snowfall, they become invisible. Even for experienced mountaineers, it can be dangerous to walk on a glacier.

In 1937 the Mundays made the first ascent of Silverthrone Mountain, which Don Munday called "the home of the snows" because of its notorious weather. They also climbed in the Rocky Mountains and the Selkirks, together reaching the summits of more than 150 mountains, and more than 40 of those climbs were first recorded ascents. After Don's death in 1950, Phyllis lived another forty years and received many awards, including the Order of Canada for her work

Don and Phyllis Munday pose on a snowy Grouse Mountain, circa 1930s. PHOTO COURTESY OF NORTH VANCOUVER MUSEUM & ARCHIVES with the Girl Guides of Canada and St. John's Ambulance, as well as for her mountaineering achievements. Mount Munday (11,010 feet or 3,356 metres) in the Waddington Range is named in honour of Don and Phyllis.

During the 1920s and 1930s the Mundays' exploratory expeditions were an inspiration for many others in the mountaineering community. Among them was Tom Fyles, who by the mid-1920s was regarded as one of Vancouver's most brilliant climbers. He was an early member of the BC Mountaineering Club (BCMC) and remained at its heart for twenty years, leading many of the club's trips during that time. While the North Shore mountains were still the main focus of the local climbing community, Fyles and his three young climbing companions, Alec Dalgleish, Mills Winram and Neal Carter, ventured farther afield, drawn northward by the unmapped wilderness of the Coast Mountains and by the accounts of the Mundays' bold expeditions. Their pioneering explorations included the peaks at the headwaters of the Lillooet River in 1932 and the mountains above Toba Inlet in 1933. Fyles's notable first ascents included Mount Judge Howay, the exposed and difficult Table Mountain and the north peak of Black Tusk, all in Garibaldi Park.

Vancouver-born Neal Carter, one of Fyles's climbing companions, joined the BCMC at the age of seventeen, and though he was given opportunities to climb throughout the world, his main love was the exploration of the Coast Mountains. Two of his notable first ascents were Mount Monmouth, the 10,440-foot (3,182-metre) peak at the head of the Tchaikazan River, and 10,249-foot (3,124-metre) Mount Gilbert in the Compton Névé region, a 276-square-mile (714-square-kilometre) icefield lying east of the Homathko Icefield and west of the Lillooet Icefield. Although he was busy earning a doctorate at UBC during these years, he also became a skilled surveyor, and known for his exploration and extensive mapping of the Coast Mountains (1920–50), mainly between Squamish and Mount Waddington. This work culminated in the production of the first topographic map of Garibaldi Park. For his mapping work he was named a Fellow of the Royal Geographical Society.

Neal Carter continued to be active in the mountains into the 1950s, balancing mountaineering with a fulfilling career as a marine biologist, and his affection for the mountains never left him: as a septuagenarian he loved to relive his adventures with young John Clarke, who made regular visits to the Carter house. Out would come the topographical maps and the old black-paged photo albums from the twenties, thirties and forties, a period that saw a huge interest in the exploration of the Coast Mountains. "My eyes were just like fried eggs looking at these images," John said years later. Carter would share stories about his favourite peaks and places he'd never had a chance to explore, hoping that young John would pick up the thread where he had left off.

Although World War II brought climbing in the Coast Mountains almost to a standstill, air access after the war drastically changed the nature of exploration, making it possible for people with less time—and to a certain extent less ambition—to do exploratory mountaineering trips. Advanced technical climbing techniques also spurred attempts on more difficult mountains, and as a result the early 1950s saw a considerable increase in the number of peaks climbed. But it was in the late 1950s that Dick Culbert appeared on the mountaineering scene that he would dominate for the next decade. In 1959, the summer before he entered UBC to study geological engineering, Culbert, just nineteen years old and in search of adventure, made a month-long solo trip to explore the Howson Range, a blank on the map equidistant between Terrace, Kitimat and Smithers. He carried a 100-pound (45-kilogram) pack, a plastic tarp and a wool sleeping bag with no zipper. However, in mountaineering there are definite rules when it comes to safety, and one of the cardinal rules is never to go alone. As a consequence, when Culbert joined the Varsity Outdoor Club (VOC) that fall, the editors of the VOC's journal refused to accept the account of his trip because they judged his solo explorations to be "foolhardy and reckless." Culbert was aware of the dangers inherent in solo mountaineering but had chosen to go alone rather than not go at all. John Clarke, who would follow Culbert with solo ventures, put this disregard of the dangers into context when he said, "You don't think about whether you're going into the mountains. You just try and figure out *where*. You pack your bag and you go. It's really that simple."

Subsequently Culbert became renowned for his incredible drive and energy. He roamed the Coast Mountains with Glenn Woodsworth, Arnold Shives and Ashlyn Armour-Brown during the summer of 1962, exploring, geologizing and ascending unclimbed peaks. They were funded through a government program intended to support prospectors. "We got these prospector grubstakes—about three hundred dollars each for the summer," Glenn explained. In the summer of 1964 Culbert and Woodsworth made the first ascent of Serra V, an elegant tower in the Waddington Range, and they climbed together again in the summer of 1967. Two years later Culbert made the first winter ascent of Mount Waddington. His true goal, however, had always been to gather as much information as possible for a mountaineering guide for the Coast Mountains, and with the publication of *A Climber's Guide to the Coastal Ranges of British Columbia* in 1965 and *An Alpine Guide to Southwestern British Columbia* in 1974, he became well known within the entire climbing community.

Culbert retired from serious climbing in the early 1970s to focus on his career as a geological engineer, but in twenty years he had made extensive explorations of the Coast Mountains, pioneered new routes, made some 250 first ascents and written two guidebooks. (In 2001 Culbert's son Vance and his companions Guy Edwards and John Millar were the first to make the 1,200-mile [1,930-kilometre], five-and-a-half-month traverse of the icefields of the Coast Mountains from just north of Vancouver to Skagway, Alaska.)

When John Clarke began climbing in earnest during the late 1960s he was already familiar with Culbert's new guidebook (from hours of studying Culbert and Woodsworth's map on the wall of the VOC club room) and was inspired by Culbert's lone ventures. With each trip to the local mountains John's skills improved, but he still felt intimidated by the BC Mountaineering Club and their "high standards," especially with regard to skiing abilities:

> I didn't join any of the clubs because I figured I didn't know much. Mountaineering clubs and proper equipment and good technique were something very far in the future for me. But I was really motivated so I started climbing all the peaks around Howe Sound and Garibaldi, all the fairly standard things that are reached from Vancouver these days. I did that from 1962 to 1967.

A young John Clarke sits on a peak in Vancouver's North Shore Mountains, circa late 1960s.
PHOTO BY ROSIANE BARIL, COURTESY OF CATHALEEN CLARKE

I was a bit stupid because—well, I shouldn't have been intimidated by the clubs. They were a really friendly bunch of people. But I just was shy about it. Consequently, I never learned anything because I didn't want to show how unskilled I was. You know how it is when you're young. So I was still out there with a Trapper Nelson and work boots and a bag of chocolate bars. 'Cause you know you have this naive notion: "Oh yes, chocolate bars—energy. That's all I'll bring."

I crossed the névé [the Garibaldi Névé is a 14-square-mile (35-square-kilometre) icefield located on the eastern flanks of the Mount Garibaldi massif] with a pair of wooden skis I got in the Sally Anne [Salvation Army]. They used to have a barrel there with these old Kandahar bindings from the forties. I just couldn't figure out how to get traction going up hill, so I got quarter-inch twine and put a loop in the end of it around the tip and just spiralled it around the ski all the way to the back and then fastened it. The glide! I don't have to tell you about the glide—Er, no glide! But terrific traction going up. It really builds up the quads, man—I'll tell you! I *walked* down from Sentinel Glacier to Garibaldi Lake—that phenomenal ski run. Well, I couldn't ski so I walked in perfect skiing conditions all the way down (I was perfectly happy to do it), then across Garibaldi Lake and out. That was my first attempt at skiing as up to that time I'd been using snow shoes. I used them a fair amount but quickly abandoned them. To me skis were just long, skinny snow shoes. But they were vastly better because they were better on side hills and all kinds of ground.

Keen to improve his technical skills, John signed up for snow school at Golden Ears Mountain under the guidance of the renowned Swiss-born mountaineer Martin Kafer. The naive participants, oblivious to the danger, begged their instructor to hold the snow school at the base of the peak at the bottom of an avalanche chute, but he was adamant they climb the 2,500 feet (760 metres) to the ridge. As John later described it:

So we're slogging all the way up there and people are grumbling. We get up there, and I don't have to tell you, in the middle of the snow school—*BOOOM!* Martin says, "There's the best lesson you're ever going to learn." The avalanche wiped everything out—right where everybody had begged him to have the snow school.

By 1966 John began contemplating more ambitious trips, having

John Clarke rappels off Castle Towers Mountain, Garibaldi Park, 1965. PHOTO COURTESY OF ANNETTE CLARKE

been all fired up by Neal Carter's descriptions of the peaks at the head of Manatee Creek. On an expedition in 1933 with Tom Fyles, Neal had seen a spectacular array of peaks from a vantage point on Polychrome Ridge at the headwaters of the Lillooet River in the Meager Group. He had never had an opportunity to explore this region, but he named the prominent glacier Manatee because its twin ice streams sported a process like the flipper of a manatee—the large, friendly marine mammal from which the mermaid legend is said to have evolved.

Then one day John read in the BCMC's monthly newsletter that the club was planning a ski expedition to the Manatee Range for the spring of 1967. It was to be the club's first major ski expedition since their founding in 1907 and a celebration of Canada's centennial year. But as John explained in an interview years later, he wasn't sure he was going to make the cut:

> I just couldn't believe it! I had no hope of going on that trip. I should have been getting more technical skills in backcountry skiing areas. I just pictured the club as being all these hard-core Swiss-Austrians … I was really, really, deeply disturbed over the fact that they were going in there and that I wasn't going to be on that trip … I had air photos all marked up and routes figured out and everything. It ran my life!

Desperate to be part of the expedition, he went to chat with Esther Kafer, who was the trip leader. Swiss-born Esther and Martin Kafer immigrated to Canada soon after their marriage in 1953, and they have been at the heart of the BC Mountaineering Club since the 1960s, leading trips, organizing expeditions, providing instruction, spearheading the building of mountain huts, editing the journal and even becoming involved in mountain rescue. In 1962 Esther became the second woman to climb Mount Waddington. In 2007 she and Martin received the BC Community Achievement Award for their fifty years of outstanding contribution to the mountaineering community.

Recalling her first meeting with John Clarke, Esther said, "I wouldn't call him quiet—but he wasn't obnoxious either. He was very nice and very, very enthusiastic, but really, I shouldn't have let him come on that trip because he had no experience." Her husband chipped in with, "But the club [the BCMC] at the time always had a policy that we would take at least one inexperienced person because all the others could teach. It was like a free school." And Esther added, chuckling, "It was impossible to refuse him—he was so eager and charming."

So John's wish was granted, but he was aghast when the group met to arrange the details and someone suggested they do a weekend camping ski trip to get to know each other before the Manatee trip. "And I'm thinking *ski* trip?" recalled John. They went into the Black Tusk Meadows in Garibaldi Park and everything was fine skiing up. John laughed, recalling what a show he'd put on. "Well, I don't have to tell you what it was like coming down the Barrier." The Barrier is a 1,000-foot (300-metre) lava dam that impounds Garibaldi Lake and falls precipitously to Rubble Creek below. It is a skier's dream or a nightmare, depending on whether you're an expert or a novice. "Just the whole process of them all waiting and watching me do head plants all the way down—out of control. They were really shaking their heads; but everything worked out fine." Esther Kafer later explained that "fine" in this case meant, "it really doesn't matter how fast a person is when they're skiing down because you are not racing. You wait—somebody falls. And of course, John would fall all the time. But it didn't matter really."

For the trip to the Manatee Range at the end of April 1967, six of the team members met in the Pemberton Valley and drove to a horse meadow where the plane was to meet them and ferry them and their mound of supplies into the Manatee Range. Paul Plummer, the seventh member and team doctor, flew to Pemberton from Prince

Welcoming Committee: First Nations kids gather in the Pemberton Valley to meet the plane, *Northern Dancer.* 1967 BCMC ski expedition to the Manatee Range. PHOTO COURTESY OF BCMC ARCHIVES

Members of the 1967 ski expedition to the Manatee Range gather in the Pemberton Valley, ready for take-off. *Left to right:* Hans-Peter Muenger, John Clarke, Brian Howard, Dr. Paul Plummer (kneeling), Esther Kafer, Judy Horgan, Alfred Menninger. PHOTO COURTESY OF BCMC ARCHIVES

George in his ski plane, *Northern Dancer*. A bunch of kids from the Lil'wat First Nation galloped across the field on their ponies to welcome the plane and the exotic party members.

During the next two weeks John was immersed in the world of mountaineering. Remote, unclimbed peaks surrounded him. He slept in a snow cave, cooked under the stars, crossed glaciers, slogged up steep slopes in the burning sun, endured snowstorms, lost a ski crossing an icy slope and watched it careen down the mountain. Then he had to climb down to retrieve it. Time after time he gazed out from the summit of a virgin peak—Remora, Sirenia, Mermaid, Oluk, Dolphin, Manatee, Dugong … a circle of marine creatures reaching for the sky. He was hypnotized by the unfolding horizons before him. "I got up there and saw these peaks and glaciers rolling off to the horizon in all directions … [and] I had to know what was beyond the next horizon." His vocation was sealed, though he didn't fully comprehend it at the time.

The group's five-day exodus from the Manatee Range carrying

weighty packs and a heavy, useless radio through rotten snow, bush and swampy beaver ponds, where they finally ditched their cheap wooden skis, did nothing to dampen John's enthusiasm. Nor was he put off by the fact that he felt cold for the entire time. "John didn't have proper equipment," said Esther Kafer. "He had one of those sleeping bags that hunters use and it was open at the feet, and at night—I was sleeping beside him—his feet would stick out of the bag." John also remembered the cold and his inadequate bag. "I had one of those cloth sleeping bags from Woodward's with the pheasants and the ducks on it ... Some of them actually have a label *For indoor use only.* I was actually cold for that whole trip. It took me a long time after I got home to stop just enjoying being warm." He recalled other members of the team having difficulties with the Manatee expedition. "I remember Paul Plummer phoning me from Prince George a week later and he said that all the skin on his feet had dropped off in one piece. Just came off. But it was a wonderful trip."

John's climbing season was cut short in 1967 when he decided to return to UBC, signing up this time for geography courses in the less hard-nosed Faculty of Arts. He would study there part-time for the next four years, with a schedule that also allowed him to work part-time to raise the money he needed to continue climbing mountains in the summer months.

John Clarke (third from left) and members of the 1967 ski expedition crossing a raging creek on their exit from the Manatee Range. PHOTO COURTESY OF BCMC ARCHIVES

But the trip to the Manatee Range in the spring of 1967 had left him with a new goal. At the end of that trip, when the group led by Esther Kafer had set out to cross the Lillooet Icefield in deteriorating weather, one peak had escaped them—the massive, heavily glaciated Lillooet Mountain. John subsequently made four attempts to climb it.

It kind of ran my life for a while. I dearly wanted to get up the thing, but at that time I was allowing jobs to get in the way. I was working during periods of *perfect* weather. [Then I] would fly into Toba Inlet, go up the logging roads and start up Mount Lillooet in a drenching rainstorm. [I would] decide to hang out as long as I could, [but] nothing cleared. I tried that peak in '67. In 1968 I tried it twice. It finally went. We [he and his French-Canadian girlfriend Rosiane Baril] got to the top of Mount Lillooet on the second attempt in 1969. So that was a major event.

Soon after this Rosiane and John split up and she returned to Quebec. But the following spring John hitchhiked across Canada to visit Rosiane and was joined by their mutual friend Barbara Handford. On their return John introduced Barbara to mountaineering.

John's account of this first ascent of Mount Crerar, as published in the *Canadian Alpine Journal*, was terse:

In August [1970] Barbara Handford and I approached from Sechelt by floatplane to the mouth of the Deserted River, site of an old abandoned Indian village. From here an obscure trail was followed along the river to a point just past Tsuahdi Creek where our route swung southeast. Cliff bands rose straight from the valley floor and made route-finding difficult for the first thousand feet. No water was found for the next 5,000 feet of steep bush, but finally a small meadow with a tarn provided a camp just after dark.

Barbara Handford's version of this venture, recounted several decades later, sounds as if the two of them had been on different trips. Just twenty years old and completely inexperienced at mountain climbing, she had only been on one previous trip with John.

The first part was easy but the bluffs were killing! . . . [There was] tons of devil's club [*Oplopanax horridus*]... We had only a little bit of water [and] we were really, really thirsty as it was a really sunny weekend. We made it to the meadow ... We were sucking up water from the moss and then found a tarn; we drank water from the tarn and crashed.

John's version continued:

Early next morning we headed for the peaks of Crerar by hiking along the crest toward the northwest peak, the lower of the two and our first objective. We were fortunate with the weather up to this point, but clouds were now boiling up from the valley to about 4,000 feet. The blocky northwest ridge of the first peak provided good class 3-4 rock, but its summit revealed that the main peak was still some distance away. The class 4 northwest face of the main peak was gained by dropping south from the crest and skirting the main divide. The peak, a sharp crest at 8,000 feet, gave a great view of the mountains northwest of Squamish and those near Mount Tinniswood.

Barbara's version of this part of the trip is decidedly more dramatic:

We had to start going up to the rocky part and the ice ... I'm not used to exposure and I'm a little bit scared of heights ... We had to do some kind of chimney stuff and go around rocks and things [but] John figured we didn't really need to rope up ... Then we came to a really pointy kind of rock, which we had to climb over, and it was two thousand feet down that way and about a thousand feet down *that* way. I'm like, "Oh my goodness!" John just walked across it in his boots because he had no fear and complete balance. I thought, *I'm not walking across that!* John said, "Just sit on it and inch along." When I got over it, John very nicely let me be the first person to stand on the first peak. We built a little cairn and that was all very exciting. Then John said, "I think it is a bit too much for you to do the second peak, but I don't want to miss this opportunity. If you just wait here, I'll be back in an hour and a half." When he eventually got back, he said, "We don't have time to go back the way we came, so the best way for us to go is down this snow chute." It was August and the snow was rock hard. John said, "You have to be *really* careful. You have to kick steps, and you have to turn around and traverse down this steep chute." We had ice axes—I'd used one a couple of times but I'd never had to save myself. So we started down. All of a sudden I slipped. I thought, *Okay, this is it! I'm going to die on this frigging mountain!* I went screaming down the snow chute. I knew there was a big boulder sticking out of the ice partway down because I'd seen it. My glasses hit the side of the boulder and went flying off into a crevice—not a crevasse, thank god! As I went down, I thought, *I guess I'm going to go over the edge!* But then I thought that this being a chute, there are probably stones at the bottom. By then, I was starting to get the axe in as John kept yelling, "Get your axe in!" I had no strength—I was a skinny thing—but I finally got the axe into the snow and that slowed me down a bit. I'm on my stomach, and all of a sudden I felt the bottom of my boots bang into the rocks. I flipped into the air and did a complete three-sixty and landed sitting up. And all I've got is this cut on my hand. I held my bleeding hand over my head and I started screaming, "God is in the mountains, God is in the mountains!" And I'm not even religious! I was just so happy to be alive!

John was so relieved because he was visualizing rescues and all sorts of crap, but then my body went into complete catatonia. I was terrified. "I just can't move," I told him.

"Well, we've got to go," he said. "We need to get down to the timber."

Finally I was able to get up and follow him. I was just in shock.

John's version of the story continued:

Stormy weather slowed our descent, so by nightfall we had only dropped to 6,000 feet where we camped in heavy mist and rain. Next morning, our third day, the long descent to the river was made difficult by persistent cloud and cliffs. An extra day was spent at nearby Stakawus Creek logging camp, waiting for our plane back to Sechelt.

Barbara did not remember it quite that way:

We got down and camped somewhere in the meadows, but we knew we wouldn't make it down [in time] to catch the plane at three the next day. We were partway down the bluffs through the devil's club again when we saw the plane. Of course, there was no way we could make it. I was exhausted. My jeans were all ripped and I'm bleeding, but when we hit the valley floor, it was like a new life, like a second wind. John said, "Let's try to run out," so we half-ran to the beach ... And the next day we got the float plane back to Vancouver.

Although Barbara did not take up mountaineering, she continued to hike, inspired by John's enthusiasm and love of the wilderness, and they remained friends.

Despite the hardships of his early ventures and his lack of experience at the time, John never held back from taking on longer and more committed explorations of the Coast Mountains. To the contrary, these trips were just the appetizers that whetted his appetite to take on more challenging and extended journeys. If a peak had eluded him in the past, his satisfaction would be all the greater when he finally stood on its summit.

4

The Communal Years

His "wife" was climbing—his passion. And although he loved the women, they couldn't compete with that passion. They just couldn't.

—Carole Kerekes

In his final year at UBC (1970–71) John enjoyed courses such as Air Photo Analysis and Cartography Design because of their relevance to mountain exploration. But it was as if his last winters of schooling were only a necessary interlude before his break from the conventional lifestyles he could see around him, and just weeks before graduating he quit school. He wanted to climb. His parents simply could not come to terms with the fact that he had thrown away a promising career. They did not, could not, understand the depth of his passion for climbing.

As a result, he walked away from his parents' disapproval and the security of the family home at 2474 Point Grey Road. He took nothing but his climbing gear, maps and skis. He first rented a room in the Arco Hotel, 81 West Pender Street, to stow his precious gear where it would be safe under lock and key. Next he checked into the Pacific Men's Hostel at Homer and Pender. There he met a bunch of similarly homeless, jobless young men and struck up a friendship with several of them, including Garry Kerekes and Dick Rogers. "John always had a crowd around him, of course," recalled Dick, a shy man from Newfoundland. "He was hard not to like." The first of the trio to land a job was Garry, who was hired by the post office—much to his surprise because he didn't think anyone would hire a homeless bloke. Soon after, he rented the basement suite in a large yellow apartment building at 4 East Thirteenth Avenue, at Ontario Street, and he invited Dick and John to join him. In their new home fake panelling clad the walls of a long, narrow hall, which was flanked by four bedrooms. At one end of the hall was a cramped living room where rumpled, scruffy old carpet barely disguised the concrete floor. The so-called kitchen was at the other end of the hall, but it had probably been used as somebody's workshop: a wooden workbench served as a counter and exposed pipes and vents drooped from the ceiling. There was only a hot plate to cook on but no wall plug, so for a while they cooked on John's tiny Svea camp stove. As an afterthought, a toilet, looking like some long-forgotten throne, had been perched on a pedestal underneath the dark stairway leading to the first floor. A tacky shower stall and laundry tub had been relegated to one corner. "Jeez!" exclaimed Dick years later, overwhelmed by memories. "It was like being in a camper." The rent for this palace was $100 per month, or $33 each when split between the three young men, but often John couldn't pay his share and had to pawn some of his few belongings to come up with the cash.

Before long the lively trio at 4 East Thirteenth began to attract friends—girlfriends, boyfriends, friends of friends, relatives of friends, waifs and strays, and their accompanying menagerie of dogs and cats—and soon the communal family overflowed to two of the three charming 1906-era wooden houses across the street. The houses were owned by Harry Dash, who had acquired all three in the 1960s for around $18,000 each. "I bought them with $5,000 down for the three of them," Harry said years later. "All I had to my name was $5,000." Over the ensuing years numbers 2911 and 2915 Ontario Street saw a continuous ebb and flow of young people.

But it was in the basement apartment at 4 East Thirteenth that John settled on the lifestyle that he adhered to for the next three decades. Even when indoors, he adopted a nomadic way of living. His "camp" was a loose arrangement of "furniture" that served all his basic needs. He fixed a sheet of plywood against the wall in a corner of his bedroom to serve as a desk. Its surface was completely buried because in his world every horizontal surface was a repository for "things." He stashed his gear and his mattress under this desk and lined the walls above it with his topographic maps. He would cut the white margins off each map and glue the maps together to produce a complete overview of the Coast Mountains, and then he carefully inked in the lakes and rivers so that they jumped out of the flat surface. (Occasionally a chosen girlfriend would be entrusted with this exacting task.) Often he would pin a map of his current mountain interest to the bottom of his desk, and at night, lying on his back with flashlight in hand, he'd peer up at the map, planning the details of his next adventure.

John's enthusiasm for the Coast Mountains sometimes rubbed off on his friends, especially when he was working on his maps, planning and drawing his routes: "I would find myself living his excitement as he spoke," said Tsippy McAuliffe. "I did not like looking at maps, but with John, his ability to describe the geographic lay of the land in what seemed to me an insignificant little curve drawn on a piece of paper challenged my naivety at reading maps." Dick Rogers, bewildered by the numerous contour lines on John's topographic maps, recalled, quietly amused, "I even learned what a medial moraine was! I'm from Nova Scotia—we don't have them there."

Carole Kerekes clearly remembered her first impression of John Clarke. She had stayed overnight at 4 East Thirteenth Avenue after a boisterous party and met him the next morning. He was about twenty-eight years old at the time.

This solicitous, enthralling guy was there, like, "Do you want a cup of coffee? How would you like it?" And I'm thinking, *They must not have women stay overnight very often.* I thought he was odd but not in a scary kind of way. He was different in what he looked like, how he dressed, how he behaved, and in his interests [from] anybody I'd met before. His hair wasn't completely grey yet, but it was very *big.* It was short at that time, but it was growing out and it just got bigger and bigger and *bigger.* And he had these shoes—he called them *wino* shoes.

John had a big enthusiasm and passion about him. He bled all over everything he did. Even if he watched TV, it was "Oh, wow!" You couldn't talk to him or interrupt him because he couldn't take his eyes off what he was doing. If he made soup, it was going to be the *best* soup ever. That was just him. Everything was just so *much.*

From his new home base John would work for six months in the winter to finance his five- to six-month summer season of exploration in the Coast Mountains. As he explained it:

> What you need for long, remote trips is, of course, huge amounts of time. If you plan a month-long trip, you need to be off work for more than a month [because] you've got travelling time on either end of it and you've got weather situations that will dictate that you start late and wind up later. You need something like six weeks off to do a four-week trip in a lot of cases.

To be ready for these trips in the mountains, he spent a lot of time preparing food. On one epic five-day trip granola was the only food he took, and Carole, by now one of his flatmates and a friend, recalled that when she first met him, "he was making granola in a big baby bathtub." He was proud of his recipe and even published it in the BC Mountaineering Club's newsletter in 1973, reminding others to "add the rolled wheat, rolled rye, sunflower seeds, coconut and sesame seeds, wheat germ and bran with raw flaked almonds, brazils and filberts." Always ready to share the detailed food lists for his trips, he

John Clarke enjoys a smoke in the communal house, Ontario St, Vancouver, 1973. Note his "wino" shoes. PHOTO COURTESY OF CATHALEEN CLARKE

would give tips on what to take: "High energy foods like pemmican and pure fat are very high in calories." He also published this recipe in the club's newsletter:

> Buy beef suet and melt it down. Strain it through a cheese cloth. Dry very thinly sliced meat at 120 degrees for four days. Insert the dried meat all through the fat; this will make it more appetizing, and form fat

into bars the size of candy bars. Wrap individually. One of these bars will give you a lot of calories and deaden the appetite.

Jamie Sproule, who lived in the communal house on East Thirteenth in the 1970s, had colourful memories of John's food habits during the mountaineering season:

> John would go for a whole season eating lentils. Then next season he'd eat oatmeal and lentils, or he'd be a vegetarian. And the next time it would be just powdered vegetables and powdered meat—add water and stir it up. John called it Glop—that's the sound it made when it hit the plate.

Even though he seldom skied or hiked much in the winter, John remained fit. To get around the city he walked or rode his bike. He also jogged to improve his endurance in the mountains. Before he moved to the communal house, he had regularly run at night from downtown Vancouver, across the Lions Gate Bridge and back across the Second Narrows Bridge and home to Point Grey Road—some twenty-two miles (thirty-five kilometres). He kept this up for most

The Clarke family 1981; *left to right*: Kevin Sr., Cathaleen, John, Brigid, 601 W.13th Ave, Vancouver. PHOTO BY JOHN MCAULIFFE

of the year. Sometimes he would run with a bunch of weights in his backpack, each time adding a little more weight to gauge the limits of his physical endurance. After he moved to East Thirteenth, he would jog up to Queen Elizabeth Park, his backpack laden with bricks. In the mid-1980s he would sometimes substitute his normal ballast for Cyrus, the four-year-old son of a close friend, and the two of them would take the BCMC trail up to the top of Grouse Mountain. In this way he combined fitness training and childcare.

Every fall, flat broke and back in the city, John would look for work again. His idea of a "good job" was one that ended on April 15, when he had completed the planning for his next expedition. Unlike many of his hard-up friends at the time, he refused to apply for unemployment insurance (UI), and over the years he had a variety of jobs—everything from driving a lumber carrier and tree planting to working with kids with disabilities and old folks.

One of his first jobs was at the old Eburne Sawmill down by the Fraser River at 9149 Hudson Street. The mill was built in the early 1900s and so antiquated that it even merited a visit by Prime Minister Pierre Elliott Trudeau. (In 1998, after prolonged negotiations with the workers who had vowed the plant would never close, Canadian Forest Products finally shut it down.) Work at the sawmill was noisy and dangerous, and John hated every aspect of it, whether he drove a lumber carrier or pulled boards off the planer chain. Of all the jobs he was assigned there, he hated the green chain the most. Workers had to perform at a back-breaking pace, pulling green lumber from a conveyor belt, sorting it and throwing it onto separate piles. This physically demanding job often resulted in severe back, shoulder and arm injuries, but green chain workers were paid the lowest wages and had the least status in the mill because the job required no special skills, only strength and stamina. But in spite of his hatred of the job and the place, when John returned from his five or six months in the mountains he'd often go back to the sawmill to look for work again, waiting outside the mill with his lunch bucket each day until someone didn't show up for the day, and he'd get the job and work for the winter.

While John's Irish charm and quick wit were legendary, his skill at dodging a topic he did not want to talk about was even more impressive. "He had this most amazing way of changing the subject without you even realizing that this had taken place," recalled Tsippy. "Before you knew it the subject was long forgotten and you were onto something else. Very few people are able to do this without making you feel like you have trespassed."

That talent fit naturally with John's easygoing approach to life in general. "John didn't worry too much about money," recalled Dick Rogers. "As long as he had enough to buy a new pair of climbing boots, he was good." He was also resourceful and would often find ways to make an extra buck. On winter weekends he cruised the pubs and downtown bars selling jewellery that was crafted by an upstairs tenant. By this time his prematurely silvering, waist-length hair was attracting a lot of attention, and guys taunted him mercilessly, but the girls he sold jewellery to in the Downtown Eastside loved him. They nicknamed him "Mona" because his big head of hair looked like a woman's wig. He would joke, "Yeah, well, it *is* a wig and I *am* a woman." Then he would grab his hair and pretend to peel the wig off his forehead. At other times he sold roses and jewellery in Gastown bars or earrings at the Pleasure Fair at the Stratford Hotel on Keefer Street.

Meanwhile, life at the communal houses at East Thirteenth and Ontario was never dull. Many of the folks who lived there were on UI

Long-haired John Clarke stokes the blazing fire, 1976. PHOTO COURTESY OF CATHALEEN CLARKE

or had evening jobs. In fact, among the group it was considered better not to have a day job. "We tried not to work," said Phil Van Gils. "We really, really tried hard not to work. But of course you had to. I was a member of what we used to call the UI Ski Team. There was always skiing in the winter." It wasn't unusual for someone to come home from work at four in the afternoon to find everyone passed out from partying all day. There was no guarantee of sleeping in the evening, either, because there would be parties all night, too. "I had the room over the living room," recalled Phil. "The ceiling would be just *puh-puh-puh*!" The house would quiver with the sounds of the Rolling Stones, the Eagles, the Doors, Pink Floyd and Boz Scaggs. But in spite of the music, Phil said, "You would just fall asleep because it was always on. It got turned down at night but I don't think anyone ever turned it off."

John didn't need a party to dress up. Always the showman, he'd don a notorious suit he'd acquired at the Sally Anne, the one he called the Plastic Suit. "It was like it was made out of rubber," Elaine Johnston remembered. "Blue and white stripes with these big lapels and it kind of looked like it was made out of asbestos but it was smooth. He'd put it on and people would just go nuts. It was so funny!"

Fun times in the 1970s at 13th & Ontario Street, Vancouver. Back row, Jamie Sproule reclines on back of couch; centre, John Clarke with braids and a cigarette; left, Vivian and her daughter, Shauna; right, Janet. PHOTO COURTESY OF THE KEREKES FAMILY

Nights could be full of surprises at the commune. Debby's dog, Brooke, knew how to open doors, and one night the dog let herself back in and left the door open. Later the cops drove by and, seeing the open door, shone their lights in the windows and then came inside and booted everyone out of bed, hoping to find a cache of pot. But they missed John, who was asleep underneath his sheet of plywood with all his laundry piled on top of him. It was his habit at bedtime just to crawl into the mountain of laundry on his mattress, throw it up in the air and subside into sleep as it swirled down around his body.

John Clarke models his infamous "Plastic Suit" for his friends in the communal house, circa 1970s. PHOTO COURTESY OF CATHALEEN CLARKE

"How many people live here?" the cops demanded.

"Three," replied two of the guys in unison.

"Where's the third?"

"In that room."

"Is he home?"

When they spied a foot sticking out from under the laundry, they gave it a big yank. "You've no right coming into this house," yelled the startled John.

Eventually the cops realized that these were relatively honest citizens and went away satisfied, having confiscated a token switchblade but no pot.

After months alone in the mountains John would return lean, hungry, starved for human contact and super-energized. The first thing he would do was visit his friends—even before he had washed or eaten. "He was rank," Garry Kerekes recalled. "I'd tell him, 'John, take off your clothes! I'm going to burn 'em!'" And Carole Kerekes remembered that when John returned to the civilized world, he

Mountain man! John Clarke's self portrait on a lone trip in the Whitemantle Range, 1972.
PHOTO BY JOHN CLARKE, COURTESY OF ANNETTE CLARKE

was "really, really stinky! Really, really dirty. [He had] really, really bunged-up feet that looked like he'd been walking underwater with blisters for a month. Just horrible looking feet. And [he was] really hyper—because he hadn't been with people for whatever length of time the trip was."

John's clothes were easily disposed of, but getting the knots out of his long, matted hair was a drawn-out affair. One season he braided it before he set out and didn't touch it again till he came back months later. But, braided or not, the young women in the household couldn't wait to get their hands on him. "The girls would sit him down and put olive oil in his hair," Dick Rogers said. "He loved that. They would spend four or five hours brushing his hair—or however long it took."

John always had a healthy appetite, but when he returned from the wilderness he was ravenous. He would go with his friends to eat at the Marco Polo Chinese restaurant on the North Shore where a ten-course meal cost $1.60, or to the all-you-can-eat hippie smorgas-bord on Main Street where he would demonstrate what high-grading meant by stripping and discarding all the breading from the mounds of shrimp and pork on his plate. "Just go for the meat," he advised his friends. "Don't take any of that filler stuff like rice. That's how you get your money's worth."

Elaine Johnston recalled her first encounter with John after she came to live at 4 East Thirteenth Avenue. He had arrived back from months in the mountains—feral, tanned, hair wild as a mountain goat's—and he craved the company of his friends. He pounded on Elaine's flimsy bedroom wall. "Hello! Anyone there?" he boomed. Not waiting for a reply, he knocked on her door, entered and thrust out a well-toned arm. As Elaine struggled up from her mattress on the floor, he announced, "John Clarke. What are you doing in bed at 1:30 in the afternoon?" Elaine took an instant dislike to this "obnoxiously enthusiastic" man, but later that day she realized she was not immune to his Irish charms.

> At supper time I watched as he prepared a meal of tinned salmon and noodles, proclaiming to everyone that the dish would be a "taste sensation." He was fun and gorgeous. Standing beside him at the workbench counter, I reached for the tea bags, just to be close, hoping we might touch by chance. I bumped my elbow accidentally on the edge of the shelf. John spun toward me in a crouch and gripped my arm. "Is there anything I can do to help?" he asked with exaggerated comic concern. Everyone laughed. With the intent gaze of his blue eyes he coddled me, leading me over to the table. He pulled out a chair and said, "Just sit yourself down and I'll bring you a meal you'll never forget."

So began the tumultuous relationship between Elaine and John. Madly in love, they moved out of the commune to live together for a while in an apartment on Hudson at Seventieth Avenue. But it didn't work out. "John was very intense and he couldn't handle conflict at all," said Elaine. "I can remember him just gritting his teeth and holding

John Clarke and Elaine Johnston at Queen Elizabeth Park, 1974. PHOTO BY DICK ROGERS

John Clarke works as a gardener for friend and landscaper, John McAuliffe, in Vancouver, 1980. PHOTO BY JOHN MCAULIFFE

it in … He would leave the apartment and not come back for a night or a day." Despite their differences, after the affair was over, they remained close friends.

In 1976 John moved to Cumberland on Vancouver Island so that he could go tree planting during the winters, but two years later he was back in Vancouver, where he moved into the basement of his parents' new house at the corner of West Thirteenth Avenue and Ash, close to the city hall. For the next couple of winters he worked for John McAuliffe, who owned a gardening business. Johnny Mac and his wife, Tsippy, had met John when he lived in the communal house on East Thirteenth. Johnny recalled how he would drive by in the morning to pick John up from his parents' home:

> I'd stop my truck by the big red house and rap on the [basement] window and a wild face would appear. John would jump into the truck full of interest as to where we were going. We had a lot of customers in [the UBC Endowment Lands], and when going in that direction, we would stop for blueberry pancakes drenched in maple syrup. Boy, that man could eat!

One warm spring day Johnny Mac and John were cleaning up after a hard day's work planting a garden on a spacious property that went steeply down to the sea. They were dust- and sweat-streaked. Just then the owner drove up in her sleek Mercedes. As she glided out of its creamy leather interior, Johnny walked over for a consult. John continued to load the truck. As Johnny Mac described it:

> She was stunningly beautiful, immaculate-looking in a black dress, her

scent wafting. I was standing with her, looking over the garden plans, when John walked behind us. I heard him give a little involuntary whimper. It was all I could do to continue the conversation.

John could be serious too. Besides sharing the magic of the Coast Mountains with his friends he would also speak about the inroads of the forestry industry that he'd observed on his journeys from tidewater to the alpine. As Tsippy recalled: "John was one of the first of the conservationists to share the rapid changes he saw taking place to the land, sea, and animals of British Columbia. He could see the greed of big business and government for natural resources."

So powerful was the grip of the Coast Mountains on John, however, that it would be more than two decades before he stepped back and turned his energy to conserving the landscape he loved.

5

Realization

When you grow up in Vancouver and climb the North Shore mountains, you look north and climb those mountains, and you look north again. Well, it just never stops. If you become interested in the Coast Range, there's no cure for it.

—John Clarke

After John Clarke put Mount Lillooet behind him in 1969, two areas of the Coast Mountains rose to the top of his "to-do list." These were the Whitemantle Range and the Misty Icefields. Whitemantle lies between Bute and Knight Inlets and derives its name from its towering snow-capped peaks. Whitemantle Mountain is the highest of them all, rising to nearly 10,000 feet (3,000 metres). The whole area is known for its wild scenery, rugged peaks, huge glaciers, dramatic icefalls and spectacular views of Mount Waddington to the north. In short, it is a mountaineer's paradise.

The Misty Icefields' romantic name provides no indication of how difficult it is to reach on foot, despite the fact that—as the crow flies—it is less than fifty miles from downtown Vancouver. This high, remote, glaciated plateau is located in the eastern part of Garibaldi Provincial Park and includes both the Stave and Snowcap Glaciers, but since the peaks within the icefields were unclimbed at that time, they had no individual names. Members of the BC Mountaineering Club had thought to penetrate the area in 1960, but their plans went awry before they got off the ground because Stave Lake, where they had planned to land the float plane, was still frozen in July. They didn't make another attempt.

In the 1960s and 1970s most mountaineers were showing little interest in lesser peaks such as those in the Misty Icefields. Once the dominant peaks in an area had been climbed, they would lose interest and protest that it was "kind of climbed out," even though the area in question might be vast and have relatively few major peaks. But John was immensely interested in those lesser peaks, and as a result he was conflicted when in the spring of 1971 the Varsity Outdoor Club announced a major expedition to the Misty Icefields and the BC Mountaineering Club planned a ski expedition to the Whitemantle Range, led by John's mountaineering mentors, Martin and Esther Kafer. Both regions were remote, with peaks unclimbed, and there were few technical difficulties to overcome, but it was the weather that would dictate success or failure. "You still might not get there on your fourth try," John said with relish.

In the end John took time off from the job he had taken at the Vancouver Airport doing airfield maintenance and joined the ski expedition to the Whitemantle Range. They were a group of just five, and they had a marvellous ski trip and climbed all the peaks. For John, especially memorable was the day he gazed from the summit of

Members of the 1971 expedition to the Whitemantle Range. *Left to right*: Esther Kafer, John Clarke, Nick Schwabe, Roy Yeates, Martin Kafer. PHOTO BY NICK SCHWABE

Outrider Peak on the northern edge of the Whitemantle Range. He could go no further but was fuelled by what he saw, and later wrote about the moment:

> Pointer Peak, a dark sugar-loaf formation, thrust out of the clouds which filled the mighty Homathko Valley. It had been like a navigational beacon to the Mundays as they relayed their packs up the Homathko River in the summer of 1926. The mist-filled void below reminded us of the long vanished Indian trails, the Alfred Waddington party, the Mundays, and the many trappers, woodsmen and adventurers who have travelled this river and fought its bush.

John would return to the Whitemantle Range many times, but throughout that first trip he found himself wondering how the four VOC team members—Barry Narod, John Frizell, Sara Golling and Roland Burton—were faring on the Misty Icefields. In fact, they had started their journey at Diamond Head and emerged nineteen days later at the head of Pitt Lake, having climbed absolutely nothing. "They were just being destroyed by weather," John said years later, shaking his head. "Couldn't look left or right—just went for the next bunch of groceries, which were again covered with snow. They were a very, very glum, grim group when they got to the head of Pitt Lake."

John, however, was elated at their lack of success as he realized there was still an opportunity to be the first to climb the mysterious peaks of the Misty Icefields. Later that summer of 1971 he had the chance to meet the unsuccessful foursome at a party held to attract new members to the fledgling Mountain Equipment Co-op (MEC); there were just six members signed up and they needed fifty to officially register it as a co-op in Victoria. John, reluctant to part with the five-dollar membership fee, protested he didn't know what he was getting in to, but when Roland Burton explained that members could buy sleeping bags and ski and mountaineering equipment cheaply, John caved in and became member number twenty-eight. This heralded the start of his lifelong attachment to the MEC.

But vastly more important to John than the start-up of the MEC was the opportunity to sit down with the four intrepid mountaineers who'd traversed the Misty Icefields that spring. He told them he was going there in July and suggested they team up. "Do you know, their trip was so grim that they still had to regain their sense of humour about anything, and they said, 'No. We're not going back in there. Go for it.'"

For his first major solo expedition, John watched the weather for weeks, waiting for a bombproof high pressure system to set up. He knew he had to cram all his climbs into a few days—the most time off he could extract from his boss at the airport was a long weekend. He was told, "You can get Friday off if you come and sign in, and then you can just take off. But you've got to come in."

John had worked out every last detail. "So I packed for the whole trip," he recalled.. "Put the pack in a locker at the bus station downtown then went home. Went to work. Signed in. Went straight down to the bus station. Got my pack out of the locker. Got on the bus. Got off at the Wild Duck Inn." This hotel in Port Coquitlam was built in 1912 as a bunkhouse for CPR workers and served as a stopping place for travellers over the decades, until it was demolished in 2008. "Got onto the Pitt Lake Express." The "Express" was a boat used to take loggers and equipment back and forth on Pitt Lake.

However, when John disembarked from the boat on that sizzling Friday afternoon, the loggers had already quit work for the day so there was no chance to catch a lift up the logging road in one of their crummies. He was forced to hike in the sweltering heat more than fifteen miles (twenty-four kilometres) to the end of the road and didn't reach the cool alpine until nightfall. Counting on fine weather, he was travelling light and fast and had brought no tent, so he slept under the stars that night and for the next four nights. In just five days he covered 200 square miles (525 square kilometres) of rugged wilderness and climbed twelve peaks that had never been climbed before, achieving first recorded ascents—quite a coup for his first major solo expedition.

All I did was do sixteen hour days for five days. Covered the whole Misty Icefields. Climbed all the peaks and just camped. All I had was a little piece of plastic [sheeting], ensolite and a bag of granola in a pillow-case, which I used for a pillow *and* ate.

To explain his absence beyond the weekend, he had arranged for a buddy who was working at the head of Pitt Lake to phone his boss at the airport on Monday morning to explain that he had been delayed by a fire at the head of the lake. "I showed up at work on the Wednesday and my face [was] all baked. He knew what was up. But I was a really good boy after that—till the fall."

When John later named the peaks and features he had explored in the Misty Icefields, he used names derived from the language of the Katzie people of the Halkomelem group of the Coast Salish, whose traditional territory includes the entire Pitt River watershed: Katzie (*Kaytzee*); Halkomelem (*Halkomay'lem*); Stalo, in honour of the Mainland Halkomelem people; Skakala, which means infant; Betstel, which means needle; Piluk, which means sunrise; Skayuk, in honour of the people of the Stave River area; Old Pierre, in honour of one of the last medicine men of the Katzie people; and Pukulkul, which means nanny goat.

Fall wasn't far off now but John had set his heart on making one more solo marathon expedition that summer, this time through the McBride Range in the heart of Garibaldi Park. Because he had promised to behave and work the rest of the summer, he used the weekends to carry dried food in to the remote McBride Range; like a squirrel hoarding for cold days, he cached it at strategic spots along his proposed route. In this way he could make a lightning-fast, four-day, figure-eight trip through the entire range.

Toward the end of August he made his escape. Again he carried no tent and prayed the weather would hold. He spent a memorable night on the summit of Mount Sir Richard (8,900 feet or 2,710 metres) in a violent electric storm. Hail, wind and lightning lasted most of the night. Then four days into his trip the weather completely closed in, and he had to use a compass to find his way through the Fitzsimmons Range as he headed for the town of Whistler. He never lost his way, although the going was desperate.

At one spot I really needed to confirm where I was, so I climbed a peak in the storm. I opened the cairn to see the name of the peak that I was on. I kept compassing then and made it all the way over to Whirlwind

Peak and spent the night on an open ridge under a piece of plastic. Just ensolite and a wet sleeping bag. I was in an awful state when I got out to the highway.

In 1972—his longest, most productive climbing season—John spent eight months in the wilderness and climbed fifty peaks (first ascents). His approach to the Coast Mountains had now taken on a pattern. His typical season of exploratory mountaineering began in May with a spring ski expedition across an unexplored icefield. This initial foray was quickly followed by a sequence of trips on foot ranging in length from several days to over a month. Then in late September or early October, when winter arrived in the alpine, he would return to work solely to finance his trips and make detailed preparations for the coming season.

For John, the mountains he climbed were not just a series of anonymous peaks. They became as familiar to him as his friends as he examined them from every angle, whether from the vantage point of other peaks, in aerial photographs or on topographical maps. An account entitled "Solitary Wanderings in the Coast Range," which was published in the *Canadian Alpine Journal* in 1973, describes his first trip of 1972:

> The idea of spending a whole summer in the Coast Mountains had always tempted me. It would be like making any Vancouver climber's dream come true. Last summer I set about finding the answer.
>
> The stormy spring was ideal for testing food and equipment for more extended trips later in the summer. The first serious ski trip was into the Ashlu-Squamish divide, to examine the southerly end of a proposed traverse from Jervis Inlet later in the summer. I got the required photos, but a sudden blizzard near Mount Amicus meant skiing back to the Elaho River leaving the tent and things to be ingested by the glacier, hoping for retrieval three months later.

In fact, this succinct account downplays what actually took place—at least according to the version he recounted many years later:

> I wound up losing all my gear that spring [so] I did the whole season

on borrowed gear. I went up to Amicus just because it had that 7,800 [foot] ski run off it from 8,300 to 500 [feet], and if you caught it in the early season, the snow took you right to the logging road at 500 feet when Weldwood was there and there was the old bridge across the Elaho [River]. I wound up losing the bloody camp altogether as I had this old cotton tent that had just a plastic sheet over it for a fly sheet, but it needed your skis and poles and ice ax and everything as that was part of the gear to hold it up. Consequently, when you left it for a day trip, [the tent] was very flat so in a storm it wouldn't be still sticking up. I wound up getting caught in a storm and ... standing in the storm all night ... I'd never seen a storm come in so fast in my life. I was crossing this névé on the other side of Amicus to get over to the proper glacier where my camp was and it just started storming. [I] never made it back, even to the valley where my camp was. I got over close to a cliff, but it was still windy and ... I had a choice of [two] equally bad spots to stand. One was a little chimney thing that either had the wind screaming up it or down it. The other one was more open but leaning against the cliff. Mercifully in the morning it didn't clear up but it stopped snowing and I got over the ridge and skied down into the valley. I know I'm on the névé where my camp is, but there's no way I'm going to find it because there's so much accumulation all night. I know the tent is covered. It snowed about a foot and that's all it would [have] needed. There was no visibility anyway to find the damned thing. So I went home and it rained and was cold for about a week, so I know this is just piling up. I flew over in June with Roy [Mason] to see if there was any little thing sticking out. Nothing. Just the névé. I actually went again in August between my long trips. Now it's bushwhacking up the damn thing—slabs and slide alder and everything. I found the camp and the sleeping bag squashed flat and wet. My down bag never was the same after that.

In June 1972 John embarked on the first of his many trips to the Toba region, a ten-day solo ski trip. Ever since his first expedition to the Manatee Range with the BC Mountaineering Club in 1967, he had wanted to explore the Toba area. On this occasion he traversed from north of Jervis Inlet, climbing the peaks along the way—including 9,200-foot (2,808-metre) Mount Elaho—and exited down the Toba Glacier to reach the logging road beside the Toba River. At the end of the trip he wrote, "It felt strange to walk under the cool darkness of the foliage as bumblebees droned in the second growth at the Toba River's edge after ten days on blinding glaciers." John would return to Toba time after time over the next seventeen years, systematically climbing every virgin peak. All but one of these trips were made alone. In the 1973 *Canadian Alpine Journal* he wrote:

> I am often asked if solo trips in remote places are lonely—sometimes, yes. But usually the uncertainty of the route ahead, the weather, [and] sheer captivation with the scenery prevent loneliness. Evenings are spent cooking, studying the next day's route on the map in candlelight, melting snow for tomorrow's water bottle, repairing clothes and equipment or just lying still and listening to the silence.

John's final climb of his first solo season was the first of his many ventures to explore the Whitemantle Range alone.

> I was broke! I was a greedy boy and I wanted to squeeze in one more trip and I wanted to climb Stanton really bad. I had this gleaming ten-speed bicycle that I was going to need all winter to get around [but] I sold it to do Stanton! I remember thinking, *I'll deal with this bicycle thing later.*

Mount Stanton is a 9,700-foot (2,900-metre) peak located in the south of the Whitemantle Range, halfway between the head of Knight Inlet and the Homathko River. John's written account of that trip read:

> At the end of August a Trans Mountain Airlines Cessna dropped me at the mouth of [Wahkash] creek, the site of an abandoned logging operation. There was no dock, so I stepped off the pontoon up to my knees in seaweed—it felt a long way to Mount Stanton! The old logging road gave fast traveling for seven miles (eleven kilometres), but it took two days to find a route from there to the high country—this was one of those valleys that look better on air photos and maps than on the ground. Finally the peaks north of the north fork of Wahkash Creek were traversed and camp placed within a good distance of Stanton.
>
> The whole region is overwhelmed by glaciers, some terminating as low as 2,500 feet above sea level. Stanton was not a difficult climb ...

Only the last 100 feet required crampons. It was crystal clear in the calm air, so I spent two hours of this glorious September evening on the peak.

The following day I climbed 8,500-foot "Wahkash Peak" by hiking across the huge 16-square-mile névé that separates it from Stanton. The surface was pitted with huge waist-deep sun cups, but the view from the peak was a reward. In every direction were ranges like a single band of white, their ridges smoothed out by the midday sunshine. The weather held long enough to return to the inlet and light a bonfire on the beach. I caught the first passing plane home—hitch-hiking Knight Inlet style.

John's later recollections of this trip while being interviewed by Greg Maurer provide some interesting details omitted from his written account:

I remember before that trip I was sitting in the airline's coffee shop ... and there's all these people slopping coffee in the morning, and a couple of guys asked me where I was going. And I said I was going to Knight Inlet.

They said, "Oh, where do you go? We go out there quite a bit."

"Wahkash Creek."

"Wow, the grizzly hunting in there is really good."

And I had an awful problem because, when I got there, there *were* quite a few grizzlies. I had a hell of a time getting out of the valley ... it actually took me a few days to figure it out ... Well, I had a few false starts, but when I finally found the actual route that I should have been on, it was a goat highway. It was grooved. There was white wool everywhere and the soil [was] all worn off. What was

John Clarke stands above a vast crevasse, 1986. PHOTO BY JOHN BALDWIN

interesting was, when you got up high where it turned into little gnarly subalpine trees, the goats were almost certainly on their bellies because these big, thick branches only left a little bit of room and the wool was there and all the soil was

> Sun cups are cup-shaped depressions in the snow that are formed as the snow melts unevenly during periods of clear, sunny weather. They vary in depth from a couple of inches to three feet or more. On high altitude snow especially they may develop into spectacularly deep depressions.

scraped off and moss and everything. So I knew they wouldn't have climbed out and over the top of it as it would have been more risky ... I had no problem route finding—just followed that goat highway.

He was to make a total of seven trips to the Whitemantle Range but this, his first, could also have been his last. He also left the following information out of his *Canadian Alpine Journal* account:

> After I came down off Mount Stanton, I was running down through the bush. It's the end of the trip, and I was coming down out of the alpine and just kind of losing altitude really fast. I got into a tumble and had my pack on and I was tumbling forward ... [when] I saw this granite flake that had sheared off. It would have split my head like a chicken, and I saw it coming up and I turned my head and it came right along my cheek. [Here John shook with laughter.] I lay there for about half an hour. Just "Whooooooooah!" You can just picture it decades later when someone arrives at the scene. They would have found a split skull. "Wow! I wonder what happened to this guy?" they'd say. "Look, there's just his belt buckle left."

Later, he would reflect on this close call:

> When you are in your twenties and thirties and you are running around the mountains, you are the king, right? Nothing is going to happen to this guy, right? You think you're invincible. It's *not* a cliché. You get kind of humbled if you are too cheeky or too indifferent to it. It'll find you.

During John's first full season of mountaineering, he began to realize his dreams: to fill in the blanks on the map and climb the virgin peaks of the Coast Mountains. All that winter he made plans for his first major solo traverse—which would become a hallmark of Clarke's future explorations.

6

Rite of Passage

Guardian spirits were also recognized by many First Nations. They were believed to bestow power during vision quests. Vision quests were usually carried out in solitude by most males and some females after puberty. During the quest, a guardian spirit would manifest itself to the individual and bestow powers that would protect the person and enhance his or her actions.
—Robert J. Muckle, from
The First Nations of British Columbia

"By travelling alone, John broke one of the cardinal rules of mountain climbing. By agreeing to fly him where he wanted to go, I became his accomplice," said Roy Mason, the prominent Vancouver mountaineer and pilot of a ski-equipped plane. A member of the BC Mountaineering Club and a professional engineer, Mason had learned to fly in 1958 so that he could access the remote regions of BC's Coast Mountains. His first plane was a land-sea machine equipped with wheels and floats so that it could take off from and land on high alpine lakes. Of course, these lakes were frozen in the winter, and in 1972, not content to be confined to summer flying, Mason traded that first plane in for a Piper Super Cub so he could install a set of retractable skis. The news spread among BCMC members and requests for flights flowed in.

Most of John Clarke's trips up to this time had been relatively close to Vancouver, so his approach had always involved catching a ride to a certain point and then travelling on foot. The availability of

Roy Mason's plane perches on the Kilippi Glacier after dropping off John Clarke on June 30, 1973. This is the start of John's first long solo traverse. It will be three weeks before he reaches his exit at Knight Inlet. PHOTO BY JOHN CLARKE, COURTESY OF ANNETTE CLARKE

bush planes had made it possible for him to fly in and land on lakes, but Mason's ski-equipped plane meant that he could be dropped off on the snow of the more remote places in the Coast Mountains, and that summer of 1972 he began taking advantage of the service Mason could provide.

Unlike the Rockies, the approach to the Coast Mountains requires as much or more skill than the climbing of the actual peaks, due to their unique geography and climate. On their steep western edge, where the snow-clad peaks are incised by deep, glacially carved valleys and sinuous inlets, John would get dropped off by boat or float plane on a barnacled beach at the head of an inlet. On the eastern, less rugged side of the range, where the mountains are more barren and descend gently into the interior plateau, John would approach on foot or charter a small plane to gain access via a nearby valley. He carried everything he needed on his back; it was only on his more extended expeditions that he might place food drops along his proposed route.

I visited Roy Mason in April 2008 at his Burnaby apartment to learn about the times he had flown John around the Coast Mountains. Spry and fit despite his eighty or so years, Mason put away the novel he had almost completed writing and showed me into his living room, where in pride of place above the fireplace hung a large, striking photograph taken by John Clarke back in the action-packed summer of 1972. In the foreground on the surface of the glistening snow is the elegant Piper Super Cub, perched on its skis like a giant bird. Behind towers ice-encrusted Mount Athelstan, startling against the backdrop of the cerulean blue sky.

Throughout John's six-month season of exploration in 1972 Roy Mason had dropped him off on glaciers and at the head of remote inlets. As Mason described it:

> I'd wave him good-bye and wonder if I'd see him again. Even though he would make his way back from the mountains on foot without my help, I felt responsible for his return. The very fact of flying him to the mountains made me responsible. Or did it? Was it anyone's business but his own if he chose to wander alone in the mountains? Was anyone responsible but himself if he fell into a crevasse? I guessed not. But I couldn't rest comfortably until he returned.

So Roy would mark the date of John's intended return with a red dot on his calendar—and wait.

In early 1973 Roy wasn't a bit surprised when John phoned to ask him for a ride to the broad pass at the head of the Kilippi Glacier northeast of Silverthrone Mountain. John's choice of destination had been inspired by the Mundays, who had become his heroes and role models. He and Phyllis were by this time good friends and they would chat on the phone and exchange letters, and sometimes he would cycle over to visit with her at her North Vancouver home. He knew every detail of the Mundays' explorations in the Coast Mountains, and she encouraged him to pick up the thread of exploration where she and Don had left off. He did not disappoint her, literally following in their footsteps and getting a thrill from standing on the summit of peaks that they had been the first to climb.

One area in particular that fired John's imagination was the vast Klinaklini Glacier. The Mundays had first seen this magnificent glacier in 1927 from a ridge above the Franklin River when they were on one of their many forays to the Waddington Range, but it wasn't until ten years later, when they made the first ascent of Silverthrone

Mountain, that they realized their dream of visiting it. In 1935 they had been foiled in their attempt to cross Tumult Creek at the head of Knight Inlet, so they returned a year later armed with a cable bridge to make the crossing of the raging creek, and thereby gained access to the snout of the glacier. A graphic description of this adventure can be found in the *Canadian Alpine Journal* for 1936.

John was impressed by their hair-raising struggles with "clouds, grizzlies and swarms of wasps," but what drew him like a magnet

Letter from Phyllis Munday to John Clarke, 1971. IMAGE COURTESY OF CATHALEEN CLARKE was the utter remoteness of the colossal, snowbound area. He felt compelled to experience for himself this howling 150-square-mile (400-square-kilometre) wilderness, to follow the glacier's twenty-five-mile (forty-kilometre) frozen course from its conception on Mount Silverthrone to its termination 700 feet above sea level. (This would be like having the entire Whistler Valley filled with a glacier.)

He planned to start his journey from the north and attempt to climb the big peaks in that area before going south, then avoid crossing the raging Tumult Creek and exit along the Sim River to the west side of Knight Inlet just beyond McMyn Creek. (See page 100 for map.)

When John asked the rhetorical question: "Is seeking remote country out of date?" his own answer was: "Not for people who want to go to a place where there's not even a hint of what century it is ... where your passing will make no difference." But whether he acknowledged it or not, this trip—his first extended solo journey—was a rite of passage. It was a complete break from conventional life and marked his transcendence into a world where he would test not only his physical stamina but his mental capacity for isolation and self-reliance. While a ten-day retreat in an ashram is endurance enough for some people, he sought something even more profound—a place where there is no escape from your inner self. "Mountaineering reconnects us with the types of natural challenges that early people had to deal with pretty well every day of their lives," he said later and then, imagining what it was like for early man, he added:

> It's very difficult for us today to try to visualize or to experience what the aboriginal people [who] lived here felt because it's almost as if we have to unlearn all our scientific knowledge to place ourselves in the situation that they were in living out under the stars.

Roy Mason was right to be concerned about John's solo venture to an area so remote that he might as well have been going to the end of the earth. This wilderness allowed no room for error. John had no way of getting help if he met with unremitting storms, cold, injury, equipment failure or lack of food. Satellite phones and cellphones did not exist. And at this stage of his exploratory career he had no back-up support, such as food drops placed along the route. For the three-week solo ski expedition he carried just 80,000 calories in his backpack and travelled on a pair of old wooden skis. He had no high-tech gear or special clothing.

Three weeks of poor weather in June delayed the start of the trip, but on the last day of the month, John enjoyed the 220-mile (350-kilometre) flight up the coast to the Klinaklini Snowfield in cloudless skies. As they neared their destination, his full attention was on the panorama spread out below, which he wrote about for the 1974 *Canadian Alpine Journal*:

> Entering the Klinaklini Snowfield in a tiny aircraft, one is drawn into a vast chamber of white space and distance—the dazzling whiteness increasing with every minute. Soon we were circling the pass at the head of the Kilippi Glacier. Mount Silverthrone (looking like other mountains would in January) rose to the southwest. We dropped toward the glacier; the skis brushed the surface of the pass once, twice, then slid to a halt. I stepped out and started wildly snapping pictures from every angle.

Roy Mason hung around, reluctant to leave the young mountaineer, so vulnerable in the midst of this vast wilderness. But soon he took off and the plane raced across the pass, rose and banked around for a last good-bye. John's gaze followed this final contact with the outside world as it departed and his head spun as he thought of all the things he might have forgotten. "The little dot got smaller and smaller, the sound died away."

John had come well prepared for any of the vagaries that the weather could throw at him—or so he thought: winter clothes, at least sixty pounds (thirty kilograms) of food, white gas, tent, stove, hefty wooden mountaineering skis. He moved all his gear to a level spot, ate lunch, then lay down in his sleeping bag "and fell asleep to dream about tomorrow," as he put it. When he awoke, it was dark and a blanket of snow covered the tent fly he'd thrown over his sleeping bag. Always the optimist, he told himself the snow would probably only last two or three days, and he set up his tent. His diary entries tell the story of the next three days:

This is July. It will go away.

Snowed today.

Boredom is not a problem. The tent is being buried in new snow at night with 40 mph winds. I don't have to worry about nothing to do. Next to 8 lb of Klim [a brand of powdered milk] and the same weight of home-made Granola, my best friend in the storm is the stack of novels I brought "in case of bad weather."

As the spindrift beat against the tent, John entertained himself by playing "food games," his objective being to extract the maximum number of dinners for the minimum amount of fuel. Granola breakfasts required no cooking. To avoid having to use fuel to melt snow, he collected water, drip by drip, from a rock face and used the water to soak macaroni, dried veggie flakes and meat for the next day. To reduce cooking time, he used a tightly fitting pot lid and allowed his dinner to stand for ten minutes after bringing it to a boil. The satisfying result: seven dinners from a third of a pint (180 millilitres) of white gas.

Then one day he awoke to an eerie silence. There was no wind lashing the tent fly. Later that morning a half-hour of sunshine and a brief visit from two hummingbirds were the highlight of his day. "How can they stand the brightness of these névés?" he wrote of these birds. "There must be so much men don't know about these tiny fellows."

Within the cocoon of his tent John's city life receded to a distant memory as the storm returned. "It's beginning to feel like I've lived like this and always will and I'm the only man in the world and everything is OK," he scribbled in his diary. "If there's anyone else in the world, they live on their snowfield and go for water, shovel out their tent and doze and read." He had found the remoteness that he sought and the inner strength to accept whatever the wilderness delivered with humour, patience and resilience.

One day John peered from

John Clarke reads in his tent during a storm day, 1984. PHOTO BY JOHN BALDWIN

John Clarke's tent: his skis serve as pegs, his equipment is laid out on the snow. Silverthrone Glacier, 1973. PHOTO BY JOHN CLARKE, COURTESY OF ANNETTE CLARKE

Snowed under: it's July on the Silverthrone Glacier, 1973. PHOTO BY JOHN CLARKE, COURTESY OF ANNETTE CLARKE

the tent as usual and was thrilled to see a hole in the clouds. He needed no further encouragement and made a dash for nearby Mount Dolter. "Lulls are *always* mistaken for the end of the whole thing," he noted in his diary that evening as the storm resumed with renewed vigour.

"Snowed all night, worst yet," he wrote the next day. "Tent buried again. Dug it out twice this morning, 1½ feet new snow since last night (no wonder this glacier is 25 miles long)." He clung to the tent poles as the wind, charged with ice pellets, battered the canvas. Next day John moved the tent back to its original site but it was now at least four feet higher. Just before dark a glimpse down the glacier revealed Mount Jubilee.

It snowed day and night for eleven days. "Only by keeping a diary did I have any idea what day it was when it was over." But those eleven days of isolation were a testament to how completely comfortable he was with himself. He had crossed into another world. What he underwent was similar to what First Nations youth experience when their elders teach them how to survive in the wilderness and take them to the horizon of their known world to be alone, to witness what is going on in the land and within themselves. Chief Bill Williams, hereditary chief of the Squamish First Nation, explained it this way:

> [T]he real problem is that most people don't know how to be by themselves ... they are afraid to face themselves ... When you go out on these types of adventures that's exactly what you do. You challenge your body—in some instances right to exhaustion. But once you are exhausted, you are still thinking about something, whether you want to or not. You still have to come face to face with whatever you are thinking about. That's what John did ... and that is something that all people should go through to know that they can survive in their own mind. That they can do things that reflect the tools that are given to them by their parents, their uncles, their aunts, the things that make them a human being and [be] able to come out at the other end and still function and be a valuable contributor to society with the experience that you learned.

One morning John's diary informed him that it was July 12. It was time to move from the glacial island where he'd been marooned by relentless storms for more than half his allotted time. He had no option but to head for Knight Inlet and hope the weather would improve. He set out early when the peaks were still wrapped in mist, but before heading down the glacial highway he made a side trip to climb Mount Triplex and Mount Fitzgerald, for he dearly wanted a glimpse of Mount Silverthrone from the vantage point of their summits. But it was not to be. Silverthrone remained coyly sheathed in clouds.

Weighed down by his heavy pack, he skied down the glacier, ploughing his way through the soft, deep snow, but the accumulated days of inactivity had caught up with him: "After the long storm my legs had a wobbly just-got-out-of-the-hospital feeling," he joked. But to be on the move again, however slowly, was reward enough, and even the dense blanket of fog didn't dampen his spirits as he used his compass to navigate his way down the glacier. When he reached the pass, the sun burst through and burned away the stubborn clouds. He sat down and soaked in the unaccustomed warmth, enjoying the views that he had been deprived of for so long. He was "preferring to think about the work ahead than start doing it," but his lethargy soon evaporated. "As soon as I rounded the corner of the pass and saw Mount Somolenko, I knew I had to climb it—rising out of ice at its feet and covered with ice right to the top." Quickly he set up camp and prepared for an early start the next morning.

The next day he lingered on the summit of Mount Somolenko for almost two hours and snapped a 360-degree panorama with his tiny Olympus camera.

I couldn't believe the view. Mount Silverthrone rose higher to the north—a perfect pyramid. In the northwest the Pashleth Glacier wound down toward Machmell Valley and even a corner of Owikeno Lake showed. In the southeast the Tumult peaks had a terrifically jumbled appearance and didn't look one bit like the route home. In the east was the junction of the Silverthrone and Klinaklini glaciers ... The route ahead was broad and flat and a long way to go—but no more beautiful place to travel! Camp 3 was made that night on a 6,000-foot pass at the southern extremity of the Silverthrone system.

John Clarke enjoys a spectacular view of the Waddington Range. PHOTO BY JOHN BALDWIN

John's trial by storm and his utter isolation on the glacier had allowed him to transcend into a different world and gave him a glimpse of the hard-earned rewards that may occur after total immersion in the wilderness. He later came to recognize the process:

> You're just focussed on the landscape, and your whole city existence and all the circumstances of your life [become] a very vague, distant memory. One thing that really accelerates that process is a storm. When you emerge from that tent, it's like you're in cold storage. Basically, you weren't needed for a while and you come out into that landscape and for the rest of that whole trip you're just floating in a dream state. You get really hooked on that whole process that takes place. It's almost as if you've unlearned everything that you knew about your city existence and you've stepped into another reality.

While on the summit of Mount Somolenko, John had glimpsed his exit route but had no intention of bolting for home. Each morning for the next eight days he hoisted his pack onto his back, strapped on his skis and set off on a new adventure. He systematically worked his way down the Silverthrone Glacier, picking off the virgin peaks along the way as he wove his way around gaping crevasses, skirted jumbled icefalls and from time to time carried his skis through the jagged ice.

John Clarke alone in the Coast Mountains. PHOTO BY JOHN CLARKE, COURTESY OF ANNETTE CLARKE

Only at sundown would he stop to camp. "There certainly was never any trouble finding a flat spot at night—just a matter of dropping the load in the snow just before dusk." One evening, exhausted after a long day, he crawled into the tent too tired to cook. "I gasped like a beached fish. I fell asleep, woke a few hours later with my boots still on."

Twin peaks rising above the Satsalla River had captured his attention and the next day, July 16, he raced off to climb them. He later named them the Shaman Peaks, after the shamans who are the intermediaries between the human and spirit worlds. The next day he ascended the 8,632-foot (2,631-metre) Klinaklini Peak, "a major objective of the whole trip" and "a magnificent snow climb of 4,000 feet, the slender top consisting of very steep ice."

The following morning he climbed his final peak—the 8,500-foot (2,550-metre) Wahshilas Peak, which dominates the headwaters of the Sim River. From the summit he caught a glimpse of Knight Inlet. "The descent was a long swim in ridiculously soft snow, many avalanches starting below my boots. This was the eighth day after the big storm and conditions still hadn't improved." Later that afternoon, at just 2,500 feet (760 metres), he called it "the lowest elevation in 19 days, and I could feel real heat and smell the forests—everything was alive." That night he placed his camp below the snout of the glacier "on the lee side of a boulder 25 feet high. I slept out and between the dark walls was a ribbon of tightly packed stars and the night was so still that a candle stuck in the sand burnt almost without wavering."

On his final morning he prepared to return to a strangely unfamiliar world:

> The battle began. The south side of the tributary was all slide alder with a swamp at the confluence with Sim River. Another five hours of wrestling brought me at last to the logging road. I sat down with the loggers who thought I was raving to be talking so much, especially after one question asking if there was "snow all year round up there."

Now, after three weeks of total isolation, his rite of passage, John was ready to re-emerge into society and was eager to share his wilderness experiences.

John's successful completion of his first major solo traverse was empowering, and made him aware of his capacity to withstand tough conditions, whether they be physical or mental. It seemed that his

John Clarke cools down at the end of the day, 1984. PHOTO BY JOHN BALDWIN

John Clarke is headed for these jagged peaks of the Klattasine Range, August 1973. PHOTO BY JOHN CLARKE, COURTESY OF ANNETTE CLARKE

guardian spirits would indeed protect him when he returned to the mountains that August of 1973.

This time he headed out to explore the area east of the Waddington Range on the western edge of the Homathko Icefield. In particular he hoped to climb the spiky granite peaks of the Klattasine Ridge at the head of the Jewakwa Glacier.

The trip started with the slow bus ride to Campbell River and a marvelous flight up Bute Inlet ending with tricky landing against the current of the Homathko several miles above the mouth. I spent that night at Bruce Germyn's logging camp and received lessons in riding their trail bike from his son Mike with their dog, Homathko, yapping behind. Next morning (August 11) I started up the road toward Jewakwa Creek, driving the bike very carefully with a 74 lb pack. Since there were no lakes to land on in the Klattasine country and everything was carried, weight

Alnus sinuata (known as Sitka alder or slide alder) seldom grows taller than a shrub. It is a highly characteristic colonist of avalanche chutes because it can regrow quickly from its shallow roots and broken stumps on poor soils, screes and shallow stony slopes. At lower elevations it is commonly mixed with shrubby willows. Slide alder's thicket of rubbery branches all face downhill, making it extremely challenging to penetrate, especially when one is burdened with a bulging pack with an ice axe projecting above it like an oversized antenna.

was kept to a minimum, but I felt I needed the 40 lbs of food in case of prolonged storms. The food featured 6 lbs Klim, 7 lbs granola, almond paste, pressed dates, 2 lbs fat, cheese, pumpernickel, dried meat and halva. I left the bike at the end of 1.6 miles of road on the south side of the river and started off. The pack felt ridiculous. In fact, the first lunch stop was 15 minutes later in easy forest. This was the first day alone yet I carried on a conversation with a small black bear who walked close by. That night I camped beside the river just above the bend and listened to the boulders rolling in the creek. "Muffled thunder" seems a good description—the ground actually vibrated.

August 12 I made about 3 miles in 9 hours—surely a good time to

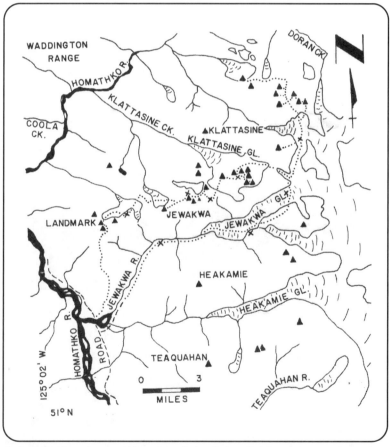

Clarke's route from the Homathko River at the head of Bute Inlet to Klattasine Ridge on the western edge of the Homathko Icefield, August 1973. (*CAJ*, 1974, VOL. 57)

appreciate the credit that climbers of former days are due. This is where slide alder was invented. Even two miles below the snout, big chunks of ice were bobbing down with the river. A family of goats was on the rocks above the snout. I stared. They were faithful to their usual (and a bit disconcerting) habit of standing motionless on a safe vantage and staring right back. The glacier was smooth going for one mile to the icefall, which cut completely across. I kept to the right but was gradually forced off the glacier entirely and camped on a bench in the moraines above the glacier. The Jewakwa glacier rises only 350 feet per mile for the first seven miles but is completely torn up with crevasses. Camp was pitched on the only flat spot anywhere—the bench was composed of dry dust, much like camping on flour.

I got up late on the 13th. You can't get up early after a day like yesterday. Followed the trough at the ice edge for half an hour on extremely loose steep gravel and sandcones. Finally the icefall pitched against a wall with no way to go but up. After climbing 1,000 feet above the glacier, I traversed above it for 1½ miles, noting that the broken ice continued up the main trunk beyond where a crossing was necessary to reach the Klattasine country. Spotting a possible route, I dropped to the ice and tried crossing but had to camp on a patch of

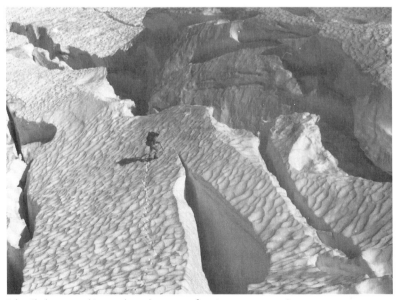

John Clarke weaves his way through a maze of gaping crevasses, 1987. PHOTO BY JOHN BALDWIN

snow in the middle. The ice groaned and murmured once or twice before I fell asleep.

In the morning an almost comically sinuous route got me to the north side of the glacier. The first northern branch was in bad shape— rotting snow covering almost open caverns. Skis were definitely needed here. Soon the right foot shot through into a small crevasse—my first ever. A second one followed five minutes later. The upper part of this tributary was easy, but I don't think I've ever been so desperately tired. Camp was placed on the 6,500-foot snow col at the head, and it immediately started to snow, turning to driving clouds of sleet the following morning. The 15th was cloudy and the 16th brought 2 inches of snow and wind. Three more inches of snow overnight was followed by a sharp drumming noise on the tent fly. About an inch of ice pellets fell in less than half an hour.

On the 18th I looked sleepily out of the tent. It was over. Glittering new snow lay everywhere and the small 7,500-foot peak one mile west of camp was a slow climb but showed glimpses of the rock peaks that lay along the route home. Fog floated below my peak. Banks of mist really add a strange beauty to glaciers. Only a fraction of the ice in this region is shown on the map.

John's camp in the middle of the Jawakwa Glacier, summer of 1973. PHOTO BY JOHN CLARKE, COURTESY OF ANNETTE CLARKE

On the 19th and 20th the storm died away, but gusts continued during climbs of all but one of the peaks south of lower Doran Creek. The farthest western 8,500-foot peak was missed through lack of time. This area showed tremendous views of Waddington country and the 16-mile-long Tiedemann glacier.

On the 21st I hiked back down the big northern tributary of the Jewakwa, then northwest over a pass to the Klattasine glacier and camp. Next day in perfect weather the 8,000-foot rock peaks at the head of the Klattasine glacier were climbed. The rock was a welcome sight for cold feet ... Camp that evening (22nd) was at a 5,500-foot flat green meadow in a side valley north of lower Jewakwa glacier.

Over the next few days John worked his way back to Jewakwa Creek, climbing the peaks along the way. "I left the pack at Jewakwa Creek bridge and walked up the creek to the little motorbike. The ride down to the logging camp was filled with the feeling that all climbers know after a stay in the high country."

John had climbed some thirty peaks (first ascents) during his two weeks in the Klattasine area, but several peaks had eluded him. The following year, 1974, he returned to climb the mountains still on his to-do list—in particular Mount Klattasine. But in his brief account of this second trip what he failed to mention was the story he told a friend years later:

The only time I could have got into serious trouble was when I was in the Klattasine. I was climbing one of the peaks on Klattasine Ridge and I poked my arm—my whole arm—into a horizontal crack ... and a block settled on my arm. My feet weren't on anything very good so they were just dribbling on the rock. It took me fifteen minutes to get my arm out of that crack. If it would have settled all the way, it would have crushed my arm. But it settled enough to pinch it in there. I left a lot of skin [but] got my arm out of there ... I was really upset for about three days over that. I was completely on my own in the middle of the Klattasine—right. That really choked me up.

John's accounts don't always give the reader a sense of just how tough it is to access these mountains. Three miles (five kilometres) in nine

hours in slide alder seems like a reasonable time, but there is no official grading system for bushwhacking and river and creek crossing as
there is for rock climbing. However, I did find a recent grading system on the Alpenglow Gallery website. According to the "Brush and
Bush Rating System" developed by a climber named Mark Dale, the
trip John made that August was right up there at the highest level of
difficulty: "Extreme brush. Multiple hours needed to travel one mile.
Full body armor desirable. Wounds to extremities likely, eye protection needed. Footing difficult due to lack of visibility. Loss of temper
inevitable." But John never did lose his temper on such occasions.
He knew that the bush was an integral part of the Coast Mountains
and beautiful in its own way. Of course, if there had been a reasonable alternative to going through the bush, he would have taken it. (I
remember my own trip with John to the Gitnadoix in 1989 when a
thrash up one valley became so excruciatingly slow that we waded up
the relatively shallow river.)

John's close call with a crevasse while crossing the Jewakwa
Glacier got barely a mention in his account: "Skis were definitely
needed here" was his only comment, meaning that he wished he had
the greater safety of skis as their relatively large surface area would
make falling into a crevasse less likely. However, there are very few

John Clarke crosses an icy, raging creek, 1987—this requires skill and fortitude. PHOTO BY JOHN
BALDWIN

mountaineers who would cross a crevasse-ridden glacier on their own because the chances of extracting yourself if you fell in would be slim. In fact, the first rule of glacier travel is to rope up. The climbing code in *Mountaineering: Freedom of the Hills*, the standard reference, says that a climbing party of three is the minimum. On crevassed glaciers, two rope teams are recommended because a climber's first unroped fall into a crevasse is often their last. Being attached to a teammate means that, in the event that one climber falls in, there is a chance of extricating them. John, however, was extremely cautious and, as in the case of the Jewakwa Glacier, if the light was poor and no route was visible through the crevasses he would stop and camp or he would walk around the glacier—even if it took him a day or so longer than going across.

Other details that seldom made it into his written accounts were about his encounters with wild animals when he was climbing alone, but he enjoyed entertaining his friends with these stories. One of his favourites occurred around 1976 when he had set out to climb the Three Sisters in the Niut Range in the Chilcotin:

About 1976 I was camped on the other side of Mosely Creek where Five Finger Creek comes in from the Niut Range. That's a big moose flat ... The problem was that moose are not particularly watching where they're going. They're just stamping around on these flats ... and I was worried about that and [having] them kind of stumbling into [my tent] at night.

But I didn't see any bears until the last morning I was there. It [was] still semi-dark and I woke up to this animal smell. The bear was right at the front door of the little tent. The claw came right down the flysheet and just ripped it. Just destroyed it. It was just straight down—slow and straight down. I'm inside the tent. What I'm trying to do is to take the lid off the white gas. You pour some outside on the ground. You bring the bottle back in. You put the lid on very carefully—tight. And you put the bottle at the back of the tent, get some matches and throw a match out.

But before I had all that finished, he'd gone around to the side of the tent and just leaned on it. All he did was just keep leaning on it, and of course it's coming in from the inside. But it's not some big attack or anything, he's just leaning on the thing and snapped one of the poles. It's an A-frame tent. He snapped the pole. When I lit the gas, of course, it was all over. BOOM! The bear just took off. So I wound up spending twenty-eight days out there with this splinted pole sticking out the top of my pack, going up about three feet above the pack. I was able to fix it, but I couldn't take it apart any more. I splinted it with nurse's tape and little tent pegs.

John's next close encounter with wild animals came just a year later. In the summer of 1977 he enticed his friend and flatmate Jamie Sproule to join him on a traverse from the ridges west of the Satsalla Glacier to the Tumult Glacier, Klinaklini Valley and Knight Inlet. (See page 149 for map.) The area features moderately high mountains and sprawling glaciers. It was Jamie's first mountaineering expedition, but John, already familiar with the exit route from his solo ski traverse in 1973, wanted to climb the peaks on the divide between Lahlah Creek and the Satsalla River.

> Rain, low cloud and the search for a helicopter kept us confined to the east coast of Vancouver Island the first ten days of September 1977. We consoled ourselves with salmon bakes, a sleep in a Native longhouse, a visit to Alert Bay and a few days camped on the magical Nimpkish River. It was at Port McNeill that we finally located the elusive helicopter giving five dollar rides at the fall fair.
>
> With the clouds still low we took off early … and flew east, navigating like a boat through the islands and channels. Over Kingcome village we broke into sunshine and the pilot dropped us off at 6,700 feet, six miles northeast of the confluence of the Kingcome and Satsalla rivers.

John and Jamie headed north. They cruised along the ridges, peering down into the valleys far below, and climbed everything along the way. Jamie climbed his first peak, built his first cairn and even enjoyed the storm days. A number of days later they emerged into the Klinaklini Valley, which is completely unlike any other on the coast. Jamie described the scene and unfolding events:

Moose have traveled through from the Chilcotin and are permanently established here. The valley is wide and flat with a big variety of animals. We charged down the valley on miles of flat gravel, easily avoiding islands of trees here and there. We saw moose, deer, bears, geese, ducks, beaver and eagles. Tall, dark columnar cliffs rose from the opposite side of the river.

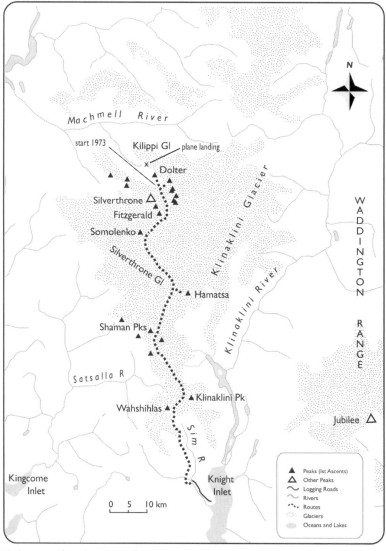

Clarke's route from the Kilippi Glacier to Knight Inlet—1973.

Toward evening something happened that we had never heard of before, let alone experienced. We were about to begin wading through a beaver pond as it was the only likely-looking route. A lean black wolf trotted out in front of us, stopped and stared. We stopped and stared, mesmerized, our packs still on. Keeping its eyes on us, he let out a few barks, ran toward us only a few steps, stopped, and growled. He then loped back to

A lone wolf, circa 2000s. PHOTO BY IAN MCALLISTER

where he was before, threw his head back, and started howling away as if we didn't exist. The howling stopped in half a minute and he repeated the short charge toward us with more growls. When he walked back and started howling again, we realized he was calling more wolves. After five or six minutes of alternating the howling and charging, the yap of a second one in the thicket behind us not only confirmed our suspicions but made us nearly jump out of our skins. I thought maybe this has happened to John before and he'll know what to do, but no, he was just as amazed as I. We had seen the remains of a moose kill earlier and felt very vulnerable. Since there wasn't enough loose wood around to keep a fire going all night, we decided to try the offensive. We threw our packs to the ground, took the ice axes and charged the wolf in front of us, yelling and waving the ice axes. We were certain this would cause him to disappear, but amazingly he only backed off about forty feet. We returned to the packs, not wanting to get too far from them. The wolf now sat farther away but still watched us. We put on our packs and plunged into the beaver ponds to try and reach the logging road. The wolf paralleled our route for about a minute and then we never saw him again. Darkness found us on the road but we marched on to try for the logging camp. At 2 a.m. we couldn't take another step and put up the tent on the gravel beside the road.

Years later Jamie elaborated on the grand finale of their adventures:

Next morning we slept late, crawled out into the warm sun and hobbled into the logging camp, still knackered. It was a Sunday morning and the guys had finished breakfast and it was too early for lunch. All they had left were these huge platters of sugary cakes and donuts. But, boy, were we hungry!

At the loggers' suggestion John and Jamie clambered into Ernie's truck as he was on his way to the dump. Jamie continued the story:

As Ernie turned the flat-deck into the dump area, a fearsome group of black bears looked up, licking their lips in anticipation. It was chow-down time. Ernie jumped into the back of the truck and started to chuck black plastic bags onto the ground. The bears crowded round, opening the bags to check for delicacies. One black bear stuck his long pink tongue down the entire length of a bottle of ketchup. Then Ernie hopped down and started to organize the bears. [John and Jamie were far too gob-smacked to take pictures at this point.] Ernie's yelling, "You want pictures? I'll get you pictures!" So he grabs a juicy T-bone steak, goes over to this bear he calls BoBo that he obviously favours, lies down

Portrait of "BoBo" the black bear, Knight Inlet logging camp, 1977. PHOTO BY JOHN CLARKE, COURTESY OF ANNETTE CLARKE

on the ground on the dump—which seemed pretty brave to me—and pokes this T-bone in the bear's face. But BoBo turns his head away ... He's full ... He'd been getting this special treatment ever since the camp opened in the spring. I guess he showed up at the dump as a skinny little bear and didn't have a chance without Ernie helping him. There is a picture of Ernie and BoBo sitting on a stump. He's got his arm around BoBo, and BoBo's wearing Ernie's sun glasses and his hat. It was just unbelievable.

After months of complete isolation, John couldn't wait to share his wilderness experiences with his friends and to show off the rugged beauty of the Coast Mountains. Telling others about his adventures was now an essential part of his return to urban life.

7

Toba Wanderings

When you step into the trackless wilderness you are making an agreement to play by a new set of rules … everything is done on the landscape's own terms

—John Clarke

By the time John Clarke started his long solo exploratory expeditions in the 1970s, there was scant appetite for his type of mountaineering. The highest peaks in the Coast Mountains, such as Mount Waddington and Monarch Mountain, had been climbed. As before, when the grandest peaks in the European Alps and then the Rocky Mountains had been climbed, interest within the climbing community shifted to finding new and more challenging routes up these mountains. Don Serl, the accomplished mountaineer and rock and ice climber from Vancouver, led the way in forging new routes at this time, particularly in the Waddington Range and the Chehalis Range, fifty miles (eighty kilometres) east of Vancouver. But he was flummoxed by John Clarke's climbing choices. In his 2003 guide to the Waddington Range, he commented that John had made only one first ascent in the Waddington Range—the 8,835-foot (2,694-metre) Martello Mountain. "This, amazingly, is the only peak in the Waddington Range that John Clarke, the master of the Coast Mountains, climbed … Mr. Clarke marched to his own drummer." And Serl continued, "Clarke said, 'It's only Class 4 'cause I could climb it.' Don't you believe it!" Serl defined the difficulty of the climb as "mid-5th Class."

And John Clarke did march to his own drummer. Back in June 1972 he had made a ten-day solo ski trip to the Toba area traversing north from Jervis Inlet and exiting down the Toba Glacier; his next visit to that area was not until October 1976. It was already wintry in the mountains, but he was determined to climb the knot of 9,500-foot (2850-metre) peaks northwest of the Montrose Glacier. His report in the *Canadian Alpine Journal* for 1977 read:

> After a ride to the main forks of the Toba River, I packed up the east side to Dalgleish Creek. I thought the stream was a reasonable prospect for crossing and even found log jams across some of the individual braids. But I hadn't yet come to the main channel. When I did, it was deep and fast. I hiked downstream to where the creek was cutting into a bank and a huge alder had fallen over and almost into the torrent. As much gear as possible was thrown across piece by piece, and the log was crossed with a light pack, camping just beyond. This is a narrow steep-sided valley with moss and water-streamed walls rising up out of the river on the south side. Moonlight in the clouds was followed later by rain, which kept me in this camp till the morning of the 3rd. Although the map shows only three miles from Dalgleish Creek to the Toba Glacier snout, this valley has *every* obstacle. For some distance the forest floor consisted of huge moss-covered angular blocks of granite and this gave way to an area of dense devil's club and then a pleasant section of virgin forest. Here the route is on a gentle bench above a canyon only 20 feet wide and 200 feet deep. Sunlight streamed through the trees onto the canyon walls, which were draped with moss and ferns.
>
> For half a mile the river roars at the bottom of this great cleft and the churning water can't be seen from the edge in many places. Dozens of waterfalls adorn the smooth faces south of the river. Following an afternoon of slide maple mixed with devil's club, I camped on sand near the river just below the outwash plain. Everywhere around is evidence of recent occupation by a huge valley glacier. Boulders balanced precariously on steep polished bedrock. Striations showed on the cliffs hundreds of feet above the valley floor which was littered with cottage-sized erratics. [A glacial erratic is a piece of rock that differs from the size and type of rock native to the area in which it rests.] The architecture of the place is awesome and water pours down the cliffs everywhere. In one

place a little creek breaks free over a 1,500-foot vertical wall dissipating into droplets halfway down.

October 4: A day of very little progress. Rain prevented an early start, and after a short walk from camp I was stopped where the river pinched against a wall. Two hours were passed looking for a route on ledges higher up, but at last I was satisfied that further travel on this side of the river was impossible. From high up I spotted an ice bridge crossing the river, the result of a glacier high up on the south side discharging ice down to the valley bottom to form a bridge over the Toba

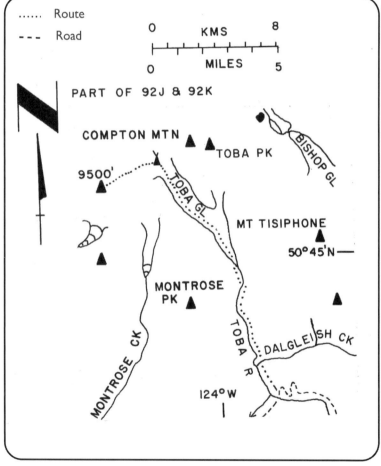

Clarke's route from the head of Toba Inlet to the peaks northwest of the Montrose Glacier. Clarke returned to Toba Inlet logging camp by the same route, October 1976. *CAJ*, 1977, VOL. 60

most of the year. One flying arch of ice remained over the river after the cool summer but only connected to a 20-foot-high boulder in the water near my side. Access to this boulder was a rappel and pendulum from a similar rock on shore. A short bit of rock and then steps were chopped in the ice arch. The whole route was prepared with a fixed line and all the gear was brought across in three loads.

On the other side the going was easy on polished gentle rocks to the flat outwash plain just below the glacier snout. I popped the tent up on moss-covered sand only half a mile from last night's camp but it was good to see the glacier up close at last. I took a stroll on the sandbars to check tomorrow's route but wet snow and rain pushed me back into the tent.

Rain kept John in camp the next day, but the following day he packed up the big valley glacier:

The anticipation of seeing over the next rise kept me moving along at a good pace ... No darkness came at sundown as a big bright moon came out, and everything sparkled in the almost daylight conditions outside. The alarm woke me at six and it was one of those incredible mornings. Nothing gets you out of the sleeping bag quicker than the first faint twilight glow on a perfect morning.

He gained the ridge in brilliant sunshine:

Distant views were opening up in all directions ... I climbed up past a huge wind cirque on the highest peak of the group, finishing the climb on steep hard ice. The reward. This was to be the only such day on the whole trip and the air was free of any trace of haze. An hour slipped by like a few minutes identifying minute distant points ... I descended and went up the second highest peak nearby—a steep snow climb ... I was back in camp before dark ... after a wonderful day.

Before dawn a storm struck and John raced down the glacier at first light.

Five hours of wet madness later I reached the protection of standing timber. I was soaking wet but not a drop of drinking water could be found among the big trees. I spent the night naked beside a fire big enough for ten people with all the clothes steaming and drying under the canopy of the giant timber. Around midnight a shower yielded drinking water in the upturned fly sheet.

A float plane drops off John Clarke on a log boom at the head of an inlet at the start of a trip with John Baldwin. PHOTO BY JOHN BALDWIN

In the morning my dry clothes were wet again in five minutes, but there were no stops in the ensuing dash to the logging road. Dalgleish Creek was crossed on the same log and two hours of thrashing around in rain brought me to the main Toba road. [But it was] Thanksgiving weekend and nobody [was] working in the woods! A "character building" eleven-mile walk with heavy rain bouncing off the gravel road ended with the camera being the only dry thing left. I arrived in camp in the usual state with everyone warming and drying the "thing" that limped in from the woods.

One adventure like that would deter even the most resolute explorer, but not John Clarke. This was just the appetizer and he was ready for the main course. The cluster of peaks at the head of the Montrose Glacier had captured his attention, and in September 1981 he set off for a "closer look." His fifteen-day traverse was as eventful as his previous trip, but in addition, when he arrived at the airdrop high up on the Montrose Glacier, he found his supplies almost unrecognizable. One empty can of white gas, torn to shreds like shrapnel, "looked like a piece of modern art." A second package revealed a "pulverized mixture of books, honey, oatmeal, flour, and the very important one-inch webbing slings for the walkout. New recipes would have to be invented." Despite this setback, he climbed the many peaks on his to-do list and took the hair-raising route across Dalgleish Creek to arrive back at the logging road just in time to get a ride with the last load of logs coming out of the woods that season.

The following June (1982) John revealed his competitive side. He made a dash to climb the peaks in between the Toba and the Raleigh–Gilbert area because he knew that Don Serl and other members of the Vancouver section of the Alpine Club of Canada were interested in scaling these unclimbed 9,000-foot (2,700-metre) peaks. John and his friend Phil Van Gils got dropped off by helicopter just northwest of the pass between the Montrose and Toba Glaciers. Phil, though ten years younger than John, was "pooped beyond pooped," his heels bare of skin, as they skied back to camp after their first try at Montrose Peak, the glaciated, triangular horn on the east side of Montrose Creek on the divide with the Toba Glacier. "I had to take about three days off," Phil confessed years later, "and John went back by himself the next day and peaked out." John's diary that day read: "June 13: I left at 5 a.m. and returned at 11 p.m. with only 13 minutes on the peak." Then, sometimes with and sometimes without Phil, John ticked off the other peaks. One morning he "went off on frozen snow and climbed Peak 9475 while Phil cooked breakfast. It was a thrill to return to the same spot as 1976, and I could see my old snow route down the other side." After breakfast they set out for the elegant 9535. On its summit they "built a cairn, made tea and took photos. Three perfect hours."

John Clarke balances on the summit of yet another unnamed pinnacle in the Coast Mountains, 1995. PHOTO BY MARKUS KELLERHALS

Days later John and Phil packed up and skied down steep slopes to the Toba Glacier. John watched with amazement as "Phil practiced his telemarking with 60 pounds of ballast on his

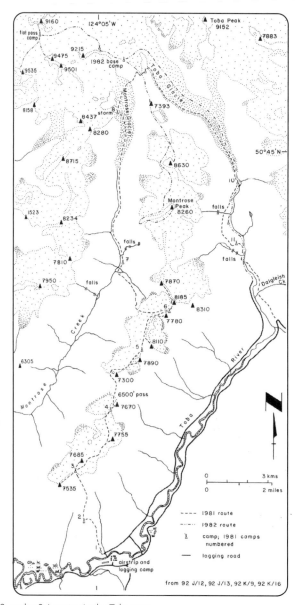

Clarke's (1981 and 1982) routes in the Toba area:

September 1981: Clarke's route from the airstrip of the logging camp at the mouth of Racoon Creek to the Montrose Glacier, and his return via the Toba Glacier to the logging camp at the head of Toba Inlet.

June 1982: Clarke and Phil Van Gils's ski routes from their base camp at the head of the Montrose and Toba Glaciers. Their exit route was via the Toba Glacier and River. (*CAJ* 1983, VOL. 66)

back." Further down they hit the bush, abandoned their wooden skis and started the walk out. Their exit down the Toba Valley left a deep impression on Phil, and twenty-eight years later he recalled that:

> Walking out was absolutely one of the hardest things I've done in my life. It's an incredibly steep valley that comes down to the Toba River, all the glaciers are melting and all the creeks were high. We had about three miles of slide alder—it took us almost two days to go three miles. You're not actually touching the ground.

Clendenning Lake at the toe of the Clendenning Glacier, 1977. Since then the glacier has receded and the lake is at least double this length. PHOTO BY JOHN CLARKE, COURTESY OF ANNETTE CLARKE

Undaunted by the inhospitable landscape, in 1984 John set up a base at the logging camp at the head of Racoon Creek, a tributary of the Toba River, and made four sorties alone to climb a series of peaks in the surrounding mountains. His first trip was to the group of granite peaks thirty miles up the Toba River, south of the main forks. Days later, storm-bound in the alpine, he wrote to his sister:

Hi Cathaleen,

I'm writing this letter at 5,000 ft. in the tent. It's pouring with rain and there's no visibility ... The ranges I'm heading into on these three trips in the Toba River were missed over the years for various reasons. I've almost climbed everything else in the whole Toba drainage and the 3 trips will finish up an enormous area that began with the Manatee trip in '67. There are 5 unclimbed peaks in the range I am in right now, all of them between 8,000' and 8,600', and none of them named.

After John's successful ascent of these 8,000-foot (2,400-metre)

One of John Clarke's messages left on a peak during his traverse along the Powell Divide in the Toba area, 1984. PHOTO BY LISA BAILE

peaks, he broke camp and started down the steep, broken glacier to the north. But his return trip was not without incident:

> I lost my frame pack jumping a bergschrund [a crevasse formed when ice and snow break away from a rock face] and watched it cartwheel down and into a crevasse. A frantic hour's work and everything was on the surface again with no more damage than ripped side pockets and a bent stove casing. Camp was on a flat slab that evening with everything I owned hung out on the rocks to dry. Next day through the timber I gorged on berries, and the insects gorged on me. After a killing ten-mile walk down the road, I was invited to fresh-caught trout and salad at the logging camp.

Dried out and restocked, he set out on his second trip. Camped deep in the valley, he eyed the only peak on the Montrose divide that he had yet to climb. Despite the evidence of bears—big grizzly droppings all around his tent—rain and kamikaze insects, he made the 8,000-foot (2,400-metre) ascent to the summit the next day and returned to camp within eight hours. "I remember thinking it funny," he remarked, "to go through all that for the privilege of standing for five minutes in a cloud on a hump of snow."

Then, his enthusiasm undiminished, he set out again, climbing almost all of the peaks in the compact range between Racoon Creek and the Little Toba River. His last sortie was to peak 7200, which he'd set his heart on climbing twelve years earlier. At the end of August he made a six-day trip to climb a very prominent 7,000-foot (2,100-metre) mountain two and a half miles (four kilometres) north of Toba Inlet at the south end of the divide between the Brem and Tahumming Rivers.

In September John finished off the season with a twenty-three-day traverse from the head of Toba Inlet to the Eldred River. Despite much new snow, the loss of one of his food drops to hungry animals and almost half of his time spent pinned down by storms—including forty-one hours of continuous rain—he made forty-two first ascents. At the end his enthusiasm was still unquenchable. He wrote:

> The country is probably the least travelled area within a hundred miles of Vancouver. It is the most beautiful arctic alpine wilderness, studded with lakes, small glaciers, and heather ridges; a marvellous stretch of wilderness, still left to the goats, wolverines, and ravens.

Five years later, in September 1989, John returned to traverse the divide between Toba Inlet and the Daniels River. This time in his report he didn't dwell on the number of peaks he climbed but instead threw out an enticement for others to follow him:

John Clarke surveys the view from the head of Toba Inlet. PHOTO BY JOHN BALDWIN

If you like scenic ridge tramping, you'll love this divide with Toba Inlet on one side and the powerful granite walls of the Daniels River on the other ... Red Alert ... Red Alert ... Rock climbers: There's a 3,500-foot granite cliff on the south side of the upper Daniels. Go do it. Red Alert ... This is not a drill.

Most mountaineers would be content to pick off one or two virgin peaks in a given area, but not John. He never did things by halves. As he demonstrated in the Toba region, if there was a peak that eluded him he would return, even years later, to climb it.

8

Heritage Vancouver

*Really! I don't get this. John's really big in the mountains—and
I'd thought of him as really big in the heritage game.*

—John Atkin

At the end of his climbing season John Clarke always appreciated his return to the city, although sometimes he found it a
little rough after such an utter departure from the "civilized
world." As he wrote in 1990:

> At the end of the season it's not so bad coming back to the city. It's sort
> of time. Although ... there's kind of an awkward two-week period of
> adjustment where you have to re-learn that there are certain sounds you
> *do not* make at the dinner table. And you're ready to be accepted back
> into the human race. But it is nice getting back to the city. I love doing
> all my rounds of visiting in the winter time and doing slide shows. I
> always take lots of pictures in the mountains and I love showing off the
> Coast Range and doing slide shows for mountain climbing clubs—and
> encouraging other people to go to these magic places. I remember hear-
> ing one guy at a slide show say, "That's it! I'm taking two years off."

John gave these slide shows wherever he could—at home, in a tiny
venue like the basement of the church or in a community centre. "John
was so passionate about sharing them," recalled Elaine Johnston, "it
didn't matter if he got paid or not. Money didn't come into it. He was
just driven. He would show slides in his bedroom—everybody would

be crammed up in a closet and against the walls, looking at John's slides."

But just as John respected and appreciated wild landscapes embedded in their geological past, so too he respected and appreciated old architecture, a reflection of humanity's past. He loved Vancouver's old buildings—the old wooden houses, ramshackle corner stores, vaudeville theatres, sprawling mansions, Craftsman houses and all the early buildings from the poorer Eastside to the city's downtown core. During his travels on his bicycle to visit friends in the winter, he would duck into back alleys, peer into ravines, take note of any remaining old-growth trees and giant stumps—vestiges of what had been there before. Always curious, he came to know the city inside out.

But his attachment and reverence for its heritage buildings didn't stop at just admiring them. Knowing that architecture was not only about providing shelter and security but also about culture, memory and history, he investigated the history of each one, who built it and when, and why it was in that particular spot. Rising early when the light was optimal and before pedestrians and vehicles obstructed his view, he would wander through neighbourhoods, tripod in one hand, camera in the other, systematically photographing the old buildings to capture the city before it disappeared. He even photographed the now-trendy Strathcona neighbourhood before it was known as Strathcona.

One of John Clarke's photos of a heritage building: Strathcona, Vancouver, 1977.

John hated to see beautiful heritage buildings torn down to make way for housing developments or more modern buildings, so he would go to city hall to find out who had taken out development permits and run out and photograph buildings that were to be demolished. His current girlfriends would often be drawn in by his enthusiasm

John Clarke rises early to photograph Vancouver's heritage buildings, 1979. PHOTO BY ELAINE JOHNSTON

for heritage buildings even if they weren't prepared to become mountaineers. Elaine Johnston remembers accompanying him on his photographic expeditions in the early 1970s. "I started taking pictures of John taking pictures [of heritage houses] because I'd have to stand around for so long, waiting while he got his pictures."

Fran Lacey, a friend who was living on Vancouver Island, would visit John in the early 1980s and recalled how he loved to show off the details of the old buildings:

> "Let's go down this street," he'd say. "I want to show you the shingles on the second storey of this house." Or he'd say, "You've got to see the posts that hold up the porch—they have this interesting carving." He'd say, "Look at the window in the attic." And there'd be this tiny stained glass window on the third storey. His attention to detail and his pleasure at the craftsmanship was just massive, and he was so excited and he was so passionate ... I began to look at things in a new way—and I do to this day.

In 1976 John joined the Heritage Committee of the Community Arts Council. (This committee split off from the Community Arts Council in 1991 to become the first independent heritage advocacy group in

Vancouver.) It was here that John Clarke met John Atkin, a civic historian and author who gives walking tours of Vancouver. What struck Atkin was John's real affection for the city even when city council was giving lip service to heritage buildings and seldom lifting a finger to save them.

> At that time the city of Vancouver had lost some incredibly significant architecture, and it was a hard place to like because it was wrecking so much stuff. The Georgia Medical Dental Building was imploded in 1989 (replaced by "Cathedral Place") and the Devonshire Hotel had just been demolished. But here was John being his usual totally optimistic self, always up on the city.

When Atkin bought his first house in Vancouver in the late eighties, John dropped by one day and handed him a photo of it taken in 1974. Atkin was amazed because, as far as he knew, no one was going around capturing images of the city in the systematic way that John was. He was also impressed with John's encyclopedic knowledge of architecture and details of specific buildings: "You know the blue house …" Atkin might begin, and before he could finish, John would say, "Oh yeah, the one at Fraser and Main …"

The house at #6 E 14th Ave., Vancouver, 1978. PHOTO BY JOHN CLARKE

The Heritage Committee shifted to a more proactive approach in the late 1980s in order to educate the public about Vancouver's heritage buildings and the need to preserve them. Informative talks and slide shows, open to the public, became a central part of the new format, and John played a key role because of his engaging speaking style, his depth of knowledge about Vancouver's neighbourhoods and his huge array of photographs of heritage buildings, many of which no longer existed. Atkin remembered those talks:

> [They were] always a lot of fun, always full of information, but they were also light-hearted. There was something about him that was quite infectious—that enthusiasm and that amazingly boundless energy … But what I really learned from John is that sense of consecutiveness—that you can't see things in isolation, and that there are the remnants, the signs of history lying all around the place. You just have to look for them.

A Kitsilano heritage house, 1979. PHOTO BY JOHN CLARKE

It is a testament to John's commitment to Vancouver's heritage buildings that for a long time Atkin thought of him only as a heritage buff. It wasn't until John slipped in a couple of his mountain slides during one of his talks that Atkin realized that he was also a mountaineer. Then Atkin read something in the newspaper about "Conservationist John Clarke." Atkin chuckled as he said, "And I'd thought of him as really *big* in the heritage game."

Michael Kluckner, the award-winning writer and artist and founding president of the Heritage Vancouver Society, also picked up a valuable tip from John's slide shows:

> When John gave his Heritage Vancouver talks, he'd show building pictures for about twenty minutes, then tell everyone he was going to take them on a trip. He insisted that everyone close their eyes and imagine they were travelling, then open them, by which time he had clicked forward onto mountaineering scenes. He then went back and completed his talk on buildings. It was a wonderful trick to break his talk. I used it subsequently for many of the ones I gave.

John gave Michael a slide of the Central Presbyterian Church at Thurlow and Pendrell Streets, demolished for the expansion of Saint Paul's Hospital—a slide that Michael subsequently used in his book, *Vancouver Remembered*. Another was of a little house in East Vancouver, which Michael reproduced as a watercolour in *Vanishing Vancouver*.

After several years of photographing old buildings John saved up enough money to buy a Nikon shift lens. Often used by architects, this lens shifts the perspective of the building so the image is more rectangular instead of having the perspective lines converge in the distance. "John was utterly thrilled," recalled Fran Lacey. "When I picture him now, I picture him cradling a camera. He lived in abject poverty but he would buy himself photographic equipment and he would look after it like mad."

In 1994 John gave a guided tour of the city to filmmaker Bill Noble, who was at work on a documentary called *Child of the Wind*, a glimpse into the life of John Clarke, which subsequently won the Best Film on Climbing Award at the 1995 Banff Mountain Film Festival. John happily showed off the city's different architectural styles while he recounted its early history, and Bill, who is from Golden, BC, was delighted to have his own private viewing of the city's heritage buildings. They ended the day on West Tenth Avenue, looking at the beautifully restored houses there. John had photographed most of the charming old Victorian and Edwardian houses before Pat and John Davis started buying and restoring them in the early 1970s, and he met the Davis family as he cycled by the very first one they were restoring—Number 166, built in 1891. "I just screeched to a halt on my bicycle and raved about what they were doing," John told Bill. "They weren't getting too much attention at that time ... [and] we've become pretty good friends."

John and Bill wandered down the tree-lined avenue while John paused to describe the architectural features of each of these lovingly restored houses. "Most of the houses on this block were built in the 1890s when there was still active logging going on in the city," John explained. "Generally the strategy in big cities is to preserve the big monumental stone buildings, but in Vancouver little wooden buildings speak a lot more accurately about the beginnings of this city than big monumental buildings do. The most beautiful way I've heard these houses on West Tenth Avenue described is 'a gift to the street.'"

The view of Burrard Bridge from SE side, 1981. PHOTO BY JOHN CLARKE

John stopped in front of Number 156, unfolded his tripod and stared appreciatively at the jewel of a house. The late afternoon sunshine set it off to perfection: the pale yellow and orange paintwork, the dark shadows on the orange fretwork. He turned to Bill:

Yep, my favourite house on the block. So we're looking at an 1895 Victorian house. The Davis family restored it to the highest possible standards. This house is highly decorated, has turned porch columns, fretwork and really beautiful windows. You can see ... John Davis used different shades of the same colour and a lot of different colours to highlight all the detail of the wood. It's a little house that speaks very eloquently about the early history in Vancouver because it shows what a small wooden town it was less than a hundred years ago.

Touring the city with Bill for *Child of the Wind*, John's appreciation of early architecture came across as strongly as his devotion to the mountains. Today, hundreds of John's slides of Vancouver's heritage buildings remain as a testament to his love of this city and his commitment to preserve the memory of its past.

Ha-Iltzuk Escapades

People are at their best when they are struggling. Mountaineering reconnects us with the types of natural challenges that early people had to deal with pretty well every day of their lives.
—John Clarke

The Cessna 172's single engine sputtered just before the propeller jammed. As the little plane skimmed the Ha-Iltzuk Icefield, veteran pilot Floyd Vaughn gripped the controls and turned it toward what he hoped was the airstrip belonging to a logging camp on Owikeno Lake. In the previous trouble-free minutes, his sole passenger, John Clarke, had successfully dropped three burlap bags of food onto the icefield below, stringing them out at intervals of about a week's walk along his proposed traverse route high above the headwaters of the Machmell River in one of the remotest areas of the Coast Mountains.

Neither Floyd nor John knew exactly where they were at this point, but they hoped the river below them was the Machmell. If so, the airstrip was at least twenty-five miles away—a short distance for a Cessna travelling at 160 miles (250 kilometres) per hour, but interminably long in a plane with a jammed propeller and a seized engine. If they couldn't reach the airstrip, their only other choices for an emergency landing were bleak. Floyd did not want to ditch the Cessna on the snow because the plane was not equipped with skis. And below them the river lay deep within a steep-sided canyon where the trees were massive and impenetrable; there were no large gravel bars visible along the river, which might have provided another option for a crash landing.

Later John would recall: "[There was] a lot of vibration and noises coming out of the engine ... So [Floyd] is right on it all the time. And full flaps, going real slow—all the way down the Machmell. So we're both just sitting there." John's hands grasped at imaginary levers as he continued the story. "Floyd's got his hands on two [levers]—like this—all the way down."

Ten years earlier, in 1973, John Clarke had stood alone on the summit of Mount Somolenko at 8,720 feet (2,660 metres), surrounded by the giant Klinaklini Snowfield, almost 200 miles (320 kilometres) northwest of Vancouver as the crow flies. He had lingered on the summit for almost two hours, imprinting a map of the surrounding snow-capped peaks on his memory. Then he had photographed a panorama of the mountain ranges around him, but one possibility for a future climb had surpassed all the others: a high traverse around the headwaters of the Machmell River, less than twenty miles to the northwest. Now the horseshoe-shaped ski traverse he had planned for June 1983 would take him around the headwaters of the Machmell River and onto the immense, 1,390-square-mile (3,610-square-kilometre) Ha-Iltzuk Icefield that surrounds Silverthrone Mountain. Canada's highest known volcano, Silverthrone towers over the surrounding peaks and provides outstanding views from its summit at 9,396 feet (2,864 metres).

All the previous winter John had worked to finance his trip and in his spare time he had planned the details of the expedition—his favourite activity after being in the mountains. In fact, "the preparation for [the trip] and the dreaming and the anticipation is as least as much fun as the trip itself." For him, his map room was everything:

> [It is] the part of the house that I have to avoid if there's anything else to be done around the place. An exploration mountaineer's life is run by maps. You look at these things and take a nice sharp pencil and start going through the contour lines. You're shopping around for remote alpine destinations.

Exploration was all about connecting the blanks on the map—not only topographically but in his mind; it was about a sense of place and his relationship to it. On the maps he played his own version of Xs and Os. He pencilled in routes and marked the peaks that had previously been climbed with an X and the unclimbed peaks with an O, then linked all the Os to form a potential traverse route.

Aptly called "The Detail Man" by his friends, John would do everything he could to remove uncertainties from any trip, because a well-planned trip could mean the difference between life and death. Once he had selected a route on his topographical map, he would check it carefully to make sure that, as far as possible, he could actually follow that route when he was out in the wilderness. But while a topographic map usually provides reliable information, the presence of a steep bluff or a 40-foot (12-metre) gap in a ridge may not be indicated on a map that has 100 feet (30 metres) between the contour lines. Lack of details such as this could be a serious problem once John was out in the wilderness, and might cause at best a huge waste of time due to an inevitable lengthy detour or at worst the end of the trip. However, air photos record all visible features on the earth's surface from a three-dimensional, overhead perspective and can provide important details that are not shown on topographical maps, so John would circle potential problem areas on the map then visit the provincial government's air photo library in Victoria. By examining their air photos of questionable areas, he could determine whether the route was passable.

Another crucial part of the planning process was choosing how much food to take and what kind. For this he commandeered his sister Cathaleen's empty basement on Slocan Street in East Vancouver—"Mission Control for the Coast Range," he laughingly called it—to organize food and equipment. Maps, air photos and climbing gear would be strewn everywhere. As for food, a shopping trip to Famous Foods, then located at the corner of Clark and Hastings Streets, was the first essential step. Items such as oatmeal, lentils and butter topped the list. John's theory was that you did not need to bring along "treats" such as chocolate because, once you were in the wilderness and ravenous, sooner or later lentils and oatmeal *became* treats. He would amass one big heap of food in the middle of the floor and then divide it up into meal-sized portions and weigh it to make sure he did not carry an ounce too much. For his trip to the Ha-Iltzuk Icefield he had packed a week's supply of food into each of five burlap bags, ready to be dropped at intervals from the hatch in the floor of the plane to the glacier below. In addition to the food, each drop contained white gas, slings (for rock climbing), matches, candles, socks, books, cairn tubes (to leave a message at the top of a peak), foot tape, soap and sunscreen. Once all of that was in order, he had only to wait for the weather to cooperate.

John Clarke prepares butter rations for a trip in the Coast Mountains, 1995. PHOTO BY STEVE SHEFFIELD

In early June he loaded his bulging pack, skis and the burlap food parcels onto an overnight bus to Williams Lake. Next day he made his way 200 miles (300 kilometres) west to Nimpo Lake in the heart of the Chilcotin Mountains. This was where he had arranged to meet pilot Floyd Vaughn, who would fly him to a logging camp on Owikeno Lake close to the start of his traverse, first dropping off the parcels of groceries at strategic intervals along his proposed route over the icefield. Although helicopters are more versatile for this kind of job, planes are less expensive, particularly if the climber has chosen a remote destination. The best sites for airdrops are over high, wide glaciers or snowfields so that the plane can get very low for the drops but still have plenty of room to manoeuvre afterwards. The pilot should fly 130 to 160 feet (40 to 50 metres) above the snow and slow to less than 60 miles (100 kilometres) per hour in the drop zone, a feat that requires skill and confidence. And, of course, the climber will not know whether the drops were successful until he arrives at the spots two to four weeks later.

John checked in with Floyd to let him know he was ready to fly anytime, then he stashed his gear in Floyd's woodshed and set up camp in the nearby woods. However, the very next day the weather turned bad, and it would be nine weeks before it was clear enough to fly and make the food drops on the Ha-Iltzuk Icefield. For John, a large part of the appeal of wilderness was its unpredictability, with the weather being a large part of that. Even if he got turned back time after time, it would only steel his resolve. On this occasion he was prepared to wait and make the most of his downtime. He became well acquainted with Nimpo Lake, which is the busiest fly-out centre in the interior of BC. Small planes fly clients in to fish in pristine lakes, to view the abundant wildlife or to simply hang out at some isolated cabin and enjoy the solitude. Adapting to daily life there, John hiked the open grassy clearings of the plateau, visited Charlotte Lake and was befriended by Geoff and Shannon Thomson at the Country Kitchen Café.

When on August 8 the weather finally cleared, Floyd and John drove to the airstrip at Anahim Lake, where Floyd's Cessna Skyhawk "JNO" awaited them. For popularity and lifespan, the docile and easy-to-fly Cessna 172 Skyhawk is considered the best of the small planes available, and since its debut in 1956 more than 43,000 have been built. With about 400 pounds (180 kilograms) of food and gear stashed away in the little plane, Floyd and John skimmed smoothly across the plateau. Once in the mountains, though, the plane was buffeted by winds while ice pellets bounced off its windshield. Airdrops are tricky at the best of times, but John always found it hard to keep his mind on the job because he wanted to gawk at the kaleidoscope of peaks and icefalls below. However, all sightseeing stopped abruptly after the third drop when the Skyhawk coughed and sputtered and then seized up. That was when Floyd banked the plane in an attempt to glide toward the distant airstrip at the mouth of the Machmell River. "It quit me in the worst place you could find if you looked all over BC," he recalled. Just after the third food parcel had been dropped, he noticed that the engine was running a little rough.

> I tried the magnetos then the carb heat and was just reducing throttle to see if that would help when there was a big bang and the engine stopped with such force I thought it would twist it out of the engine mounts. The prop was locked solid and it was very, very quiet with no place to go that I could think of. There was no use going east so I headed down the

canyon to the west and what I hoped might be the Machmell logging camp. I was still up at 10,000 feet, so when we cleared the glacier, we had quite a bit of altitude, and with the prop stopped, the plane seemed to be gliding real good. John in the back was real cool, which confirmed what I thought about mountain climbers (*that they are all nuts!*), and he wanted to know if I wanted him to throw out the rest of the gear. I told him not to throw anything out and to pile everything on the right side of the airplane then buckle himself tight behind me.

I had flown this guy quite a few times before into Waddington and other places where these nuts go. I was thinking, *We may need all the food for ourselves.* I didn't know where the canyon I was in would come out, but anyplace was better than where we were because below was big timber on 70 percent slopes except in the creeks, where the rocks looked like they were as big as houses. There was a twenty-mile-per-hour inflow so I found that if I put my right wing up against the rock cliff and held the airplane at eighty miles per hour, I was going up a thousand feet a minute.

After a long time I seen some logging roads on the steep hillsides that looked better than them big rocks, but not good enough to try yet. After about twenty minutes I came out at Rivers Inlet Camp [but] I was still over a thousand feet in the air. Not being used to the sea level air and with the prop stopped, I was S-turning to lose altitude and wasn't going to get down—so I did a 360-turn, which I was always told was a no-no. Anyway, I got lined up with the runway and still just about overshot, and was thinking, *Christ, after all this I'm going to run off the end of the runway!* But I got it stopped and heard this clanking sound. When we got out, there was a lot of valves and metal pieces laying on the ground under the engine.

John, recalling this flight later, said, "He's flown all his life—I don't think he's ever had a serious accident."

A few moments after they landed a logging crummy appeared from the shut-down camp. It was driven by Dago Walker, a local First Nations man who is the grandson of one of the chiefs of the Owikeno tribe; he was taking care of the camp while the full-time caretakers, Weldon and Penny Munro, were on holiday. "Hey," he called, "that plane of yours didn't sound too good when it was coming down the valley!" Dago collected his tools and helped Floyd take the engine apart to assess the damage. Meanwhile John, who was sitting in the crummy reflecting on his narrow escape, glanced up to see a big grizzly bear walk out of the bush, cross right in front of the truck and amble back into the bush again.

Once the cowling was off, Floyd radioed for his partner and a mechanic to fly out from Nimpo. An hour and a half later they arrived to look over the damage; apparently, "JNO" had "swallowed a valve that had jammed one cylinder and locked the engine up." This did not come entirely as a surprise to Floyd. After trading another plane for "JNO" in Vancouver a while earlier, he had stopped at Springhouse to have the mechanic there inspect it for commercial operation. When the mechanic saw the registration number, he said, "Oh, that's the one with the bad engine." Apparently that particular plane had a "throwaway engine, and after one cycle it was not to be used again." Floyd had not believed that it could be that bad, even though the mechanic had said, "That damned thing will quit you someday."

The partners arranged for the Cessna to sit on the logging camp's airfield for a few days and then flew home over the mountains to wait for the necessary parts to arrive. John was left to contemplate his dilemma. Months of planning had gone awry. Three food parcels had been dropped high on the Ha-Iltzuk Icefield, but to get up there, he needed to have the two remaining parcels placed between them and the logging camp. And without the plane that was impossible.

Dago and his girlfriend Vee invited John to stay with them while he reorganized his food and gear and made new plans. He was torn between two major objectives: one was to make the first ascent of Mount Willoughby—the mountain that he called "the apex of the whole range"—and the other was to climb Silverthrone Mountain and the high peaks on the Ha-Iltzuk Icefield that he had failed to reach on his stormbound trip in 1973. Finally he decided the mountain he most wanted to climb was Mount Willoughby (8,406 feet or 2,560 metres), a striking, broad peak with a pyramid-shaped summit. In 1964 two young geologists, Tony Ellis and Montry Laserre, had climbed all the satellite peaks around it while they were working for the federal government, collecting rock samples. Serendipitously, their work had taken them up one side and down the other of all the summits along their route, but Willoughby had escaped their efforts. They had attempted two routes, but due to lack of time they had not reached the peak. (Perhaps it had been a Friday afternoon.)

Willoughby is situated at the head of Ankitree Creek, which was at least a week's hike away from the logging camp and near the

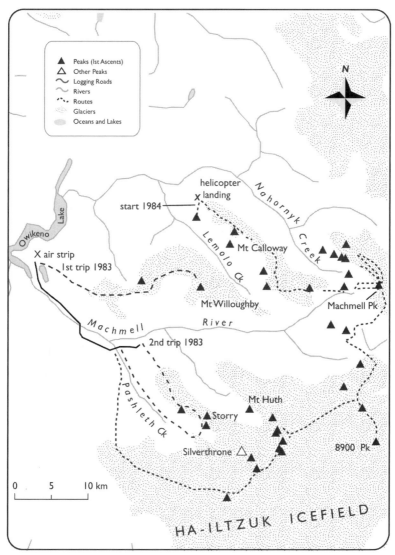

1983: Clarke's routes from the logging camp at Owikeno Lake to Mount Willoughby (first trip) and to Mount Storry (second trip). **1984:** Clarke and Baldwin's route around the headwaters of the Machmell River.

beginning of what was to have been John's traverse route. However, even though he chose it as his primary destination, he was unable to completely abandon the idea of doing the entire horseshoe traverse he had planned. As a result, he decided to start out carrying his skis so that, when he reached Willoughby, he would still have the option of continuing and completing the horseshoe.

> I really wanted to get to those high peaks on the icefield—there's an 8,900-footer [and] about thirty unclimbed peaks on the icefield. I wanted to get those. But I didn't know whether I could do the circle or not [because] I didn't know what the hell I could do with that little grub on the route. So what I decided to do was load up as if I was going to go on and do the whole horseshoe—as I was heading for Willoughby anyway.

At noon on August 10, Dago and Vee crammed John and all his gear into the crummy and drove him to the end of the Genesee Creek Road, which is barely 1,000 feet (300 metres) above sea level. (See page 129 for map.) It was still a long haul to Mount Willoughby. Genesee Creek is one of the many salmon-rich creeks that flow into Owikeno Lake, so the valley in which it lies is prime grizzly bear habitat. John set off up the logging slash staggering under the weight of his pack, his skis and two weeks' supply of food, and soon entered the muffled world of moss and big trees. He was just packing up through big standing timber when a black bear rushed at him. John later described the incident to his friend Elaine Johnston:

> It was only a small bear, about a year old—a couple of hundred pounds—and it was playful. It just looked at me like a dog that wanted to play ... It made a beeline straight for me and it was going to bowl me right over. [It had] no bad intentions or anything but it would have knocked me right off my feet. I was just ready to step aside [when] I made a big loud sound and it stopped right in front of me. Its nose was about two feet from my face. There was a tree right beside me and it just started to hug the tree and slap the trunk. And I was telling it to take off—go away and stuff. So it just walked off—but it hung around, it followed me. Then when it was walking away, it would turn around every once in a while and look at me. I kept packing up the ridge and

it followed me—hung around during supper while I was cooking. I wasn't able to sleep all night—as it hung around all night. Then in the morning it just wanders off—and I'm supposed to go packing after no sleep! I never saw it again.

Rain and lack of sleep kept John in his tent till noon, then he broke camp and continued upward through wet berry bushes. He paused at a tiny jewel of a lake at 2,800 feet (850 metres), where he noticed a snow-depth gauge nailed to a tree. However, there was no snow at that elevation so he could not put on his heavy skis. He continued upward until he reached the subalpine area at 3,800 feet (1,160 metres) and set up his second camp. He had barely made two miles that day. In his log he wrote: "Bugs incredible."

He endured another two days under the crushing weight of his pack and skis, although he would shuffle along on his skis when he came to the occasional snowfield. The bad weather continued. Views were smothered by cloud, often until late morning, so he was unable to see the beautiful Neechanz River down below, which was "a real untouched grizzly hide-out." High in the alpine, pikas called through the mists, and marmots whistled urgently across the valleys at their "new neighbour." A family of goats raced off as he donned crampons and headed up a small glacier to a pass at 6,300 feet (1,920 metres) where he was rewarded with views of Mount Waddington, Mount Bute and Silverthrone Mountain.

But the going was gruelling and the pace too slow, so after five arduous days John stashed the skis and skins and everything else he didn't need. Of course, this meant that he could only climb Willoughby and could not continue on his planned traverse route high above the Machmell River. "I was disappointed but sure loved the new, light pack!" Now he sped along the ridges, negotiating creeks, sodden snow "swamps" and crevasses. Later that day the wind was so severe he had to drop down to the 6,200-foot (1,890-metre) pass to find a sheltered spot for his tent (camp six)—but still the wind howled and black clouds pressed in. Once in the more protected lee side of the pass he dug a platform in the snow for his tent, while ravens, the sentinels of the high peaks, patrolled overhead. As he wrote in the *Canadian Alpine Journal*, "They spotted me, folded their wings and plummeted down for a look, landing on the rocks above. They watched while I worked away. I got everything inside [the tent] just as the rain started in earnest."

Icy rain pounded the tent all night. For the best part of the next two days John was tent-bound, and shrouded in the swirling mists he allowed his senses to become attuned to the surreal world outside: the plip-plop of water seeping from the crevasse behind the tent, the filtered calls of pikas, the tweeting of tiny birds as they passed through the col. His entertainment was the sound of a marmot's whistle in the wind. "Lentils with curried dumplings beat the boredom in the evening."

In the afternoon of day eight, as the clouds parted, John got his first glimpse of Mount Willoughby, a still distant but "fantastic" peak. When the sun appeared later, he dragged all his gear up to the col to dry out. "It really looks like I've got my weather—I only hope it's the long awaited good stretch." From here he could make out the highest points on Mount Willoughby that the young geologists Ellis and Laserre had reached back in 1964. The next morning, as affirmation of the cold clear weather, he found his boots were frozen solid as a block of wood. He thawed them over his stove while he made porridge and got ready to climb a snow-capped 7,300-foot (2,225-metre) peak that rose close to his route. He broke camp and eased his way up the heather ridge and followed the easy summit ridge. It had taken eleven weeks of perseverance to reach this first peak of the trip. He lingered on the summit, built a cairn and then descended to the glacier below and followed his lengthening shadow across the snow to set up camp seven in the 6,100-foot (1,860-metre) pass. "At sunset I bundled up, sat on the rocks with another bowl of lentils and dumplings and watched Willoughby and Silverthrone change colours. When I settled in for the night, the sky was still perfectly clear and a three-quarter moon came up."

He woke dismayed to hear rain "furiously bashing the tent" and then remembered he had left his boots "drying in the sun." He hastily retrieved them and retired to his inadequate sleeping bag to wait out the rain. By early afternoon it was just clear enough to travel. He packed up and sped across the flat snowfield to put up his eighth and final camp, close to the south ridge of Willoughby. It was still cloudy at 9:00 p.m. when he gobbled down another batch of lentils and dumplings. He was poised for the next day's summit bid.

On wakening at 5:30 the next morning, his first thought was "I definitely have to get a new sleeping bag; this one's a rag!" He was shivering and did not know if he had even slept. "I couldn't believe it was so damned cold till I looked out and saw it was clear. I was sure glad the boots were inside." He lit the stove to warm up, excited about finally tackling the big peak. It was a clear, crisp morning as he negotiated his way over ice and snow around the toe of the south ridge of Willoughby to gain the sun-warmed rocks higher up on the ridge. He used the huge boulders to protect himself from the fierce, icy wind as he ascended to 500 feet (150 metres) below the peak, where snow covered the ridge, and he turned toward the south ridge of the summit pyramid. At 8,406 feet (2,560 metres), the peak was an airy perch that fell away steeply in all directions. John recalled:

> It was a fantastic climb, [a] beautiful big mountain feel to it—you're above everything—I could see the whole icefield just sitting there; every peak on the icefield. All the ones I wanted—but I couldn't go any further than Willoughby round the circle.

He lingered on the summit for an hour, built a cairn, left a message and dreamed of his next journey. Nearly 2,000 feet (600 metres) below was the tiny dot of his tent. Now he had to turn around and head back to the logging camp in perfect weather, thinking all the time, "I should have kept going." His return journey was as swift as the outward one had been slow. The sun blazed down as he slithered around in the sun cups, swatted horseflies and wondered when the cool weather would return. Spectacular views across the Machmell River left him shaking his head in disbelief: "Kilippi Creek, and Mount Silverthrone remote, majestic and draped with ice . . . the best peak the Mundays ever climbed." Time after time his gaze was drawn to the icefield and the peaks he most wanted to climb—especially Mount Huth. He thought about his parcels of abandoned groceries on the icefield and wondered if he would ever reach those airdrops. That evening, he watched the changing sky:

A big orange full moon rose up over the southwest ridge of Silverthrone and as the peaks and glacier turned pink and mauve, the moon rolled like a ball up the edge of the ridge, perched on top of the peak for a minute before floating away into the sky.

As luck would have it, when John collected his stashed skis there was still just enough snow to make skiing possible. All went smoothly until he paused for a dip in the lake in the midst of a flowery meadow, then had to dance a jig all over the meadow to keep the ravenous horseflies at bay. The next morning after a breakfast of porridge and raisins left over from the previous night's supper, he escaped before the bugs stirred. He cruised along the high ridges with short grass and heather underfoot and found goat trails, grooved deeply into the soil, that served as a welcome highway. "The entire depression of Machmell valley, Owikeno Lake and Rivers Inlet was filled with cloud. Tight flocks of small birds let themselves be blown around in the warm breeze." A mere four days after leaving Willoughby, he thrashed his way down through windfalls to the logging road beside Genesee Creek. Stifling heat rose from the valley floor as he hiked the final stretch to the logging camp, tired, dirty and starving after a two-week diet of porridge and lentils. He got a warm welcome from Weldon and Penny Munro, the permanent caretakers, and their six kids, aged two to seventeen—five girls and one boy.

> The way they put me up was unbelievable—homemade bread, spaghetti and stew. I came staggering in off the logging road, just knackered. I've been eating raw oatmeal and lentils and sesame seeds, and [Penny] says, "Would you like some leftover spaghetti? I'll warm it up in the microwave."

The kids instantly recognized that John was "one of them" and had a great time playing with him. He even helped out with their "homework." Alone in the middle of the wilderness, the Munro kids learned by correspondence and each day went down to study in the vacant office of the logging camp. "They're just barrelling through the work—going way faster than they would if they were in school," John recalled.

For Penny and Weldon, who liked the solitude that wilderness brings, it was a good life: decent pay, grizzly bears in their backyard and unlimited fishing—part of daily life in the boarded-up logging camp. They showed John photos of 500- to 600-pound (230- to 270-kilogram) sows with cubs in their vegetable garden. "One sow took up their whole vegetable garden—this big fat bear and her two cubs."

John made himself at home in Dago and Vee's empty trailer with the luxury of unlimited scalding hot water, and he washed everything—clothes, tent and sleeping bag—and left them in the sun to dry. The trailer was also equipped with a fifty-channel TV, and when TV was available, John showed no restraint, no matter how trashy the program. He recalled the abysmal movies: "just terrible ... and those beach movies, terrible trash. I watched them though! Lots of them. I think I permanently hurt my eyes!"

But he did not relax for long as he was already planning the next leg of his trip. His three food parcels were sitting on the icefield, it was only late August and there had been no snow in the past week, even as high up as 10,000 feet (3,000 metres), so climbing conditions were ideal. He was anxious to head up to the Ha-Iltzuk Icefield before "winter" set in, and always the eternal optimist, he had his route all planned.

> I'd figured out a pretty good line to get me right onto the icefield; a gorgeous route, just beautiful ... There's a ridge going straight into the alpine, and when you get into the alpine it just skylines, no drops—little minor ups and downs. At 7,000 feet the alpine goes straight into the icefield. When you get close to the icefield, there's a 2,000- to 3,000-foot drop and back up the other side and then you're in the icefield. [By way of comparison, the famous Grouse Grind on the North Shore has a 2,800-foot or 850-metre change in elevation.] It was nothing. Maybe five to six days in.

Weldon Munro drove John fifteen miles (twenty-four kilometres) up the logging road to a point upstream from where Pashleth Creek flows into the Machmell River. (See page 129 for map showing the route

Ice Worms

The first ice worm species (*Mesenchytraeus solifugus*) was discovered in 1887 on the Muir Glacier in Alaska. Since then they have been found on glaciers in British Columbia, Alaska, Washington and Oregon. The name *solifugus* is Latin for "sun-avoiding," as ice worms come to the surface of glaciers in the evening and morning, looking like little dark brown to black cotton threads, and retreat beneath the ice before dawn. They are about one centimetre long by one millimetre wide. One study on the Suiattle Glacier in the North Cascades estimated that over seven billion ice worms lived on that glacier alone—more than the entire human population of the Earth!

of John's second trip in 1983.) John's pack was much lighter this time, and he soon made his way through the steep slash and bluffs and sped up the grassy ridges to camp in the subalpine meadows. He recalled that it was "like putting the tent up on the front lawn at home ... I couldn't take my eyes off the glaciers across the valley—I could have spent a week in this camp." From there he peered through "clouds and swarms of insects" for a glimpse of Mount Willoughby to the northwest. In the morning "high clouds created a pale, flat light on the glaciers higher up. The huge nameless glaciers on the other side of Pashleth Valley were incredible." The next day he continued up the ridge to camp on snow south of Mount Storry in a "high, gloomy ice basin ... as dense, wind-driven, black clouds quickly consumed the peaks." At midnight it started to rain. The date was September 1. He wrote: "I looked at my watch in the dark—it was 12:05 a.m. Five minutes into September and the rain! Heavy, heavy rain—couldn't sleep for the noise of it. Then it started blowing."

John's gamble had not paid off. Winter had arrived early in the Coast Mountains. For the next six days it stormed, and beyond the thin walls of his tent loomed a black-grey world of cold and damp. Hours of deafening wind and rain were interspersed with absolute silence when the wind briefly abated. He wrote: "A glance outside showed me what this precious little tent is protecting me from and the idea that hot meals are possible here seems almost hilarious." But mealtimes were his only highlight, punctuating the otherwise timeless days. "My appetite must have been good this evening, as I gulped down a lentil, flour and oatmeal soup with chicken soup stock and bran!" That night he picked an ice worm out of his soup—it had stowed away in one of the snowballs he'd brought into the tent to make water.

John was worried about his food parcels high on the icefield, but his optimism still held:

At least I'm glad it isn't snowing as the first fall will make the glaciers impassable, [but] I'm worried that it may be snowing on the icefield. I know it's not snowing on the [food] drops, though, as they are the same elevation as here. Really hoping I reach one of the drops as I want to climb the three highest peaks on the icefield. Fabulous peaks everywhere around here. Just need the damn weather.

During a lull in the storm he raced to climb Mount Storry, which was on his to-do list. On his return he hastily moved camp, but he was not wearing crampons and he sprained his little finger when he slipped while ascending smooth glare ice. The new campsite (camp four) was a vast improvement as it was on a heather bench near a little stream, and he was in heaven for a full five minutes. But driven back to the tent again by another wave of the storm, he wrote: "A single 'eh' from a pika failed to cheer me as I pictured the airdrops being consumed by the glaciers on which they were resting."

The storm continued with renewed vigour, and now fine snow began to "sandblast" the tent and formed high-walled wind cirques around it, making it tricky for John to unzip the tent door to toss out his pee-filled plastic sandwich bags. As John commented in an interview for *Climbing* magazine, "These things are great. They are light and cheap and you don't have to go outside to pee in a storm. When it clears, you just go out and pick them off like so many decorations on a tree."

He consumed more food on storm days than on packing days because he would get into long sessions of "recreational eating" for something to do. When his supplies began running low, he reviewed his situation. He wrote in his journal:

Dreams of pancakes and tea. There are still heather, flowers and grass under the tent floor. Can hardly see over the big drift in front of the door. 5 p.m.—wind dropped—still snowing heavily. Then followed the first complete lull in 21 hours. It's bright. This might be it. Bright for a full 30 seconds! When I get home, I can have all the raisins I want in my porridge; and milk too! Love to see some horseflies and mosquitoes now.

As the storm continued, he wrote:

> Can hardly open the door to throw out the pee bags. Fine powder blown under the tent last night but it's just sitting there now doing no harm. Tent flapping constantly and fine ice crystals are making a sifting sound as in a sandstorm. One p.m. Had a few mouthfuls of sesame seeds. Wondering what my table manners will be like for the first week at home. I'm going to have to go out eventually as tent walls are pressing in and straining the seams.

But still he refused to give up his plan to climb those remote peaks. It simply was not an option. The hardship for him was not about going without food, enduring an inadequate sleeping bag or carrying a crushingly heavy pack. The real hardship was to forego climbing the peaks he had set his heart on. It was only when he was down to his last crumbs of food that he had to abandon his quest to reach the icefield. He dug his way out of the buried tent and staggered through deep snow to the Pashleth Glacier 2,500 feet (760 metres) below. His route was strewn with broken logs from avalanches, and by noon he had only reached the glacier's snout, where the headwaters of Pashleth Creek emerged.

> The river went over a falls inside the glacier just before it charged out of the cavern at the snout. It was a roaring streaming place and surface streams poured over the open mouth of the cavern.

Throughout the day there was not a moment for him to relax: loose boulders and quicksand interspersed with large eskers—long, sinuous ridges of layered sand and gravel—made travel all the more dangerous, and his progress was further slowed by being forced up a steep-sided valley. When he paused briefly to nibble a few sesame seeds and dry out the tent fly beside a little creek, he noticed big bear footprints in the sand. Then, in his haste to get into the big timbers to make a fire, he fell up to his chest into icy Pashleth Creek. When he finally reached a grove of ancient spruce, he made camp and dried out in front of a hot fire.

Two days later he hit the logging road and after a fifteen-mile (twenty-four kilometre) trek he hobbled into the logging camp at dusk to "another heart-warming welcome from the Munro family. I knew I was going back to the Silverthrone country soon, but I sure wasn't going to think about that now."

John Clarke gazes at the peaks floating above the cloud-filled valley, 1996. PHOTO BY JOHN BALDWIN

10

The Two Johns

We both thought exactly the same way. I don't think we ever had a question about the route. It was always just obvious to both of us.

—John Baldwin

Reading about John Clarke's solo expeditions in the *Canadian Alpine Journal*, you might conclude: "This guy is nuts, he's a recluse, a social misfit. How can he be out there alone for weeks on end, year after year, in some of the remotest, wildest country on earth?" Yet it was not by choice that he usually went alone. In the 1960s and 1970s most mountaineers were not interested in the relatively low, remote peaks of the Coast Mountains. They were not "fashionable" like the Himalayas and did not provide enough kudos. In addition, most climbers could not take the time off work for extended trips, and they worried about the unpredictable nature of such expeditions—the notoriously bad weather, failed routes, dwindling food supplies. But most importantly they had no interest in doing long exploratory traverses from horizon to horizon—a hallmark of Clarke's expeditions.

It wasn't until the early 1980s that John Clarke discovered John Baldwin, a young mountaineer who had grown up in North Vancouver and been fascinated with every aspect of the Coast Mountains. In 1974, as an engineering student at UBC, Baldwin had joined the Varsity Outdoor Club (VOC). He read articles in the *Canadian Alpine Journal* about trips that others had done and was gripped by Clarke's accounts of his solo traverses. When the VOC invited Clarke to speak at a banquet in 1977, his talk and slide show of his adventures in the Coast Mountains left a lasting impression on Baldwin. "There were incredible pictures from places in the middle of nowhere—and he went by himself—and there was all this talk afterwards: 'Did he have a pole across his pack for the crevasses?' You know—this sort of myth."

Baldwin soon embarked on longer and more ambitious trips with his friends. Then, intrigued by the huge icefields that dominate the Coast Mountains, he led four friends on a 140-mile (220-kilometre) traverse on skis from Ape Lake, southeast of Bella Coola, across the Monarch and Ha-Iltzuk Icefields to exit at the head of Knight Inlet. Clarke read about this mammoth ski traverse in 1983's *Canadian Alpine Journal* with incredulity: "Wow! You mean someone else is actually doing this stuff? I've got to meet this person." They arranged to meet in the basement of the United Church at Larch and Second Avenue where Baldwin was to give a slide show to the Alpine Club.

Baldwin, thrilled to see Phyllis Mundy at his show, didn't recognize the guy she was chatting with. "Not a mountaineering type at all," he recalls, "but like an accountant, with his short cropped hair, large owlish eye glasses and serious demeanour." As Baldwin approached, the "accountant" spun around. "John Clarke," he said to Baldwin. "Great to meet you." And he extended a powerful hand. Baldwin was flabbergasted. He had formed this vague image of Clarke, a larger-than-life, eccentric, wild man with a huge head of long, hippy-length white hair. But as soon as the two Johns started talking, each instantly recognized a kindred soul.

It was as if a thread ran between them that had always been there. They never felt the need to explain why they were drawn to the mountains. "It was a given. *He* felt like that—*I* felt like that," says Baldwin. "Why wouldn't the whole world feel like that? When John was talking to me, it was totally obvious. He didn't have to explain *why*." After that instant recognition of kindred souls, the Johns never looked back. They would explore the Coast Mountains together.

If you were to enter a room where Baldwin and Clarke were present, Clarke would always steal the limelight. He was gregarious, fun-loving, whacky, the constant comedian and deliverer of self-deprecating jokes or one-liners, with his face-splitting smile never far away. He'd come bounding into a room with a "Woop-woop" or "Pssssst" or "Did you miss me?" Bum and legs would lead his long, lean upper body—well honed but not muscle bound—as he swung through the door with uncoiled, palpable energy and optimism out of control, his head crowned by his white mountain-goat shock of hair and seasonal white beard, a gleam in his blue eyes, set off by crinkle lines from years of laughter. His large, heavy-rimmed eyeglasses sat squarely on his somewhat aquiline nose, secured by an elastic band at the back. There was no hint of machismo here, though one of his characteristic poses was a parody of Charles Atlas, the world's most perfectly developed human specimen.

His film-star good looks were balanced by large ears (a barometer of his body temperature, as they could generate their own sunrise glow at times). Those famous size-eleven feet, seemingly large on his moderate 6-foot (1.8-metre) frame, were also sensitive feet that required taping to protect them on long trips; agile feet that could scale loose, exposed rock faces even when encased in heavy leather boots. Perhaps it was because of his expressive exterior that it was rare to get a glimpse of the private, inner man. He didn't reveal his inner self easily or to many, but his facial expression and body language

John Baldwin prepares lunch on the rocks during his 1986 traverse with John Clarke around the headwaters of the Tahumming River. PHOTO BY JOHN CLARKE, COURTESY OF ANNETTE CLARKE

reflected his emotions. Like the mountains, if you accepted him on his own terms, the rewards were great. Try to contain him and he would simply walk away.

John Baldwin, twelve years younger than Clarke, was quiet and reserved with an air of complete innocence about him, and still has that quality about him. Even now in his mid-fifties he is youthful: dark hair, dark eyes and angular features. Of slight build, he is lean, flexible and muscular—hard core. Everything about him is well proportioned, but he has the appetite of a horse. And underneath his quiet exterior he is playful, curious, smart, full of fun and excels in whatever role he takes on: father, mountaineer, skier, handyman, cook, writer, cartographer, log house builder. On his feet Baldwin is less articulate than Clarke was (but who isn't!). However, his writing is full of poetry and wonder and reveals his deep, enduring love of the Coast Mountains.

Their first trip together was an ambitious ski expedition in the spring of 1984 to the epicentre of remoteness in British Columbia—the sprawling Ha-Iltzuk Icefield, which includes the massive Klinaklini and Silverthrone Glaciers. (See map, page 149.) Both men had been rebuffed in their previous attempts to reach the high peaks in this area, and "with a craving for more punishment" they were going back. Then just weeks before their departure Clarke reinjured his back. Baldwin showed up at his house one day to assess the damage and found Clarke crooked over like a windblown tree. "It'll be fine," Clarke said, laughing. His punishment had arrived a little earlier than usual, that's all.

After days of hectic preparation the Johns relished the long drive to Bluff Lake in the heart of the Chilcotin Mountains, home of the King family ranch and Whitesaddle Air. Mike King, an experienced helicopter pilot, would fly them to the start of their month-long traverse after dropping off their parcels of food at predetermined spots along their route. Although spring had already arrived in Vancouver in mid-April 1984, winter was far from over in the mountains. As if to get them in the mood, it snowed in Cache Creek as Baldwin's yellow Beetle trundled through. That night they camped in the Kings' cow pasture alongside the helicopter hangar, ready for an early morning start. They awoke to a brilliant, crisp Chilcotin morning with cows ambling nearby. "To put up with the fearsome storms in the Coast Range, it really helps to have a cow-like attitude to life," remarked Clarke as they crammed their gear into the helicopter.

Soon the helicopter was spiralling away across a world of wild, cold beauty. "Beyond, Mount Whitesaddle crowned the scene. The giddy excitement of the flight took hold as we shot across the wintry Pantheon Range," Clarke wrote. But there was little time for sightseeing. This flight would provide them with a one-time snapshot of crucial information while they placed their food drops. The helicopter, dwarfed by the immensity of the peaks and sprawling glaciers, landed three times at predetermined sites, so that the Johns could extricate the food parcels from the bowels of the noisy machine amid a vortex of swirling snow and set them down with unswerving faith that they would find them again in a few weeks' time. And as if to placate the mountain gods, they marked each of their boxes with a tall wand because it is always winter in the Coast Mountains. (See map, page 129.)

The final time Mike set the helicopter down, he delivered Clarke and Baldwin into their pristine world of snow and ice. The umbilical cord cut, they stood dazed and bemused on a snow hump in their bright new world as the helicopter became a receding speck in the blue sky. Then came deafening silence. This marked the first

The Tahumming-Klite divide in summer, circa 1980s. PHOTO BY JOHN CLARKE, COURTESY OF ANNETTE CLARKE

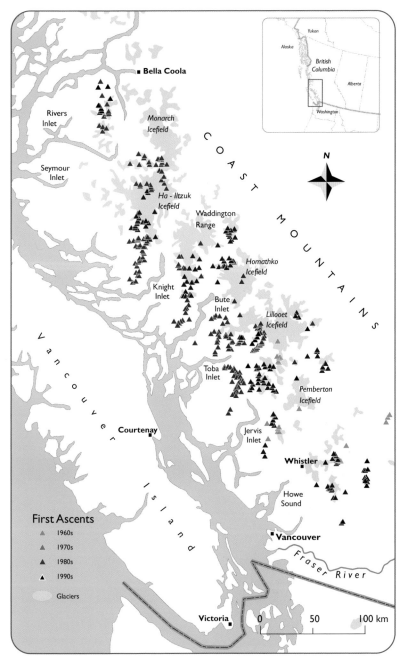

John Clarke's first recorded ascents of peaks (in the Coast Mountains) located between Vancouver and Bella Coola. Peaks are colour-coded to indicate when Clarke first climbed them (green-1960s, blue-1970s, red-1980s, black-1990s). Clarke also made roughly 180 first ascents of peaks located north of Bella Coola and south of Dease Lake, which are not shown here.

John Clarke has no problem in finding a flat place to camp on the Silverthrone Glacier, 1973.
PHOTO BY JOHN CLARKE, COURTESY OF ANNETTE CLARKE

John Clarke in his element, 1992. PHOTO BY STEVE SHEFFIELD

John Clarke and John Baldwin called this striking peak "The Apple Spire" because it is located at the head of the Apple River, 1978. PHOTO BY JOHN CLARKE, COURTESY OF ANNETTE CLARKE

Next to his and John Baldwin's camp above Burke Channel, John Clarke wanders along the rocky slabs, peering through the mist below, 1989. PHOTO BY JOHN BALDWIN

John Clarke pauses to enjoy the flowers in an alpine meadow during his traverse with John Baldwin from Burke Channel to Chuckwalla River, 1989. PHOTO BY JOHN BALDWIN

The beauty of the alpine is reflected in this tiny tarn, 1993. PHOTO BY JOHN CLARKE, COURTESY OF ANNETTE CLARKE

Randy Stoltmann is first to reach a summit in the Kitimat Ranges, 1994. PHOTO BY JOHN CLARKE, COURTESY OF ANNETTE CLARKE

In 1998 John Clarke guided Witness volunteers from Princess Louisa Inlet to Sims Creek. Here he approaches Mount John Clarke (then known as Sun Peak). PHOTO BY GREG MAURER

PREVIOUS PHOTO: There is no divide between peaks, forests and ocean in the Coast Mountains. Here a happy Bill Noble leaps from rock to rock during the filming of *Child of the Wind*, 1994. PHOTO BY JOHN CLARKE, COURTESY OF ANNETTE CLARKE seconds of twelve seamless years of climbing together—perhaps the closest partnership in the history of exploratory mountaineering in the Coast Mountains. "We stood bewildered on a snow hummock at the beginning of a long journey." Over the next twenty-nine days they would travel 110 miles (180 kilometres), make twenty-four first ascents, watch ten feet of fresh snow fall and be tent-bound for ten days—ample time to get to know one another. As the days unfolded, they realized just how well they related and how much fun it was. "We got along instantly," said Baldwin. "We were totally on the same wavelength and wanted to do the same things. It was fantastic."

The sun shone the day that Clarke and Baldwin stood together on the summit of Mount Calloway, the first of hundreds of peaks to come. Clarke gazed at the north face of Mount Willoughby—"something I'd wanted to see since climbing it from Owikeno Lake eight months before," he recalled, when he had been forced to retrace his steps. He'd been longing to get a glimpse of the wild side of Willoughby and now there it was.

Days melded as they glided onwards, climbed peaks, gawked at the fantastical scenery and read the constantly changing form of the clouds. Below them lay the Machmell Valley, "a dark corridor where no lights ever twinkle, that sliced into the snowfields to frame their

John Clarke prepares supper for John Baldwin. PHOTO BY JOHN BALDWIN

flat light in somber hues." Beyond stretched the deep blue of Owikeno Lake. As in dreams when the dreamer steps effortlessly from past to future, so time ceases to exist for mountain climbers. With one glance they see the peaks ahead and those behind, future and previous friends. The journeys of Clarke and Baldwin were like that.

Each evening they camped and, appetites out of control, brewed up steaming pots of soup and downed huge cups of rice and lentils. Occasionally Baldwin's youth and enthusiasm outdid Clarke's. They had planned to climb Machmell, but a heavy snowfall had "completely dampened" Clarke's ambition: "I wanted to get inside [the tent]. Not so with John! He was grinning through his frozen beard and pointing up! We started. It was a wild climb as six inches of snow fell in under two hours."

They also shared moments of hilarity and unbridled joy: one crisp morning after a storm had passed through they unzipped the tent to find a glorious slope of fresh fluffy snow stretching out below them. Baldwin, an accomplished skier, gobbled down porridge, strapped on his skis and linked graceful turns down the perfect 900-foot (270-metre) slope. Clarke followed "murdering the hill with kick turns." A photo of their tracks shows Baldwin's perfect linked turns and then another set of zigzags, which look like an uphill track. Then it becomes apparent that the zigzag track doesn't continue to the bottom and somebody (Clarke) is skiing *down*. Baldwin explained:

> John could do good stem Christies and he was solid on his feet. He could edge on ice and all that kind of stuff, but he wasn't a keen skier. He used skis on trips even later in the summer—June and so on—when the snow is not that great anyways. [But] he wouldn't ski all winter. Back then there was no such thing as telemark skiing lessons.

Clarke later explained why he never learned to ski:

> Right from the start it was just a religion to stay out of trouble … I was terrified by anything that would prevent me from not being able to go out and explore—if [I] get hurt, make it above the waist. Please! So consequently I never learned how to ski. I probably hold a world ski record—the longest time on skis without learning to ski.

Ski tracks in the powder: John Baldwin's perfect linked-turns; Clarke's zigzags across the slope look like uphill tracks! Ski traverse around the headwaters of the Machmell River, 1984.
PHOTO BY JOHN BALDWIN

The two men also shared moments of fear: one afternoon while skiing down from an abortive attempt to climb a peak, the whole slope beneath Clarke collapsed into a bergschrund. He fell about twenty feet, and when he stopped he was buried up to his chest in soft snow. He brushed the snow off his face and squinted up out of the abyss to see Baldwin peering down from above. "I was standing right there—he could have got hurt," says Baldwin. "He was sticking out from the waist up and could move around a bit, [but] I had to shovel him out and get his skis out." Another time when the weather turned sullen and savage, a sudden gust of wind knocked Clarke right off his feet. He reported: "In three minutes of absolute terror, I was blown fast and wildly out of control off-route down a gentle icy slope."

After nearly two weeks out, the two Johns' excitement rose as they closed in on the big peaks that they had both wanted to climb for so long, and the main focus of their expedition. They panted as they skied up the final slope, so eager were they to reach the pass and the view. Suddenly they were there, staring across at the 8,900 foot (2,700-metre) peak—the highest and most distant of them all. Clarke wrote:

I must have looked at it on the map and in photos a hundred times and now we would be on it in two hours. First we circled around to the east face of the 8,700-foot peak where a steep snow chute led up to the summit ridge. The enclosing walls of this gully were thickly crusted with gleaming ice feathers, the royal blue sky above them completing an unearthly scene. From the summit we floated in a vast confusion of peaks and in the north Mount Monarch rose out of a woolly ring of cloud. In the south the snout of the great [Klinaklini] glacier was 25 miles away, and beyond it a band of cloud wrapped itself at half-height across Klinaklini Peak. In front of the Pantheon Range tongues of cloud oozed up and poured like waterfalls through broad snow passes and dissolved. We clambered down to the skis and schussed over to the 8,900-foot peak, the last 2,000 feet of which was climbed in an hour, so eager were we to see the view from its top. The Ha-Iltzuk snowfield was at our feet. The view toward Mount Silverthrone showed a land overwhelmed with snow. It almost seemed the many upper branches of the glacier could hardly carry it away fast enough … The ski back to camp ended a day that was a gift to us from these elusive mountains.

Clarke relished every moment of Baldwin's companionship. They actually enjoyed a couple of days of complete "bedrest" forced upon them by an early storm. "There was a full moon up there somewhere that we never saw," Clarke wrote in his journal that evening. "John started reading *How Green is My Valley* while I patched gaiters and greased boots … Shrimp curry and rice capped an afternoon of loafing in manky socks and underwear." And later when another unrelenting storm rolled in, Clarke could not believe his good fortune at having Baldwin as a partner. "It is a marvel for me to be out in the Coast Mountains with someone who can actually enjoy these storms." When snow and wind made it next to impossible to keep the stove alight, he worked for two hours to produce two bowls of porridge. "After lunch and a snooze a new drift had plugged the door and outside there was no sign of the six-foot hole dug that morning." But neither man showed any hint of frustration or boredom, accepting that they were here on the mountains' terms, and Clarke wrote: "We must have discussed the complete reform of the whole world during this storm!"

The last food drop had been attacked by a hungry wolverine, but fortunately the animal "had chewed through one of the boxes but stopped on reaching a soup packet he didn't like." The unsettled weather and tent-bound days cancelled any further climbing after their successful climb of Mount Huth, a peak that had eluded Clarke for so long. "I thought about my nineteen days tent-bound trying to reach this spot. I couldn't have been more satisfied." At this point,

> the shrinking food bags resulted in a wild dash to get close to the Machmell River ... Leaving our snow and cloud world, we skied into

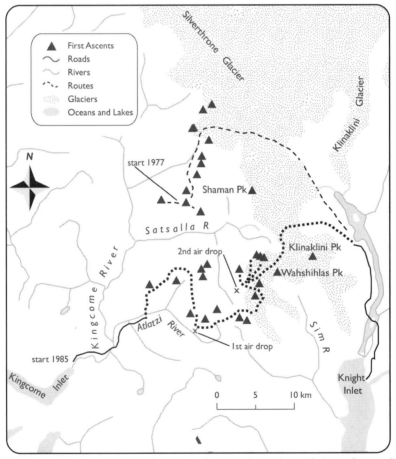

- - - - Clarke and Sproule's route from (6,700 feet, six miles northeast of) the confluence of the Kingcome and Satsalla Rivers to Knight Inlet—1977.
• • • • • Clarke and Baldwin's route from Kingcome Inlet to Knight Inlet—1984.

The village of Kingcome, or Gwa'yi village, lies about two and a half miles (four kilometres) from the head of Kingcome Inlet on the shore of the Kingcome River. It was a summer home for the Tsawataineuk First Nation for centuries, but today is the year-round home for about 150 people. The only access is via boat or plane.

Ernest Halliday arrived in Kingcome Inlet in 1893 and, along with his brothers, pre-empted land at the mouth of the inlet where the First Nations women used to gather food. He developed a 900-acre (360-hectare) homestead on the fertile delta land and built a modest house where he lived with his wife, Lilly, and three children for more than twenty years.

In 1912 the Powell River Company discovered the rich forests of the Kingcome Valley and set up a large, well-equipped logging camp. The Hallidays benefitted from the proximity of the camp, which provided a convenient market for their beef and dairy products. But more importantly, several married women and their children arrived with the company, and a school was soon opened, which ran until about 1940.

The Halliday family moved to a spacious new ten-room house nearer the head of the inlet in 1918. Other settlers came to Kingcome over the years, but eventually most of them died or moved away until only the Hallidays remained. Ernest Halliday and his sons worked the ranch until Lilly died in 1955. Reginald, the oldest son, then took over, but as changing technology and job opportunities drained the coast of its people, it became increasingly difficult to sell the ranch's produce. Ernest Halliday's grandson, Alan, reluctantly abandoned the family home in December 1986.

the woods where the smells of spring hung between the trees … Marmots played on the spring snow and grouse hooted in the pockets of trees … We camped on cupped snow and listened to the unfamiliar sound of wind through the forest.

The next day, after many hours' march along the logging road, Clarke and Baldwin poked their "baked faces into the cookhouse of the logging camp."

After their first exhilarating journey around the headwaters of the Machmell River, Clarke and Baldwin pulled out the maps, pencilled in routes and prepared themselves for another season of exploration. Like a couple of racehorses fresh out of the starting gate, there was no holding them back. Having completed their three-week ski traverse of the vast expanse of the Homathko Icefield in the spring, in July they turned their attention to an area that fascinated them simply because there was absolutely nothing known about it. This was the mysterious terrain between Kingcome River and Knight Inlet, 180 miles (290 kilometres) northwest of Vancouver.

In July, Baldwin and Clarke arrived at Port McNeill on the northeastern coast of Vancouver Island. They disgorged the contents of Baldwin's yellow Volkswagen into a nearby Beaver aircraft, "JFQ," which was equipped with both floats and wheels. For this flight, pilot Jack Scholefield had replaced the three-passenger rear bench seat with a single seat and removed the round camera hatch in the aft belly of the plane so that the food parcels could be dropped through it. Scholefield knew that the "fair load of equipment and foodstuffs" plus his two passengers was going to put a strain on the plane's ability to gain altitude, and he was also aware that the glacier on which his passengers wished to make their food drops was "indicated in bold print as 8,050 feet" on their map.

Clarke's description of the flight indicates that neither he nor Baldwin was aware of Scholefield's anxiety:

> Beyond Malcolm Island the expanse of Queen Charlotte Strait gave way to the labyrinth of inlets and lagoons on Broughton Island. Then came the chalky grey glacial waters of Wakeman Sound and Kingcome Inlet.

Scholefield would later tell writer Sean Rossiter, the author of *The Immortal Beaver: The World's Greatest Bush Plane*:

> My estimated time-to-climb worked out pretty good, and we arrived at the corner of Wakeman and Kingcome at about five grand [5,000 feet] and still climbing. I felt a little sorry for the engine along the route and had leveled off several times to permit those hard-working cylinders to cool off ... The aircraft was [now] showing signs of reluctance to climb, and the time to gain the next 3,000 feet was greater than the first leg. I persevered in pampering the engine to that height, where it became essentially tapped out, with the throttle to the wall ... [After the first airdrop] I turned around and yelled to my passengers over the rush of air from the hatch: "I won't go lower than 300 feet above the ice and we will climb out of the descent before reaching the bottom of the glacier ... "
>
> It is hard to say who was the more reluctant to climb back and do it again—me or the airplane—but JFQ did what was asked of her once more. She handled it like a marshmallow. I was terrified. JFQ wanted to go home and so did I. We just barely got out of that canyon. I never heard from those climbers again. But I've got a hunch they're still up there on that glacier, digging like maniacs, trying to find their lunch.

Clarke wrote only that:

> We placed two air drops on high snowfields along the intended route, the second from 1000 feet. We wondered if the food pulverized on impact. The plane then floated down through thick summer air to the shimmering green floor of the Kingcome valley and landed on the river beside the logging camp.

Baldwin would later explain:

> [The pilot was] really nervous and wouldn't come closer than 800 feet or so above the snow. It was hopeless [so] we just chucked [the packages] out. Surprisingly they weren't too bad—once you're more than a little ways up, they're going as fast as they're going to go anyways. The best thing is if they have a bit of forward speed and then the drops can roll rather than impact.

The arrival of two mountaineers at the Kingcome logging camp was a novelty. Clarke wrote:

> The camp was dead quiet with the loggers on the early shift because of the heat. [But] we found four fellows who were quite surprised at the appearance of a couple of tourists. After a chat and some advice about the merits of "coming to this place on your holidays," they told us to find Sam, the super. We tracked him down and he immediately gave us bunks and invited us to supper and breakfast. After supper we all sat out by the river, drinking, swatting flies, and talking about the surrounding country. Al Halliday dropped by and we had a grand talk about the ranch at the inlet head, which has been in his family since 1893. There was a big island in the river just across from us, and John and I stared in disbelief when a 2,000-pound black bull came out of the forest and ambled down to the river's edge. Al told us he had sold 25 cattle five years ago and the new owner put them on the island. They've been surviving wild and fighting off grizzlies and wolves ever since.

Next morning, Sam dropped them off near the end of the logging road where they forded a creek to gain access to the steep bushy route from the valley. Clarke wrote: "The valley fog burnt off, revealing powerful sun-bathed walls above the main forks of the Atlatzi [River]. The first air drop was only two miles behind these forks but our winding route would take us four days to get there." Once they were in the alpine, all sense of time faded as they "fiddled away the afternoon with laundry, spaghetti, putting pine tar on boots, and just gazing around."

After they retrieved their first food parcels—which, given their 1,000-foot (300-metre) plunge, had suffered amazingly little—Clarke noted: "We repacked burst bags and wiped up butter that had spread through everything on impact." There is a Zenlike quality to the rest of his account, as he and Baldwin continued their journey from Kingcome to Knight Inlet almost as if they were floating through the exquisite, magical land, so in tune with the wilderness that there was time to enjoy and reflect on every detail:

> It rained during the night but in the morning we were in the clear, sandwiched between two layers of cloud. The ranch, the logging camp, and the Indian village lay somewhere under a fleecy sea of fog ... After [we started] up the ridge, a raven circled and croaked then lazily spiralled down till the musical beat of his wings was audible. John returned the call—the bird floated close by, did a few rolls, and started a long glide toward the inlet. It was beautiful travelling over the next few bumplets—I had a bath in a tarn on the ridge crest. Then we dropped down to an easy level granite ridge where a heavy drenching mist closed in."

Later, when they stumbled on the most wildly beautiful campsite imaginable, Clarke wrote:

> No amount of map and air photo studying prepares you for many of the surprise beauty spots. Clouds poured over the ridge tops to the south and dissolved among the little shelf glaciers on the face below. The heather around the tent was in bloom and beyond it the glacier snout was broken and blue. Waterfalls completed the scene of absolute isolation.

On the first 8,100-foot (2,400-metre) summit of their three-summit day they built a cairn, relaxed in the sunshine and played their

John Clarke would seldom pass up an opportunity to swim in a mountain tarn, 1987. PHOTO BY JOHN BALDWIN

favourite game of identifying specific mountains in the maze of distant peaks. The perfect day was rounded off with "hot food, a golden sunset and oblivion." And Baldwin mused:

> There is a tremendous feeling that comes on a trip like this, with so much to see and so much to do and all of it unknown. Have you ever taken a dog on a hike? Well, imagine yourself as the dog. As a dog you don't worry about the weather or the route; the details of the hike are not concerns of yours; your only concern is to swim in every tarn, climb over every rock and experience every moment of this mysterious hike that you are being taken on. But who, you might ask, is taking you on the hike? The mountains! Who else lays out the route? Who else decides when it is sunny and when it rains? And who else do you sidle up to panting, hot and exhausted?

Days later, from a "tiny meadow perched on a promontory on a ridge," they enjoyed their last high view of the traverse before they descended to camp in the meadows below. Clarke wrote:

> Lazy morning. Porridge. Tired. Very tired. Mosquitoes staring through the mesh. They know you have to come outside eventually. Down into

the shadowy timber. Blueberry bushes stirring in a breeze. Lower down we ran into orange tape on the trees, then a loud air horn. It was a surprised group of timber cruisers who thought they'd heard a bear. After the drive down the valley we scouted around, looking for the cookhouse to put the reputation of logging camps for hospitality to the test.

It was a given that Clarke and Baldwin would continue to do trips together as they had the same passion for exploration, and although they differed somewhat in their objectives, it was of no consequence. Clarke could never bypass a mountain that had never been climbed before, whereas Baldwin has always kept going back because of his innate curiosity and the desire to explore every aspect of the wilderness, even peaks that have been climbed before. For him it is the sheer joy of discovery, of being out there. It's not as if there is usually any sign that someone has been there before—except perhaps a summit cairn holding a damp note from John Clarke with "Greetings from the 20th century" written on it. Baldwin acknowledges their differences:

> John definitely had more of a thing for peaks than I did, but I love climbing mountains. Whenever you're out there, it's fun just to climb mountains. But he [Clarke] wanted to get certain peaks, and if he didn't get them, he'd come back—plan another trip. He had that framework, but once he was out there he loved every part of it.

Mountaineering is not for the faint of heart; it brings out the best and the worst in people, especially when out in the wilderness for weeks at a time. One aspect of it that invariably produces discussion, arguments and even friction is the choice of route. In this respect Clarke and Baldwin were exceptional—they had very different personalities yet never disagreed over which way they should go. "We both thought exactly the same way," Baldwin recalled. "I don't think we ever had a question about the route. It was always just obvious to both of us."

The 1986 Clarke–Baldwin season was exceptional—in fact, it was one of their best. By then they had their turnaround time down to an art: within two or three days they could restock with groceries from Famous Foods, wash up, pack up and head out again, so that year they strung together a series of trips with only a few days between them. They had also realized the fantastic nature of their long traverses from inlet to inlet—during their long partnership, they would complete more than fifteen of them—because each trip was not just about the peaks anymore but had evolved into a rich, fascinating, beautifully intricate journey in its own right.

That year they crafted what they both later agreed was their most magical trip of all: a traverse around the headwaters of the Tahumming River. As John described it: "Every day for three weeks you're clobbered with the best. I'm not kidding, every minute of every day for three weeks, you're hit. All the time. Around every corner." Their route has been described as one of the most outstanding alpine traverses in Canada, and it is one of their few trips to have been repeated. The traverse was the creative offspring of two earlier aborted ventures: the first was a foiled attempt to encircle Klite Peak and continue along the east side of the Tahumming River, and the second occurred in July 1984, when they failed to reach the west side of the river after John Clarke fell ill. This happened shortly after an exhilarating climb of an impressive 7,907-foot (2,410-metre) rock spire they later named the Orford Tower. The ascent was notable first because it was Clarke's first lead, despite his years of experience and agility on rock, and second because Baldwin pointed out that the pitches were "at least 5.6 class!" Clarke thought about that fact for a moment and then said, "Maybe not all those Class 3 peaks I've climbed over the years *were* Class 3s!"

But the euphoria of that climb faded when, nearing their camp, Clarke developed chest pains and a rapid heart rate. The next morning, after a restless night, he was no better, so Baldwin hiked out to find help. After a gruelling thrash through the bush he returned by helicopter late the same day accompanied by the Comox Search and Rescue team. Clarke was whisked off to St. Joseph's Hospital in Comox for a thorough examination, but they didn't find anything really amiss.

So it was from these leftover scraps that their famed skyline traverse encircling the drainage of the Tahumming River evolved in 1986. Their sixteen-day journey proved idyllic despite the sweaty climbs, the inevitable bugs and the tiredness at the end of long days.

They were more than compensated by the unusually cooperative weather, the endless magical moments—peaks floating above the clouds like lost continents; dark, horn-shaped summits rearing out of glistening icefalls; crevasses split open like stars; a glimpse into the narrow gorge of Headwall Creek, where a falling rock takes twelve full seconds to hit anything; thousands of feet of polished rock; frigid pools connected by warm granite slabs; snoozing goats; and far below, the sun-struck braid of the Tahumming River snaking its way toward the infinite blue of Toba Inlet.

But the unimaginable surprise of the entire traverse was the glorious reward at the end. Eight days after splashing across the icy headwaters of the Tahumming River, a wild and desolate place ringed by 3,000-foot (900-metre) cliffs, Clarke and Baldwin broke out onto a long promontory of solid rock jutting into the valley west of the Tahumming River. Bare slabs of granite swept down until engulfed by trees 1,000 feet (300 metres) below. The gently curving top of the whaleback was sprinkled with stunted trees and tarns of every imaginable size and depth. Baldwin and Clarke experienced heaven that day, scampering around, swimming in the deep tarns, whooping and hollering, and looking back from whence they had come. Two days later they reluctantly dropped down to the mouth of the Tahumming River via old logging roads flanked by wild raspberries and thimbleberries in order to end up exactly where they had started two and a half weeks earlier.

In July 1989 North Bentinck Arm was the starting point for Clarke and Baldwin's traverse (map, page 159). This was the place where, almost exactly 196 years before, the great Canadian explorer Alexander Mackenzie had finally reached the waters of the Pacific Ocean. There, the mountains cling to the outer edge of the range and rear up from the ocean's depths like mythical sea creatures, constantly lashed with moisture from the sky above and the ocean below. The upside of all this moisture is revealed in a proliferation of cascading waterfalls and lush vegetation. The sprawling alpine meadows on the south side of the modest peaks are a rich contrast to the glaciers and icefalls on their north side. The terrain is complex and appears to be almost an island as the serpentine waters of Burke Channel, South Bentinck Arm, Rivers Inlet and Owikeno

Lake encircle and isolate that part of the Coast Mountains from the higher, central area of the range.

On Mackenzie's journey to the Pacific he had travelled from the headwaters of the Fraser River along established Native trade routes or "grease trails," so-called because they used them when trading eulachon oil with their inland neighbours, and arrived at Bella Coola, the territory of the Nuxalk Nation—or the Bella Coola people, as they were also known—on July 20, 1793. His attempts to reach the open ocean were foiled by the warriors of the hostile Heiltsuk Nation, and he went no further. He commemorated the now historic spot on Dean Channel with his name and the date. It is now the site of Sir Alexander Mackenzie Provincial Park.

John Clarke's account covered in great detail the events that unfolded over the first week of their journey, after they'd been dropped off by float plane on the beach at Jacobsen Bay in Burke Channel.

The stove won't work!

What do you mean?

I mean the stove won't work!

John Baldwin and I had driven from Vancouver to Bella Coola, placed three airdrops along our intended traverse route, and were now trying to cook supper on the rocky headland where a floatplane had dropped us a few hours earlier. Scanning the horizon we concluded that these northern waters sure are quiet. Our first day of the simple life!

We had always been intrigued by the 1800-square kilometre area southwest of Bella Coola, bounded on the north by South Bentinck Arm and Burke Channel and on the south by the deep east-west trench of Owikeno Lake east of Rivers Inlet. Hours of map gazing at home resulted in the decision to traverse the whole area from north to south. Despite a high point of only 2,256 metres, the region has many challenging peaks and glaciers that come down below 1,200 metres.

The day before, we had driven down from the Chilcotin Plateau to the Bella Coola Valley, boxed up the air drop parcels at the Hagensborg Store and headed for the airport. The first pilot we spoke to sounded cautious about doing airdrops, but then miraculously he was replaced by a more sporting one! We took the seats out of the Beaver, loaded it up, and flew down our intended traverse route.

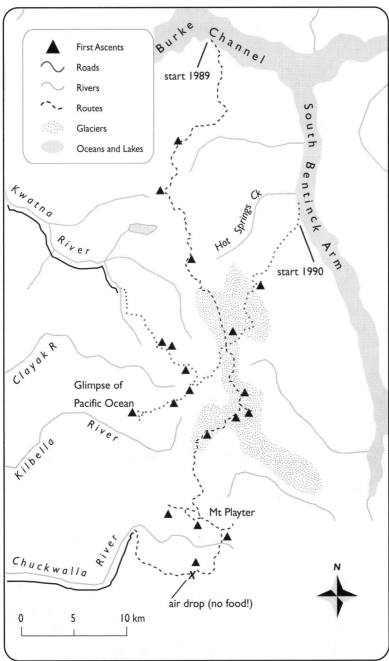

Clarke and Baldwin's routes from Jacobsen Bay in Burke Channel to Chuckwalla River (1989) and from South Bentinck Arm to the Kwatna River (1990).

Once again we realized that no amount of staring at maps prepares you for what you'll see when you get there. Dozens of new peaks, snowfields, icefalls and impossibly green valleys paraded by the windows of the airplane. Our pilot was fantastic, coming in low and slow over all three drop sites—one of them with the floats cruising only 30 feet over the sun cups! Then the Beaver glided down into the thick ocean air, landed on the choppy sea, and deposited us, our packs, and our useless stove on the beach of Jacobsen Bay.

In the morning we hung around, wondering what to do, listening for planes and gaping out into the ocean. Then a Beaver flew right over our heads! No chance of hailing him. We were just about to light a fire out on the tip of the point when a logging barge, looking like a Normandy invasion craft, showed up and came ashore in answer to our hysterical arm-waving.

We decided that I would go with them to get a new stove somehow, and John would wait on the point. "You might want to put some pants on, though," said Rein, the skipper. "There's a woman on board." I looked down … a pair of high-mileage long johns weren't going to do for a trip anywhere. Even in Bella Coola they're not quite that casual! I

Peaks, glaciers and alpine meadows are juxtaposed. Here John Clarke crosses the heather meadows on the divide between the Clayak and Kilbella Rivers, 1990. PHOTO BY JOHN BALDWIN

grabbed a pair of shorts, jumped aboard and waved John goodbye, still with no clear idea where the boat was going.

It didn't matter. I needed to get to Bella Coola somehow to either buy a new stove there or send to Vancouver for one. Meanwhile John would be patiently waiting my return. When the boat got a couple of miles from shore, he looked pretty lonely standing on the tip of the point still looking out to sea. On board, I discovered that the crew was going down to Kwatna Bay; unloading a pickup truck there, going fishing for the rest of the day and then heading for Bella Coola that night.

There was nothing to do but relax, enjoy the cruise to Kwatna Bay, fish for rock cod and wonder how John would react when we came back past him on the way to Bella Coola. Well … we picked him up on the way and we all arrived in Bella Coola in time to phone Vancouver to have a replacement stove sent up by plane the next day.

In the morning, after breakfast of porridge and rock cod, we picked up the stove at Bella Coola airport and chartered a plane back to Jacobsen Bay. The pilot had to veer the plane just before touching down in the bay to avoid three whales that appeared in his path.

In the morning we followed deer trails through easy timber to a

This mountain goat stares at Clarke as if to say "My, what a poor design!", 1989. PHOTO BY JOHN CLARKE, COURTESY OF ANNETTE CLARKE

small lake, had a swim and pushed on up to timber line, camping at 1,400 metres. Next day, the climb up south of camp revealed the best inlet views we had ever seen. The deep forest-clad trench of Burke Channel lay at out feet with the winding "S" curves of Labouchere Channel stretching north off into the Kitimat Ranges. Views came and went along with sun and cloud, and we camped on a grassy knoll on the crest of the ridge, a mile south of peak 6532.

Next morning we scrambled up the 6,200-foot peaklet near camp, came away with no view but had a grand glissade back to camp. We hiked all day in fog and rain—never enough fog to stop us or enough rain to completely soak us. From the col at the head of Oak Beck Creek we could see down into the wonderful greens of the valley. We climbed up and camped in a sheltered nook on the ridge. Rain pounded down like mad all night.

The morning was still cloudy but we packed up and pulled on our slickers, which were now becoming permanent ridge-walking garb. Apparently people on the North Coast put their rain gear on in the morning and then look out to see what the day will be like! We were enjoying the blustery weather though, as the sudden rain squalls always stopped before we got too wet. During a short stop to tape up my foot, a hummingbird hovered for half a minute right in front of my face.

With so much wind and rain we didn't go for the airdrop parcels that were probably only 50 yards away in the fog. We put up the tent and fiddled away the rest of the day and night drinking soup and listening to the rain lashing the fly sheet. Breakfast consisted of a half-ration of porridge and half a shrimp dinner—definitely time to go "grocery shopping".

It's a strange feeling tramping around on a foggy névé searching for airdrop parcels, looking for any darks spot in the white void. The first box we found had blown open on impact and dinners, oatmeal and paperbacks were strewn on the snow. There was no water damage though, except for one waterlogged loaf of bread which we fried later to make it somewhat edible. We spent the rest of the afternoon in the tent, re-bagging everything, stuffing ourselves and listening to a new rainstorm drumming on the roof and walls.

Baldwin recalled that:

John was never going to complain because it was raining or we were bushwhacking or whatever happened—that was part of the trip. Some people get grumpy, they get tired, they want to go home, they don't like the conditions, but John is just constant all the time, cracking jokes, having a good time.

When the rain stopped the next morning, the two men packed up, headed south and "sauntered" along the divide for the next eight days. From Clarke's account it was idyllic: they climbed peaks, hobnobbed with goats, collected wool, swam in dozens of tarns, some icy cold. As they closed in on their final food drop, located on a small névé between the heads of the Inziana and Chuckwalla Rivers, the Johns experienced the usual delicious anticipation of a new pile of groceries. But when the drop site came into view Clarke said, "John, shouldn't there be only *four* parcels? It looks like there are about *twelve* down there!" Clarke wrote:

> Grizzlies had ravaged the boxes so thoroughly that not a crumb of food remained, and even our spare clothing was ripped to shreds. I have a tuna tin as a souvenir at home that was chewed flat as a coin. Grizzly droppings dotted the whole area, tooth marks punctured thick paperback books and even the fuel tins were chewed up and empty.

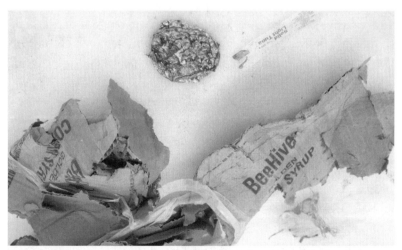

Remains of the food drop ravaged by grizzly bears. Note the punctured and flattened tuna can. PHOTO BY JOHN CLARKE, COURTESY OF ANNETTE CLARKE

They began studying their map to find the shortest way out.

The following summer, having been bewitched by this ruggedly magical land with its total isolation, Clarke and Baldwin were drawn back. This time they planned to cross from east to west along the divide between the Clayak and Kilbella Rivers (map, page 159). The float plane dropped them off on South Bentinck Arm near the mouth of Hot Springs Creek, and they headed up to the ridge through scruffy wind-bent trees. Once in the alpine, they followed the ridges toward the headwaters of the Clayak River. Baldwin wrote:

> It is only when you are looking that the goats and tarns, the glaciers and meadows, the mist and the fog can seep into your bones. And only then can you realize just how deeply you are connected to these endless miles of nameless mountains in the rain.

Days later Clarke and Baldwin noticed a narrow ridge snaking southwest to separate the upper reaches of the Clayak from the Kilbella River. Intrigued, they deviated from their planned route to investigate the divide and climb the two peaklets joined by a small snowfield. Even the sweltering midsummer heat did nothing to dampen the thrill of that day: the easy ramble along the undulating ridge crest with massive slabs and sheer gunmetal cliffs on one side, icefalls cascading into oblivion on the other. And then the moment of magic as they stood on the furthest summit of the two peaklets.

> We found ourselves looking out, not to more mountains on the horizon, but instead to the Pacific Ocean dimly visible through the afternoon haze. We almost felt that this ridge was the culmination of our years of climbing.

For Clarke and Baldwin, the mountains were in control of their lives and directed their movements. At the time their journeying seemed haphazard, but in the end they could see that they were being drawn inexorably to the northwest as they pieced together the jigsaw puzzle of the Coast Mountains going from inlet to inlet—Jervis to Toba to Bute to Knight to Kingcome to Burke Channel—from horizon to horizon, from peak to peak. Then came this day, when they looked out from the high ridge and realized they could go no further west. There were no more mountains and, like Alexander Mackenzie, they had finally glimpsed the endless blue of the Pacific Ocean.

11

Reflections

I'd look back at him in this white outfit with this white beard—
more Merlin than Merlin. And what he was doing was magic.
　　　　　　　　　　　　　　　　　　　　—Peter Croft

In his published accounts John Clarke consistently downplayed
the true nature of his explorations and provided few or no details
of the hazards he encountered along the way. He never thought
of himself as a rock climber, and he invariably underestimated his
abilities and overestimated the ability of others to follow in his footsteps through this rugged land. In addition, because he was so profi-
cient at living out in the wilderness, he tended not to see how arduous a mountaineering traverse might be for the uninitiated. This was
the case for David Boyd, environmental lawyer and author, and my
friend and neighbour on Pender Island.

David first met John in 1984 and was inspired by his "amazing
slide shows with photographs that made you laugh and cry—mostly laugh. John was so exuberant about his experiences that you just
couldn't help but want to go and follow in his footsteps." John's description of Racoon Pass sealed the deal for David. "I had to see that
spot and there was no other way to get to it than the long journey."

David was not a mountaineer but he enjoyed backpacking
and had grown up in the foothills of the Rockies. He arranged to
meet John and get his advice on the traverse from Meager Creek to
Princess Louisa Inlet. "I remember sitting in a café just off Cordova
Street in Gastown. John had his maps out and I said, 'Look, I've done

backpacking trips but, … he goes, 'Don't worry! Of all the Coast Mountain traverses, this one is *dead* easy!'" Reassured, David talked his brother Sandy, a park guide, into accompanying him.

David bought the necessary maps and John dropped by to show them the route. John pencilled in a line across two topographical maps. "Right," he said, "this is the Stoltmann Traverse." David told me:

I don't know how many times I cursed John Clarke during that three-week trip because it was anything but *dead easy*! We parked at the end of the Forest Service Road near Meager Creek Hot Springs and strapped on our backpacks. It was the heaviest thing I've ever carried—probably sixty pounds. Within the first hour we reached Devastator Creek … It was unbelievable. The water was pounding down. John had said, "Well, just look around—you'll find a log that you can get across on." There was nothing in the immediate vicinity, so I said, "Okay, look, Sandy, why don't you go that way for half an hour and I'll go this way for half an hour and we'll leave our packs here. I'm sure one of us will find something. So I went walking upstream and my brother went downstream. The water was coming down so fast and furious that there was nothing that would stand in its way. There was nothing to get across on. So I walked my period of time and came back, really hoping that my brother had found something. Meanwhile, Sandy was having the same thoughts. There was nothing we could do but peel off our boots, put them around our necks and walk across this incredibly cold, just-melted-that-morning, glacial water that was moving really fast. As soon as we got into the creek, within seconds our feet went numb. So we are walking on rocks that we can't even feel because our feet are completely numb and carrying these heavy packs above our heads—we stood beside each other for balance. It was terrible. It probably only took thirty seconds but it seemed like about an hour. It was really scary and cold and we were super happy to get to the other side of it.

So that was the first time I was cursing John Clarke. Then, later that day we came to a section of the thickest devil's club that I've ever had to whack my way through to get up [into the alpine]. It was wet and slippery and just brutal. I kept falling down. I had these hiking boots that were not up to snuff, and I kept slipping. At the time I was running ultra marathons—Iron Man triathlons—and those were a piece of cake compared to the first day of this traverse. We finally got up onto this snow-field where we immediately pitched our tent in sheer exhaustion.

I sat in the tent that night thinking, *Okay, that's day one of a twenty-one-day trip.* And I actually sat there and cried, thinking, *I don't think I can do this.* It was so frigging hard. I'd never been on a glacier before. I've got a harness in my backpack I've never worn, and I've got crampons in my backpack and I've never worn crampons before. I just sat there crying and cursing John Clarke. Then my brother remarked, "You know what, David? If we turn around, we have to go back across that creek." So we kept going, and from there on it got better—for the most part.

However, two weeks into their three-week traverse David and Sandy were unable to locate their second food drop.

The thing that actually saved our bacon was another one of John's tips: "Instead of carrying the extra weight of a tripod," he advised us, "just take a bag of dried lentils. You can put that on any surface and nest your camera in it." So for four days mostly what we ate was watery lentil–cream of mushroom soup.

"When we came back we had dinner with John and told him the stories," David told me, rumbling with laughter, "and we all had a good laugh together." Then he added:

To be fair, John viewed the world through his own eyes and so this traverse, compared to some of the other trips he'd done, was relatively easy. But for someone who'd never done a traverse, *easy* was the last word in the *Oxford English Dictionary* that you'd apply to that trip ... But doing a trip like that gives you the confidence to do anything else in the future ... John enabled people to do things that they wouldn't have thought possible ... That's a pretty special gift to be able to give that to people.

John Clarke's two trips to the Klattasine Range in 1973 and 1974 had left him with a craving to climb a spectacular granite tower northeast of Mount Klattasine in the northwest corner of the Homathko Icefield. However, since he didn't think of himself as a rock climber, he waited for someone else to climb it. "All through the years I've been looking at faces and buttresses [like that one] and thinking, 'Wow! I wonder when anyone will come and climb that.'" Finally he decided to have a go himself and looked around for a partner to lead the way up the tower. One young man immediately came to mind: Peter Croft, who had made an indelible mark on the Squamish climbing scene. He had grown up on Vancouver Island and started rock climbing as a teen, having been inspired by the book *I Chose to Climb*, written by world-famous mountaineer Chris Bonington. There had been no doubt in Peter's mind about his chosen career—rock climbing—and around 1976 he started climbing on the Stawamus Chief, the 2,303-foot (702-metre) granite dome on the southern outskirts of the town of Squamish, BC. His unbounded enthusiasm would find him climbing long after his partners had packed up for the day. He would climb up and then climb back down just for the sheer joy of it, and he developed an extraordinary ability to climb unroped to astonishingly high standards. Peter's free climb of the University Wall on the Chief in 1982 established him as Canada's leading rock climber. Today, he is hailed as one of North America's greatest living climbers. In 1988 he moved to California where he could climb to his heart's content free of the West Coast drizzle, but two years earlier he spent one memorable week climbing with John in the Klattasine Range. In a conversation in 2009 he recalled:

> John called me out of the blue because he'd spotted this really cool-looking rock spire and figured he needed somebody who knew how to use the gear and stuff like that. Before I actually met him, I thought he was some kind of a social outcast to spend so much time alone ... I thought he was going to be so weird, but on the phone he sounded really charming, and once I met him, [I discovered that] sun or rain or whatever was going on, he was a really good mountain companion, fun to chat with, cook up dinner, and go climbing all day long ... I think the very best people I've been with in the mountains are the ones who, no matter what's going on, they realize they can't control everything and they enjoy just being there.

John was incredibly good with people—just bubbling with enthusiasm. Everything that I had thought about him was pretty much the opposite of what he was. He was extremely careful when he went into the backcountry. I went on a very short trip with him—only a week long—for him that was a really short trip. For me it was a really long trip. He just seemed so at ease that he never seemed at a loss to me.

Because of time constraints, they flew in to the Klattasine Range and camped in a gentle rocky basin to the west of the peak. Next day they ascended the tower with Peter leading across the final airy traverse to put them on the peak. John wrote: "If you want to climb a remote peak and need someone to lead a short 5.8 traverse, then Peter is definitely the man to have along!" That evening they moved camp to prepare for their five-day walk out. In his account John describes himself as the "mule" and Peter as the "acrobat." As Peter recalled it, this was far from the truth:

Because so much of the climbing John did was exploratory, he really had no idea how good a climber he was. For instance, he'd done tons of climbing that was fifth class climbing, but on the tower he was completely surprised when I said it was high fifth class. He thought it was class three because he'd done lots of other climbing on other mountains that was probably around that grade. He just didn't think it was very hard. It was one of those things [that he told himself]: "If I can do it—it can't be that hard."

John Clarke ascends this rock face in fine style despite his heavy mountaineering boots, 1986. PHOTO BY JOHN BALDWIN

The day after climbing the tower they crossed the crevasse-riven Jewakwa Glacier in a complete whiteout. Peter recalled that:

We couldn't see anything—no floor, no ceiling. It's drizzling and it was really hard to tell which direction we should go. So John starts directing me with the compass. I'm walking straight ahead in front of him. There is nothing to see. I might as well be walking with my eyes closed. So he's walking behind me with the compass, keeping me on a line. He's dressed in his white cotton anorak with this pointy hood and these white cotton pants and he's got this white beard. So I'd be walking forward, and every once in a while I needed to give my eyes a rest, to have something I could actually focus on. I'd look back at him in this white outfit with this white beard—more Merlin than Merlin. And what he was doing *was* magic. I knew how to use a map and compass but not like that. I would get worried that we'd get lost. We've only got a certain amount of food, but he was really positive and at the same time he had really kind of old-fashioned gear. Finally when we got to the other side of this glacier, we were exactly where he was aiming us.

John's own daily summary read: "The mule and the acrobat left a long line of tracks across the foggy Jewakwa Glacier to a camp at 2,000 metres, a mile northwest of Pelorus Peak."

Two days later they gained the crest of the main massif of Mount Heakamie. For thirteen hours, in swirling clouds and drizzle, they made their way along the slippery knife-edged ridge, the rope still in the pack. They were having the time of their lives! "A wonderful traverse," John recalled. "Once in a while a hole in the clouds would reveal the terrible beauty of the icefalls buried in the depths of the Heakamie Glacier thousands of feet below." The drizzle persisted and inevitably John's sodden cotton long johns crept toward his knees. Unfazed, he removed them. Peter, laughing, described what followed:

He's got these little white underwear and these white legs poking out of them, and he's going for these wild manoeuvres over this huge abyss. Every once in a while I had to stop on a ledge and watch and just laugh! It looked so ridiculous—his big boots, huge pack, [and he is] bridging, jamming and mantling in the rain thousands of feet above the glacier; his white legs sticking out of his briefs like mushroom stems.

Two days later they were enjoying the warm hospitality of the logging camp, "stuffing their faces with real food":

> I'd never been with anybody who really had reached that level of being able to travel in bad conditions and deal with whatever came up. From my point of view—from the whole climbing perspective—John was the greatest exploratory mountaineer certainly in the Coast Range. And as far as I can tell, in his lifetime he was the most prolific and important exploratory mountaineer ... that I know of anywhere, not just in western Canada or just in Canada ... and that wasn't for a certain season, like the summer of '86. It was year after year; going back again and again and again.

Climber Don Serl, the author of *The Waddington Guide* (2003), met John Clarke at a slide show in the late seventies and was impressed by this legendary yet modest guy whose life was inseparable from the Coast Mountains. However, although the two men were both avid Coast Mountains climbers, they weren't motivated by the same challenges and ambitions—Don being more of a technical climber who sought out the bigger peaks and dramatic routes. It wasn't until the summer of 1988 that they set out together to climb the southeast buttress of remote Klite Peak. They never even reached the base of that climb, though, as they were marooned for days in their little camp among the rocks due to remorseless rain. Don became frustrated but John was unperturbed. Don reported:

> He doesn't care. That's the most impressive thing. It doesn't matter to him very much. He just goes out to live in the mountains. He was just the best at that. If a mountaineer is a person who has the ability to live in the mountains, John was the best mountaineer of any of us. He just settled right in, and when the mountain said it was time to go climb something, he would climb something, and when the mountain said "not doing that today," he just went into neutral and didn't get fussed by it. He just enjoyed it anyway. He was living the way he wanted to live and in the place he wanted to live.

Mountaineer and writer Chic Scott remarked that:

There probably isn't anybody in the world [like John]. Most mountaineers are drawn to striking spectacular peaks and difficult lines on peaks. They are also drawn to things that get them some fame and notoriety. Although climbers talk about being modest, they are essentially egotists and they do like to be special and recognized. I can't think of anybody in the mountaineering world off-hand who is like John ... [He] is really, really unique.

Glenn Woodsworth doesn't agree with Scott's appraisal of the average climber as "drawn to things that get them some fame and notoriety," nor does he feel they are "essentially egotists"; instead, he says they are generally "pushing some inner personal boundaries." However, he does agree that John Clarke was unique among climbers. And Peter Croft, recalling his week in the mountains with John Clarke in 1986, said, "John seemed almost like someone out of a different age as far as his approach to the mountains and what he was doing—like Eric Shipton." During the 1930s Shipton (1907–77) was a key member of four expeditions to Mount Everest. A proponent of self-reliant and simple travel, he was perturbed by vast, cumbersome expeditions and instead lived simply for months at a time in some of the remotest, most inaccessible regions in the world. Like Clarke, his real passion was exploration rather than the ascent of a mountain for the sake of standing on the summit, and in 1937 he was drawn to an 1,800-square-mile (4,700-square-kilometre) area of mountainous territory in the Karakoram simply because it was marked on his map as "Unexplored." His book, *Blank on the Map,* describes his expedition to the Shaksgam area of the Karakoram Mountains—the highest concentration of 23,000- to 26,000-foot (7,000- to 8,000-metre) peaks in the world—just north of K2.

Shipton's book was one of John's favourites—probably because his fundamental approach to exploration was similar to Shipton's. Their affinity for remote, unexplored regions completely outweighed their desire to climb mountains that might provide them with fame and kudos. Of course, there was the thrill of standing on an unclimbed peak, but there was an equal thrill in exploring unknown territory. Both men were humble in their achievements and did not seek attention from the outside world. When out in the wilds for weeks at a time, they appreciated the sense of timelessness, of becoming one with their surroundings, and valued the simplicity with which they lived. As Shipton writes in *A Blank on the Map*:

> How satisfying it is to be travelling with such simplicity. I lay watching the constellations swing across the sky. Did I sleep that night—or was I caught up for a moment into the ceaseless rhythm of space?

Compare that to Clarke's words:

> You're completely focused on the landscape and you're just floating in that landscape in kind of a dream state. You get really hooked on that.

But for both men even wilderness had its limits, and in time they missed the company of friends—especially women. As Shipton put it: "In spite of my love of wild, remote places, I am not very good at coping with long periods of isolation … I am, in fact, a gregarious creature and crave the company of my fellow men—and of women." And Clarke: "This is day 35. We are anxious for it to clear up as we would like to get out to the Skeena, have some fresh vegetables, and see some WOMEN!"

Clarke and Shipton also shared charm, and intense blue eyes— they were both loved by many women

The ridges, peaks and valleys of the Coast Mountains shaped Clarke's destiny and formed the backbone of his life. By accepting the mountains on their own terms he crafted an approach to exploration that defied classification. As is clear from the observations of his friends and fellow alpinists, Clarke was unique.

12

Family Matters

My main mission in life is to make you laugh.
—John Clarke

n Bill Noble's award-winning video documentary *Child of the Wind*, John Clarke commented on his personal life, and how it was affected by his dedication to mountaineering:

> The result of all this tramping around the Coast Range has put quite a few awkward gaps in my employment resumé. I remember sitting in a restaurant listening to somebody in the booth next to me and he was in an awful state because he had a three-month gap in his employment resumé and thought this was a terrible problem. And I was kind of sitting there smiling to myself. I'd have to say that over the years I've got no regrets about it. Other things that I've left—except with women [and] I shake my head once in a while—but I always walk away from it. Sometimes it's very hard to do. [But] there's a lot of women out there that I'm keeping very happy by not being married to them.

For years John Clarke's life as a mountaineer far outweighed his desire to settle down and have a family. He loved women, but every time a relationship looked as if it would interfere with his season of exploration, he would take off. "Anything that I saw coming towards me that was going to get in the way of climbing," John would tell me, "I blew out of the water before it even got near me."

His relationship with Theresa Lammers is a case in point. They met in Vancouver in the spring of 1969 when he was giving a slide show in the hall across the street from Holy Rosary Cathedral, where she volunteered. His show and talk were about the street people of the Downtown Eastside and she was also working with the poor. "He just poured out his heart, and of course I thought he was the most wonderful thing in the world." She soon discovered that they also shared a love for the mountains; she had grown up in Keremeos in the narrow Similkameen Valley.

Years later Theresa recalled the times she and John would visit her hard-working parents at the family home and how he charmed them. One night her mother washed his clothes and, seeing there were no pockets in his pants, stayed up late to sew two into his tatty jeans. Next morning John pulled on his pants, put his hands in his pockets, pulled off his pants and examined them closely: "Oh! They *are* my pants!" He couldn't believe that someone would stay up to sew pockets into his jeans.

In August 1969 Theresa left for a year in Europe but her love affair with John resumed when she returned. They would go hiking to places like Golden Ears and Singing Pass, but they never did any extended mountaineering trips together. And even though he would be gone for five or more months, she tolerated his absence and supported his passion. "I thought what he was doing was wonderful and I really admired him." They talked about getting married, having children and where they might live, but after several years she realized what she was really up against.

> His first love was mountain climbing. He would say: "Okay, I'll be over at two o'clock." Then I would wait and wait and he would come at six o'clock or seven o'clock because he would start looking at his air photos and his maps and he would just completely forget about what we had planned to do. But of course, he was just so, so charming that you had to let these things go.

One day, heartbroken, Theresa told him, "It's not going to work. You can't have two loves. You can't be married to mountains and married to a woman. It's just not going to work because neither one would fare well." They split up in the fall of 1972.

And that was how most of John's relationships ended. When I

> -NOTES-
> OH MY GOD, I COMPLETELY FORGOT TO HAVE CHILDREN!
> get new pair MEC white thin long johns
> dried green lentils
> black beans better
> canned sockeye good.
> don't do long lying around - move a bit!
> make good head sun gear.

One of John Clarke's famous to-do lists: "Oh my god—I completely forgot to have children!" heads this one, circa 1990s. PHOTO COURTESY OF CATHALEEN CLARKE

was researching for this book, though, I came across a telling note in John's neat script. It headed one of the many lists that he made. In capital letters he had printed: "OH MY GOD, I COMPLETELY FORGOT TO HAVE CHILDREN!" Beneath these words his list continued: "get new pair MEC white thin long johns, dried green lentils, black beans better, canned sockeye good," etc. He was, of course, being his usual comic self by putting his note about children right above his need for long johns and canned sockeye, but to anyone who knew him, it was obvious that he adored kids. And it was small wonder that kids adored him because he would pull out every stop in his repertoire to keep them amused. He had no nephews or nieces to play with and be an uncle to, so he gravitated toward other people's children. He had several families he regularly dropped in on, but when he visited friends who had kids, they all accepted that he would spend much more time with their children than he would with them. He would barely get over the threshold before the kids were in a frenzy of excitement, immediately sensing that this guy was fun. He would play hide-and-seek, act goofy and wind them up, and always seemed surprised if the kids got out of control and had a total meltdown.

Love at first sight: John Clarke with baby Sarah McAuliffe, Vancouver 1981. PHOTO BY JOHN MCAULIFFE

John's relationship with his

friends' children left a lasting and indelible mark on their lives. His close friend Jamie Sproule moved to Vancouver Island in the 1970s and bought a house a mile (two kilometres) outside the historic coal mining/hippie town of Cumberland, where he lived with his wife, Gwyn, and two daughters, Flora and Annabelle. Flora simply doesn't remember a time before John as he was always part of the Sproule family, and one crisp winter's day in 2009 she entertained me with her vivid memories of the times he visited their home. He would arrive in the driveway in his beat-up grey Volkswagen Rabbit with a screen projector hanging out the back because he often tied his visits with them in with bookings to give slide shows at community venues. She remembers him as being quite a bit younger than her parents, but he was, in fact, five years older than her father. John's secret weapon was his huge affinity for kids and an uncanny gift for blending in with them, chameleon-like, so that they simply recognized him as one of their own, and age didn't come into it. He never talked down to kids, and he gave them his undivided attention and made them feel special. "He was one of our more favourite people," Flora said, "because he was so crazy and energetic and funny. He always put on an act. I don't remember him ever being very serious—maybe when he was giving his slide shows—but the way he talked, he was always kind of breathy, kind of like a young kid. He was always so excited about everything." Flora took a photo out of her purse to show me. It was of John peering into the girls' dollhouse—a short-sighted, absent-minded professor, tugging at his glasses. A total ham.

First thing in the morning the girls would rush into the guest room where John was sleeping, jump on his bed and get him up to play or go for a walk or a hike. "He devoted most of his attention to us," Flora recalled. "I don't remember playing any specific games. It was just that he would do whatever *we* wanted to do. If we wanted to play dolls or games, he'd go along with it ... He never got boring or businesslike, you know? He never seemed to get tired of playing with us either. He had such terrific energy." John would share stories of his adventures: how he'd been stuck in his tent for ten days during a storm, how a bear or ravens had eaten his food, the thrill of exploration, of standing on an unclimbed summit, the sheer beauty of the Coast Mountains. "We always knew that there was somebody up there," Flora said. "Every time

Left to right: Flora, Jamie and Annabelle Sproule and their dog enjoy a rest during an outing with John Clarke, 1994. PHOTO BY GWYN SPROULE

we looked at the Coast Mountains from Mount Washington, we knew that he had been up in those giant peaks and that he was strong enough and could carry all his gear and live in the wilderness." They appreciated how he lived in the moment, and always seemed happy despite, or because of, his unconventional lifestyle.

> It definitely inspired me to spend lots of time outdoors. My parents were already inclined to that, but I think that having people like John in our lives made us, as kids, really excited about all our family camping trips. We never wanted to do anything other than that. My parents didn't have a lot of money and every spring we'd sit down and decide what trips we wanted to do, and having people like John around made it seem more normal ... We were perfectly happy going on canoeing and backpacking trips every summer. That makes a big difference in your life. I remember going through first year college and it being really stressful. When I'd be having a bad day, I'd just go out and stand in the woods and listen to the birds; so it all kind of ties in to what I've turned into.

John seldom revealed his deepest hopes and longings, even to his closest friends. To the outside world he remained the same crazy explorer who spent weeks and months alone in the wilderness, a man who was determined to stay single. And he would laugh it off. Then in 1992, in the last paragraph of a letter to close friends (the McAuliffe family who'd moved back to England in the 1980s), he revealed what was happening in his private life:

> When I was talking about women earlier, I left something (someone) out! There was a girlfriend I had in '77—Catherine Stafford. Well, I'm visiting her now again. She has two gorgeous boys and she's on her own. I take the boys on Sundays and some week nights. I love them (and her) very much and would walk away from climbing for good if she would marry me—but we'll see. The four of us have a grand time together but I don't think she likes me THAT WAY ... I miss them when I'm not with them and it makes the mountains lonely now. The boys' names are Will and Cyrus. Will is 9 and has physical problems like walking but is as smart as a little lawyer. Cyrus is 7 and says he "hates hiking!" Last hike he said, "We could have driven up here in 5 minutes!" Catherine has her hands very full and is very glad to see me when I come to take the boys swimming or whatever.

When I asked Catherine to tell me about her memories of John, she found it difficult as he had been such a constant in her life for so many years. In 1977, when she was in her early twenties, she had lived in a hippie house on Quebec Street close to 4 East Thirteenth and met him at one of the many parties at the communal houses. "I just fell in love with him," she said, "but he was all about his mountain climbing ... I was devastated when he left." He disappeared into the wilderness and she went travelling in South America. They lost touch.

When Catherine, now a single mother with two boys, moved back to Vancouver, John returned to her life. At first he would simply show up at the door and stay for dinner, as he characteristically did with many of his friends, but gradually he became part of the family. Whenever he was in town, he'd take her two boys out every weekend and do something different with them—swim, fish, go to movies, draw—and always have fun.

Cyrus and Will are now in their mid-twenties, and as we sat at

Catherine's kitchen table in 2009, Will laughingly summed up the brothers' very different personalities: "I'm the intellectual and he's the artist—nerd and media." They remember how thrilled they were to see John whenever he returned from the mountains, brimming with enthusiasm and regaling them with stories of his adventures. The boys would watch wide-eyed as he pulled treasures out of his pack—railroad spikes, the crushed tuna can that a hungry grizzly bear had popped into his mouth, a sliver of wood from a thousand-year-old tree, a fistful of mountain goat wool. Cyrus explained, "Instantly he'd be back into our lives, we'd be hanging out in the pool or going to play soccer. Literally, three to four nights a week he'd be here—even if it was only for an hour or two. He was *always* there. He was always there when we needed him ... I still refer to him as 'my dad.' When I was younger, he *was* my dad. I didn't have any positive male influence. I never played soccer with my real father, [but] I played soccer for hours and hours every night with John. We'd just relate to him so well and he was so funny. He'd have this entire arsenal of funny noises he'd make in different situations. He was like a walking cartoon character."

Will shifted his wheelchair closer to the table. "John built our first slingshots—he knew how to do it with surgical tubing." And Cyrus butted in: "He had a piece of plywood and he cut out a 'y' ... and added surgical tubing."

"And we'd go up to the gravel pits near Squamish."

"He brought these giant cardboard boxes with light bulbs stuck in them and we'd go up to these giant gravel pits and we'd just fire our slingshots. It was the best thing you could ever think of. And then we'd be in the bottom [of the gravel pit] and he'd climb up and push giant rocks off the cliff for us," Cyrus said, back in that moment.

When I later checked John's handmade, briefcase-sized calendar, I found an entry for this memorable event: April 14, 1996. John also made it possible for Will, restricted by his wheelchair, to go fishing. "If it wasn't for him," Will said, "I wouldn't have been able to go out into nature and fish ... Whenever he'd ask what I wanted to do, I'd always say, 'Fishing.' He didn't look at it like a challenge to take me along to do all those things." Cyrus's passion was drawing and making comic books, and he and John "would sit at the kitchen table and

I'd just tell him to draw stuff for me—for hours on end," says Cyrus. "We'd have giant pieces of paper and in the end they'd just be covered, and we'd save them all." And sometimes John would take him to see his cartoonist friend Tami Knight and she would give Cyrus lessons.

Catherine placed a box of photographs and other memorabilia on the table and found a couple of John's cartoons for us to admire. Cyrus pulled out a photo of John, himself and his brother in Halloween costumes, Will as a gorilla, Cyrus as a vampire and John, in the middle, as Richard Nixon. "Halloweens were huge! John would always have the Nixon mask," Cyrus explained, and Catherine said, "John took them out every Halloween, even in the pouring rain. He would wheel Will for miles in the rain and run up and down the stairs carrying Will up the stairs, carrying him down. And come home with bags of candy, and they'd just sit and feast on the candy and then he'd help put them to bed, and then he'd be gone until the next weekend, the next adventure."

John never confined himself to conventional forms of entertainment, whether it was a visit to the local junkyard—a favourite—or the game they loved to play with a plate full of melted gummy bears. "We'd just go nuts," Cyrus said. "Play with it, eat it. It was so much fun!" Cyrus and Will treasure the trivia collected in their childhood: John's U2 *Rattle and Hum* T-shirt, his favourite Gary Larson cartoon.

And they remember John's favourite TV shows: *The Simpsons* and *Kids in the Hall*. "I was probably too young to be watching that show," Cyrus said of *Kids in the Hall*, "but I still watch it. I have all the episodes on my computer."

A sticky and delicious game: Will Stafford makes cat cradles with Gummy Bears melted on the hood of John Clarke's car, circa early 1990s. PHOTO COURTESY OF CATHERINE STAFFORD

John and the boys would go to the wave pool in North Vancouver as swimming was one of the few forms of exercise that Will could really enjoy, and it helped his arthritis. When Cyrus spoke of his hikes with John in the North Shore mountains, Will held up a picture of Cyrus, a miniature mountaineer with John's red pack on his back and his long ice axe in his small hand. When the going got steep, Cyrus would "crawl into [John's] backpack with just my head sticking out, and he'd climb all the way up there."

Neither Will nor Cyrus can remember John disciplining them. According to Cyrus, this was "because it was always so fun. The way it should be … He just had that knack for seeing what you were interested in and then going from there." He ad-

John Clarke and Cyrus Stafford during a hike in Vancouver's North Shore mountains, circa early 1990s. PHOTO COURTESY OF CATHERINE STAFFORD

mitted that John's approach helps him to raise his own two-year-old son: "I can relate to my kid a little bit better because I had somebody do that for me."

Unfortunately, when John asked Catherine to marry him, she was unable to take that step. "I knew that I cherished him, but I couldn't bring myself to be with him emotionally," Catherine explained. "Part of it was I was afraid he was going to die on me. I was afraid every time he left [for the mountains], afraid I was never going to see him again." But for years afterwards, he continued to be a father for Will and Cyrus and was always supportive of Catherine. Much later she realized how deeply she cared about him, but it was too late. He had met somebody else. He stayed in touch and phoned her when his son Nicholas was born in January 2002 and promised to bring him over. That was the last she heard from him and she didn't learn of his illness and subsequent death until February 2003. Will and Cyrus were heartbroken by the news. They had assumed that John would always be there when they needed him. They had been rebellious teenagers in the last few years of John's life and, like normal adolescents seeking independence from their parents, had seen little of him. If he had the opportunity now, Will would say to John, "Thank you for everything you did for me and accepting me the way I am."

In later years, after I had come to know John well, I would sometimes remark, "John, you'll get married one day," and he would deftly sidestep the issue with "Clarkes never marry" or "I'm too poor." And that would put an end to the conversation.

13

Mount Mason Mania

*I don't think motivation and drive have ever been a problem
'cause frankly I don't think I'm the one in control here.*
—John Clarke

John's heroic efforts to climb Mount Mason in the spring and summer of 1990 illustrate key elements of his character: his focus and determination and his patience in the face of obstacles. Although he was always colourful in every sense, when it came to mountains his personality was black and white. There was no grey scale. Once he'd set his mind on climbing a certain peak, he gave it everything he had—and then some. If scaling Mount Mason had been straightforward, then we would not know how desperately he wanted to climb this peak. But the more he was rebuffed, the more it consumed his thoughts; Mount Mason ran him ragged for over three months. Everything else on his agenda was tossed aside.

John was smitten with Mount Mason the first time he saw its prominent dark rock horn curving into the sky. He didn't know for sure if the peak was virginal—his research showed that it was likely unclimbed—but he just knew the horn was too tempting to ignore. (Like falling in love: it is immaterial whether she already has a boyfriend.) In fact, Mount Mason is a relatively minor peak, 7,677 feet (2,340 metres) high, to be exact. It is situated at the headwaters of Douglas Creek, east of the head of Harrison Lake on the divide between the Nahatlach and Mehatl Rivers.

Although less than 60 miles (100 kilometres) from Stanley Park in Vancouver, Mount Mason's appeal for John was its remoteness: "Mount Mason is the mountaineer's perfect challenge. Surrounded by unlogged valleys and complex ridge systems, its ascent involves valley travel, creek crossings, high level navigation, and rock climbing."

By the early 1990s John Clarke was a legend within the climbing community, his name synonymous with the Coast Mountains. People were eager to join him on his adventures, among them Sandy Briggs, a mountaineer, Arctic explorer and academic at the University of Victoria. His opportunity arrived one day when John was giving a slide show in Victoria to members of the Alpine Club of Canada. After the show Sandy more or less invited himself to go on John's next ski traverse, which was scheduled for the coming spring. Although John would often take an untried partner with him on a trip, he might advise the novice against it. He would warn, for instance, that:

> The person you left the end of the logging road with on day one is not the person that you're sharing a tent with on day twenty. It's like some mad experiment. It's almost like someone's looking through a little hole at this crazy experiment ... That's something that really speaks for doing trips with proven people and people that you've done long trips with before. You would *not* want to do a four- to six-week trip with someone that you haven't done a trip with for longer than two or three days. You can only imagine!

In this instance it was Sandy who should have been worried that sunny May afternoon at the start of their three-week trip, in the first moments of their first trip together. After days of hectic preparation they sat at the end of the logging road on a huge sun-warmed log relaxing after work done and mentally readying themselves for work to come. Over a decade later Sandy wrote to John and described that indelible moment:

> One thing I do remember is the first day of our *first* trip together. We drove to Pemberton and put in the food drops by helicopter, then got let off at the end of a logging road in some creek valley. I didn't know you except by reputation and a couple of days of food-packing together. We sat there in the hot sun at opposite ends of a log, getting psyched

up for shouldering the heavy packs and heading up through the bush. You turned sideways to look at me (as the helicopter rattled off into the distance), you contorted your upper body into an odd shape, assumed a very twisted expression involving wild eyes and quietly said, "Have I told you about my *problem*?" But soon followed the smile that follows a good joke, and we set off uphill. I found out what your *problem* is. It's that you love the Coast Mountains so much that hardly anybody else could understand.

For the first six days the fickle weather kept the two men guessing as the sun and clouds played games of hide-and-seek. The snow was perfect for easy skiing—hard enough to stay on top of the firm, powder-coated crust. They cruised along the ridges, climbed every peak along the way, built cairns, left notes and changed campsites to provide fresh views each day. Before them rose the impressive bulk of Mount Judge Howay and distant Mount Baker, and behind lay their route from the Lillooet River up Gowan Creek. On the fifth day they glimpsed Mount Mason and their route ahead. As dusk fell, the magic of the wilderness was enhanced by the haunting cries of ptarmigans and the orange glow of the full moon suspended over the next day's peak.

Day six stood out as a "fantastic day." John and Sandy romped up four peaks grouped at the headwaters of Gowan and Livingstone Creeks, each one different from the previous and providing new challenges and excitement. They climbed the first on skis, the second on foot, and once they had to use the rope to safely cross a yawning gap. On the third climb they glimpsed a goat silhouetted against the leaden sky. And while they were ascending the graceful crest of snow to the summit of Mount

Intrepid mountaineers: John Clarke and Sandy Briggs, 1990. PHOTO BY SANDY BRIGGS

John Clarke examines Sandy Briggs's gift of Fart Plugs—an antidote to a diet heavily laced with lentils and beans, 1993. PHOTO BY SANDY BRIGGS

Gowan (their fourth peak), the tip of Sandy's ice axe buzzed in the electricity-laden air. In high spirits from bagging four peaks that day, they skied back to their snow dome home in flat light. John's last entry in his diary that evening read: "The more meat and potatoes you eat, the more dessert you get!"

Then the weather that had kept them guessing for five days resolved into drizzly snow flurries, and there followed a series of what Sandy called "library days," when the poor visibility and unsettled weather confined them to their tent for much of the time. Fortunately, they were getting along just fine. Any lingering doubts that Sandy might have harboured about John's sanity had long since disappeared. Indeed, as the days passed he increasingly appreciated John's wealth of experience and attention to every detail:

> John was the first person I really ever met for whom camping was an art form. It was not something that you just went and did, but everything had a reason and nothing went unnoticed. For instance, John's washcloth ... was for mopping up spills in the tent and wiping down condensation. But it wasn't just any old cloth. It had to be cotton and it had to be black because it dried quicker in the sun.

For a while they enjoyed the luxury of hanging out in their warm and dry tent, listening to little ice pellets spraying on the fly, with nothing more strenuous to do than read and answer the call of nature. In his diary John wrote: "As soon as we're finished our porridge in the morning, we get contractions and dive through the door, clutching rolls of toilet paper." That chore out of the way, they'd go back to their books. Sandy, the academic, had definite ideas about what constituted acceptable reading material. As he wrote in his trip journal:

> John usually puts cheap, I mean *really* cheap, novels in the air drops, the argument for this quality being that they are useful for soaking up condensation and spilled soup, and that they may ultimately be torn up and burned (which they deserve) and thus not burden the long-distance traveller. My counter-argument is that the burden on the mind of reading vacuous soap-opera pulp is at least equivalent to the burden on the body of actually carrying home a more artful volume. During those long library days, as the snow swirled and the cloud rolled outside, the contrast between Margaret Laurence and some lesser authors was, shall we say, stark indeed.

John loved to entertain Sandy with riddles and jokes: "Why are people so down on economists?" But he'd quickly supply the answer: "Because they've predicted fifteen out of the last twelve recessions!" And after a day of complete bedrest out of the silence would come: "Museum curator to visitors: 'These dinosaur bones are twenty million years and seven months old.' 'How can you be so exact?' asked a visitor. 'Well, they were twenty million years old when I started at the museum, and I've been here seven months!'"

Sandy soon began to grasp the subtleties of John's humour:

> He could deliver those one-liners and you could never see them coming. Some of them were just invented for a particular thing that was going on in provincial politics, a particular time or current event, and sometimes they were more general. I was lying there high-grading my snack bag when John looked over and remarked: "We are tubes—food tubes." Various things like that would just come out all the time and sum up a situation.

At the same time Sandy's dry, well-honed sense of humour never failed to delight John, and his aphorisms punctuated his diary: "Sandy says there's no way I can be cured now from climbing peaks since my condition has gone untreated for too long!" And, "Sandy says I'm almost due for early retirement. I just have to figure out from what."

Nine days into their trip they began to speculate whether Lewis Kaiserseder, the third member of their party, would show up as planned by helicopter the next day. During a lull in the storm, they crawled outside and stamped out a big arrow in the snow, mainly to get some exercise but also to direct Lewis's helicopter. That evening John cooked up the notoriously pungent *tswan*, or wind-dried salmon, that he'd bought in the First Nations village of Mount Currie, but it was so dehydrated that it didn't reconstitute very much, even when boiled for a long time. "Good-rich food though," he wrote in its defence. There were two camps as far as John's culinary skills were concerned: those who appreciated his cooking and those who didn't—there was no middle ground. Sandy was definitely in the first camp and commented, "John would say 'If it's costing us $15 a pound to drop this [food] up here, then it had better be good.'" It wasn't just the dinners that Sandy appreciated but the "truly awesome nature of the snack bags John had prepared. I counted fourteen ingredients, including such exotic fruit as pineapple, papayas, and mangos."

On the tenth day, when Lewis was supposed to join them, the morning dawned clear and cold with windblown powder. John and Sandy began their day in their usual leisurely fashion, which was much appreciated by Sandy, who was used to the traditional pre-dawn departures of mountaineers. "No frenetic alpine starts for these boys!" They slowly packed up camp and headed south toward the col where the helicopter would deposit Lewis, and they soon heard the chatter of John Goat's chopper. Then, almost magically, amidst a swirl of snow, there was Lewis bearing gifts of strawberries and apples.

The trio skied across steep, windblown snow slopes and set up their camp six near a 7,300-foot (2,225-metre) peak for an easy ascent the next morning. From this vantage point there were spectacular views into the Nahatlatch Valley and to their proposed route beyond. When Mount Mason made a brief appearance through boiling columns of cumulus clouds that evening, John was elated and felt that nothing would stop him reaching his cherished goal.

After ascending the peak near their camp the next morning, they packed up camp and headed east to the main glacier feeding

Livingstone Creek and their food parcels. In worsening weather they deftly placed camp seven on the edge of a wind cirque, and with pre-science Sandy made a broad track in the snow to the airdrop boxes nearby in case the weather socked in. While John fashioned a snow cave to escape the reverberations of Lewis's nighttime snores, Sandy demonstrated his digging skills, acquired as a young boy during snowbound New Brunswick winters. His artistry with the snow shovel was revealed in the form of an incredible sunken kitchen, a biffy and a high wall around the tent to protect it from the fierce wind. John was terrifically impressed by the beauty of Sandy's creations: "The place looked like an Aztec City!" The pristine kitchen was officially opened that evening with a steaming pot of tuna and macaroni and cheese. But soon clammy fog enveloped the new settlement, and even the rocks beside the camp became invisible.

The next day the sun filtered weakly through the fog and John, damp from his night in the snow cave, optimistically set everything out to dry while Sandy perfected his architectural creation. Afterwards, they climbed the 7,000-foot (2,100-metre) "bump" just north of their camp. Stubborn clouds obscured the view and the only real excitement was when Sandy started an avalanche by bowling a rock down a steep slope. Back at the kitchen it was spaghetti night.

Sandy Briggs's snow wall helps to protect the tent from inclement weather, 1990. PHOTO BY SANDY BRIGGS

Fog and drizzle enveloped the camp next morning and produced major lazing around. John described the scene: "Sandy is outside making an igloo and Lewis is sewing his raincoat. I'm reading a paperback called *Why Rock the Boat* by William Weintraub. 'Wacky, ribald, hilarity,' good book. Light reading for the 'hard of thinking!'"

John was annoyed when Sandy didn't finish building his igloo as he'd been anticipating an undisturbed night. He wrote: "The snoring is driving me crazy. Like a goddamn bull moose! All night. After supper I got in the tent and I went to SLEEP. Then Lewis wakes me up and starts snoring loud only three minutes later. I got mad as hell." John's usual method of dealing with confrontation was to walk away, but that was hardly possible. Instead, he gritted his teeth and after yet another sleepless night couldn't believe it when his unfailing good nature took over. "If that wasn't crazy enough, now I get up and cook breakfast for the guy who kept me awake all night! It just doesn't get any more cockamamie than that! Sandy even brought it to him in bed!"

Wet wind changed to "wet snow with wind" and another round of library days ensued. At one point John remarked: "We feel like we're being kept in storage until we're needed!" Sandy's masterpiece kitchen was mightily appreciated: "It's a bloody marvel. The high walls cut the wind and there's a nice high work bench for cooking." Meanwhile, completing the slanting inward roof of the igloo in the fog kept Sandy and Lewis busy for hours. John hunkered down in the tent reading *The Black Sun*. "Typical pulp," was his succinct review. Once in a while he'd peek outside to check on the igloo's progress: "Lewis is quarrying the blocks from the steps down to the kitchen and Sandy is inside the igloo with his head sticking out of the shrinking hole in the roof. Much shaping and climbing goes on with the placement of each block." That evening, to celebrate the completion of the igloo, John cooked supper in the new "dome home." Steam billowing from the bubbling pot made the inside as foggy as outside. Later, installed in his new bedroom, John savoured a quiet read by candlelight and a silent night, marred only by his mattress skating around on its icy platform.

After four days of inaction the men were anxious to move again, and a brief clearing in the afternoon had them scurrying out to stretch

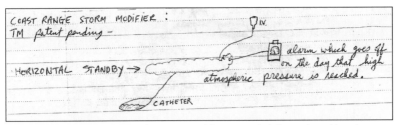

John Clarke's innovative design of a "storm modifier" created while tent-bound by "the worst weather in 25 years," May–June 1988. SKETCH BY JOHN CLARKE, COURTESY OF ANNETTE CLARKE

their legs and climb the 7,400-foot (2,250-metre) peak close by and enjoy the enticing views of Mount Mason and John's old friends the Misty Icefields, Mount Pitt and the McBride Range. Back at camp John masterfully repaired his broken ski binding, using the tip of his breadknife and a red-hot wire to drill new holes in the ski to relocate the binding. But despite his optimism, the weather refused to cooperate and the adventurers were pinned to their camp for another round of fog and wet snow. One afternoon John retreated to the relative warmth of the igloo and melted a big pot of snow to provide hot water for a luxurious bath: "The first in two weeks," he wrote. "Felt great but I itched like crazy after. Can't get all the soap off! Clean shirt and underwear too!" Two more stormy, tent-bound days convinced Lewis to cut his losses. He skied out the next day accompanied partway by John and Sandy, but he was quickly lost from view as he headed down into snow-covered forest. He'd arrived dramatically bearing gifts of strawberries and apples and departed silently with a fistful of phone numbers and a package of garbage, surely meagre gleanings from a week-long "holiday."

John and Sandy followed their own ski tracks back to camp and consoled themselves with "second extraction" cups of tea, chatting, library time and Sandy's much appreciated aphorisms. John, the eternal optimist, led the way the next day when they resumed their quest in flat light and marginal conditions. From a col they were mocked by fleeting views of Mount Mason, but John remained entranced: "Mount Mason looked outrageous! A fantastic peak." They made a detour to avoid a gaping step in the ridge and set up camp eight down in the trees in the Nahatlach Valley.

John's carefully planned agenda had disintegrated as precious days dribbled away, but so powerful was the lure of the black granite horn that he was already anticipating his next trip to Mount Mason. Two more days of confinement and the situation seemed bleak: "We are low on grub and out of all luxuries—and there is a huge grub cache on the shoulder of Mount Mason that we haven't a hope of reaching. Some country! Some weather!" However, the humour of the dismal situation did not escape him: "It's way past my bread time. We just have bread and butter for breakfast—with "tea" made from water, brown sugar, powdered milk and cinnamon! Not bad. At least it's hot and wet. Only one slice of bread at lunch instead of the usual two. We're going to waste away." It was now day twenty-one and there was heavy rain until noon then light rain and fog. Sandy quipped, "I was in shape till I came on this trip!"

The following day they packed up and headed for the valley and home. John's mind seethed with plans for phase two of the siege of Mount Mason. Departure time was only five days away. In high spirits he dashed off a note to the McAuliffe family in the UK:

> I'm just going out the door to go off on a two-week trip to the mountains northeast of the north end of Harrison Lake. There's a granite spire hiding back there that hasn't been climbed. Wild! When the good Lord made the world—he forgot only one thing ... CAIRNS on the peaks! So I'm doing God's work—and my work is not yet finished.

For his second attempt to reach Mount Mason, John decided that he and his friend Dave Lammers would approach on foot and bushwhack up the Douglas Creek valley from the south. The trip began inauspiciously on June 2, 1990, with the two men camping in a deluge at Skookumchuck Hot Springs in the Lillooet River valley. Next morning they peered out of the tent to find themselves marooned in the middle of a lake. "Trip is definitely off to a slow start," muttered John after he inadvertently dropped a hefty pipe from the hot tub on his foot. They retreated to spend the day in Pemberton's cosy laundromat.

Dave Lammers worked for BC Tel and had known John since the late 1960s, when John had been dating his sister, Theresa. He was not a mountaineer but one day in April 1990 when John popped in to chat, Dave mentioned that he had recently done the renowned Spearhead traverse on skis. John immediately said, "Well, if you can do the Spearhead in January, you can come on one of my trips." So it had been settled that they would climb some peaks in the Misty Icefields in Garibaldi Park. Of course, that plan changed after John returned from his abortive twenty-three-day venture to Mount Mason in May. "So John's all excited about putting a whole shitload of food up near Mount Mason," recalled Dave. "'We're changing the plans,' John told me. 'We're going up [to Mount Mason].' So we didn't do the Misty Icefields." John's own understated version was: "Dave wanted to go somewhere in the Coast Mountains—he didn't care where."

This was to be Dave's initiation into the Coast Mountains, an opportunity of a lifetime, an event not to be passed up. "I've always looked at these ice-cream-covered mounds on a calendar. You always wonder what it would be like to be there—it was really something to be as old as I was—I was 47—and I'd had ankylosing spondylitis my whole life."

That first evening, warm and dry once again, the two men drove to Port Douglas at the head of Harrison Lake and stayed in an abandoned house on the edge of the Douglas First Nation reserve. Next day they left the car with Sam Peters, a First Nations man who was the caretaker of the logging camp there, and began tramping along an old logging road up the Douglas Creek valley to enter dense, seemingly endless logging slash punctuated here and there with huge stumps—ghosts of another age. The going was slow, but the next morning they emerged into glorious ancient rain forest. Sun

David Lammers camped in Douglas Creek valley on his 1990 trip with John Clarke to "conquer" Mount Mason. Here David tentatively holds out his two-cupper for supper. PHOTO BY JOHN CLARKE, COURTESY OF ANNETTE CLARKE

filtered through the rich canopy of giant cedars and Douglas firs, and beneath them were thickets of slide alder and lacy vine maples, lush ferns and soft green moss. John sauntered along, but Dave, less fit and unused to the heavy pack, was already exhausted. That night when they camped on the only tiny flat spot they could find under the overhanging branches, Dave was too tired to eat supper.

They were greeted by a grey sky and gentle rain the next day. John wrote: "Couldn't believe it!! I was convinced that yesterday's sun was the big turnaround in the weather. Fooled every time!" They pressed on until steep ground and pelting rain forced them to seek shelter in a dry cave where John re-taped his feet: "My feet are nearly covered in tape. My right foot is sore from dropping the pipe on it at the hot-springs. It fell on the tendons just behind the smaller toes." Later that afternoon Dave, exhausted and sodden, could go no further, and they made camp on a snow-covered dome at 4,800 feet (1,500 metres). Twenty years later he recalled how desperate he felt at the time:

> Especially when we came right out of the creek and we went all the way up onto that dome. I was finished. I almost crawled to the tent to get in there. I was cramping up trying to get my clothes off. I was soaked from rain. I got into my sleeping bag and John was eating my last night's supper. I was throwing up, and he didn't care! Nothing bothered him. He was so hard core.

But John did care. He wrote: "We can't leave this camp in either direction until Dave gets his appetite back because he won't have any strength until he eats." Then, while waiting for Dave to revive, John wandered off to explore and quite by chance came upon a little miracle—a newborn fawn nestled in a mossy hollow. Knowing the mother would be observing from nearby, he took a photo and crept away. (That photo was one of his all-time greats.)

Next morning Dave drank some water but couldn't eat the porridge John had prepared. Later, when a few blue spots appeared in the sky, they hiked up to the top of a knoll and stared at the clouds blowing through the peaks and the gorgeous stunted trees near camp. "This is monumental granite country and looks rugged as hell for casual backpacking," John observed in his notebook. "We want sun-shine really bad but it only comes in fleeting little bits. Maddening!" He calculated they had only three days left, and needed one to climb Mount Mason and another to collect food from the airdrop for the hike out. They hung around camp all day, waiting for a glimpse of the route to Mount Mason, but it was late that evening when Mason, freshly coated with snow, glowed through the parted clouds as if to taunt them. "Is this the big clear-up?" John wondered.

That evening he dressed for dinner in a tie and white shirt. "He packed it along for the occasion," said Dave. "That was the type of thing he did. Just for the heck of it. He could climb all day and keep a white shirt clean. He shopped for everything at Value Village and he burned them at the end of the trip because they were so filthy."

For the entire trip Dave struggled to keep food down:

> I couldn't even eat nuts and chocolate as they'd just go into a ball in my mouth. That's how bad it was. I couldn't eat anything. I'd spend all night trying to eat—so I ate more than John thought. I couldn't sleep either because of my back and being on a hard surface. I'd wake up and I'd take a spoonful of food and wash it down with water—glug, glug—and by next morning I'd have three-quarters of it in me. But John remembers it as me not eating anything as I'd just sit and look at my food.

If chocolate was on the tolerable end of Dave's hard-to-eat scale, then John's pungent *tswan* (wind-dried salmon) was off-scale on the intol-erable end. Dave remembered that:

> Oh! It was awful! But John loved the Indians so much that he didn't want to admit that this was awful stuff. He said, "It really doesn't do anything to the taste, does it?" I said, "John, it doesn't do *anything*." That fishy oily taste went right through the *whole* meal. He finally stopped putting it in.

Next morning the pelting rain on the tent fly did more than damp-en the tent. John's carefully planned season was unravelling, and he began contemplating a siege of Mount Mason in the likelihood that this trip was unsuccessful. The trips he had planned for the rest of the season could wait. Mount Mason had to be climbed: "If I come in here a third time this season, it will be open-ended time-wise so I can siege long stretches of bad weather ... The worst thing is having to be out on a certain date. That's lethal!"

The conditions were atrocious the next day but it was their last chance at Mount Mason, and they headed for the steep southeast ridge.

> The snow got very steep near the top and big bucket steps had to be cleared in the soft snow. The rock at the top of the gulley we were in was plastered with ice and fresh snow and all the rocks were wet. We couldn't get to the ridge crest to see what the final ridge was like! We were 20 feet short of the ridge crest, just below a notch and stopped only 250 feet from the summit of a 7,600-foot peak!

John spent a futile half-hour bashing at the ice feathers and clearing snow from ledges with his ice axe, but it was pointless because everything was so smooth and iced up. Dave marvelled, "I was amazed how I could trust John like that and follow him. We just couldn't go any further. You'd have needed a rope and pitons."

Reluctantly, John turned round in the driving snow and they headed for home. That evening a watery chicken and macaroni dinner did nothing to dispel the gloom of the slushy rain pounding on the flimsy tent fly. Dave recalled the miserable conditions: "I had no clothes left that were dry. I had to go out [of the tent] without any clothes on to go to the bathroom because I wanted to keep that one last pair of socks dry." By now Dave's boots were completely water-logged, so as they hiked out the next day, each time he raised a leg to climb over a fallen log, the water poured *up* his leg. "The wet! My feet were totally covered with band-aids where I'd been rubbed raw by the wet boots and wet socks. For a first trip it was quite something."

As dusk closed in on them late the next day, they were still marching onwards like zombies, but when they began to scout around for a campsite, something magical happened. John remembered:

> We were pretty desperately tired. We were starting to think, *Let's just stop and put the tent anywhere.* Then I saw this enormous rectangular

boulder about the same size and shape as a city bus. It was so big that there was actually a small forest growing on top of it. I thought, *Down on one end of that thing there might be a flat spot to put the tent.* So we walked over to it, walked all along the edge of it, and when we got to the end, we came to a perfectly flat spot to put the tent. There was a roof that extended out from the top of this enormous boulder and on the wall, under the roof, was an image of a face and an animal's head imprinted onto the forehead of the face. We both turned around and looked at this thing. We must have stood there like statues for about five minutes just staring at it—looking at it, thinking, *Is it an image? Is it lichens? What is it?* Of course, it was a beautiful old image. No one knows how old it was. It was a beautiful thing to find.

Curled up in his sleeping bag that night, John thought of the ancient peoples who had carved the petroglyph. As he explained it in *Child of the Wind*:

> I always try to imagine who were they, what was it like, what was the ordinary everyday existence for them? I can just picture these guys out there in 1300 and something, or older. I always try and think what it might have been like in their societies. I can picture them walking up that valley in the old-growth forests. They had some reason for going up there. It wasn't really an economic reason so it may have been some kind of a religious pilgrimage; certainly in the case of Douglas Creek.

Two days later, back at Port Douglas, John told Sam Peters about the petroglyph. One of the last of his people still living in Port Douglas at that time, he knew nothing about the pictograph, even though his dad had trapped in Douglas Creek.

Back at Dave's place in Surrey, John prepared for what he hoped was the final siege of Mount Mason. "It seems I've spent most of this spring lying down in my sleeping bag," he told Dave before dropping off to sleep.

As soon as he returned to Vancouver, John phoned friends Emily Butler and Kobus Barnard to see if they "wouldn't mind" coming along to Mount Mason the following week, instead of climbing Peak

8503 in Bute Inlet as they had planned. Apparently they didn't. They also knew John would simply go on his own if they didn't join him.

John and his fresh young crew met at Whistler Air on Green Lake and waited for the weather to improve in order to drop the food parcels. The next day Mike, their pilot, flew them through cloud to the head of Harrison Lake and up to the col at the head of the big eastern tributary of Douglas Creek, where he skillfully manoeuvred his little fixed-wing craft, and all the parcels were thrown out successfully. By the next evening John, Emily and Kobus were well on their way up Douglas Creek and camped on a flat, mossy bench in a storybook forest, the creek pounding loudly near the tent. John could hardly believe this was the same route that he and Dave had slogged up the previous, soggy week.

In the morning Kobus taught John, who was very proud of his porridge-making abilities, a new breakfast trick—chocolate chips in the porridge. "It makes it so you can eat it," explained Kobus, "but overdoing it is simply gross." Nursing head colds, the trio then headed into the dewy bush, boots disappearing in deep-pile moss. "We looked like bugs, with dripping noses and horrible growths on our backs," observed John, "sliding and sinking in a giant, wet salad."

Emily Butler and Kobus Barnard catch a glimpse of the elusive Mount Mason, 1990. PHOTO BY JOHN CLARKE, COURTESY OF ANNETTE CLARKE

The next afternoon they came across a black bear tucking into a large bag of brown sugar, a sure sign they had arrived at their first airdrop. The bear refused to be hurried and only moved on when he'd finished the last sticky grains. But eventually they rounded up the rest of the parcels, and a base camp gradually materialized on the beautiful pass. John, prepared for a siege, was leaving nothing to chance this time. They divided the food into three separate piles, and Emily cached one in the snow and marked it with a wand; to which John attached some mothballs to keep the bears away. Kobus deftly strung the second pile high up on the rocks. They stashed the remaining parcels in their packs and headed for high camp, a col just two miles southeast of Mount Mason.

That night they placed their tent in the lee of a big oval boulder cracked in half like a colossal egg. It was now June 21, summer solstice, and it lashed rain all night. Once more, they had to wait for the weather to clear, but after forty-nine days of his non-stop love affair with Mount Mason, John felt he was within reach of his goal. "We only need one day of clear weather from this camp and we'll get up it at last. Kobus has loads of rock gear, so only the weather can stop us." Two days later the big day arrived. It was a sunny morning and spectacular columns of cumulus clouds were rolling up above the snow-capped peaks. Armed with rock-climbing gear, Kobus led the final assault on Mount Mason. As they crossed the snowfield southeast of the summit ridge, John could make out the cracks and ledges he had tried to clear of ice feathers barely fifteen days earlier.

This was the culmination of his siege of Mount Mason. Every time the mountain had rejected him, his resolve and determination had grown. A few more steps and he would stand on the summit of this feisty, elusive horn. They scrambled up to the summit on the best possible granite. John crested the ridge and approached the demure little snow-capped peak—and then he saw it. A cairn! "An old pile of stones but, maddeningly, no record! A wonderful effort, whoever you are, on this grand peak, a classic granite horn!" John was gracious in defeat and conceded that "To be truthful, I'd actually become a little obsessive about Mount Mason since seeing it last September from the Nahatlatch Lakes, and gawking at the distant peaks that appeared briefly through the boiling cumulus, the effort felt worthwhile."

According to Glenn Woodsworth, it's likely that Mason had been climbed by a prospector, possibly as early as the 1800s, as there had been a good deal of prospecting in this region, and Mason stands on the route to the Fraser River via Harrison Lake and Lillooet. Prospectors weren't in the habit of leaving records of peaks climbed.

John's three-month affair with Mount Mason only left him more determined to complete his climbing season as planned, and he pushed the saga to the back of his mind.

Three years later, however, John developed a similar determination to climb Mount Desire but he couldn't find a partner for the climb as by now John Baldwin had married and started a family. "By that time I'd started to feel lonely in the mountains on my own," he said later, "not like the old days when I didn't give a damn, [though] obviously that never stopped me from going." On August 27 Clarke made a note to himself: "Mount Desire must be climbed!" Two days later he had completed detailed plans for the climb—including options in case his primary plan was scuttled by weather:

> August 29: I want to climb Mount Desire and Big Snow Mountain so have decided to put an airdrop near Big Snow, get dropped on logging roads in Smitley River, climb Desire, traverse over Big Snow and hike out via Clayton Falls Creek ... If the weather stays good (and this morning was brilliant) I [will] climb Desire from the Smitley River (est. 3 days return). Then if I could cross the Smitley, [I will] go up Brynildsen Creek, turn right up its tributary with the lake, hike over Big Snow and on to the head of Clayton Falls Creek. If the crossing of the Smitley [is] too much and the weather stays good, I would continue up the east side of the Smitley, cross it three bits at a time at the headwaters, pack up the glacial valley east of Big Snow, then pack over Big Snow and beyond. If the weather changes, then I [will] go down the Smitley to the Noeick and South Bentinck Arm.

Within days he had bought supplies, packed his gear and set off for Bella Coola—"reluctantly on my own," as he put it.

Packed the West Wind tent and the two-man Sierra Design stretch dome in case I found a partner in Bella Coola, but I never did … I told Wilderness Air to watch for smoke coming from the Noeick River mouth and that would be me waiting to fly back to Bella Coola. We loaded up the helicopter and flew up Thorsen Creek and put in a food drop at the base of the west ridge of the 7,200-foot peak NW of Big Snow. I put it here instead of E of Big Snow in case I couldn't get up the Smitley after doing Desire. W of Big Snow it would be useful for a separate trip in from Clayton Falls after the Desire trip.

While he would go on to climb Desire with few problems, the most memorable part of this trip happened soon after the helicopter had dropped him off on a sandbar in "the bowels of the Smitley River":

I had breakfast by the river and then headed for a shoulder at 6,200 feet. The forest lower down was nice—not steep and good going. Beyond that it got steeper and I finally got into the dreaded thick "berry bush zone." At about 4,500 feet I heard this loud exhalation of breath mixed with a guttural sound. A bear! But I didn't worry too much even though I knew the bear was very close. I thought all I had to do was find the closest rock, bang the ice axe off it and he'd run away. Bears usually react to that metallic clang— that's why the old-timers used to use bells. Not this bear! I made a big racket, but he moved in closer and repeated the aggressive sounds.

This huge cinnamon-coloured head comes up out of the foliage and looks at me—a healthy grizzly in his prime. He was deciding what to do and, believe me, so was I! All I had was a day pack, [but within it] I had some IGA book-matches and some toilet paper. And it was dry. So I figured I could get a little fire going and just throw some sticks on it really quickly. But what he decided to do was to move around really slowly. He's doing this breathing in and out thing and head going back and forth. What he was doing was getting the very slight wind, to get right in line so that he'd get my scent. While he was moving around over there, I was getting the light and the toilet paper and getting some twigs going. He was only about fifteen feet away [now]. It was so funny because he'd positioned himself [downwind of me]—Well, where does the smoke go? Lazily it just goes straight over right into his face. Then he left. Whew! I would have had no chance [among] those snotty little trees in the alpine—there's no way.

A trio of grizzly bears, circa 2000. PHOTO BY IAN MCALLISTER

I waited for half an hour, fanning the smoke so it would spread as widely as possible over the whole slope. I put one stout stick into the fire and scorched one end thoroughly so as to carry it with me for a while. I continued on up, carrying this clumsy stick through steep scruffy trees and berry bushes and finally got out into the open. It was a long haul but I got to the 6,200-foot shoulder on the west ridge of Desire before dark and camped. Full moon came over the south ridge of Desire. I never saw that bear again.

Typically, the account he wrote for the *Canadian Alpine Journal* contained only a single line about his grizzly encounter:

In mid-August [1993] I drove out to Bella Coola to climb Desire Mountain from the Smitley River. This was an adventurous trip, as the rugged peak had taken a good bit of fresh snow, and at about 1,200 metres on the west ridge, I ran into a cheeky grizzly who didn't go away until I lit a fire right in front of him.

However, John's first scheme for scaling Mount Desire went just as he had planned:

From the high camp at 1,890 metres on the west ridge, I traversed onto glaciers west of the peak, gained the crest of the south ridge at 2,315 metres and crossed over to the glacier southeast of the peak. An awkward climb on rock and in a bergschrund put me on the south ridge again, this time at the base of an easy 150-metre scramble to the summit. Ecstasy! Many thanks to Glenn Woodsworth who suggested I go to this grand peak!

John's ability to accept the mountains on their terms and his persistence and optimism in the face of adversity were essential ingredients to his success. John didn't view his trips in terms of wins or losses—at least in the long term. Rather, he got satisfaction from the fact that the mountains would still be there when he was ready for another attempt. As was the case with Mount Silverthrone, where he at last stood on the summit—wearing a tie for the occasion—nineteen years after his first attempt to climb it.

14

Randy Stoltmann

The best tribute we can pay him now is to maintain his vision of preserving wild places as a celebration of his life.
—John Clarke

Carrying his skis, John Clarke walked cautiously to the edge of the cliff where just moments earlier he had watched helplessly as an avalanche swept Randy Stoltmann over the edge. He peered down. Nothing. No sound, save for the *wooosh-wooosh* of the powerful wings of a lone raven circling in the dark blue sky above. As he stood on that cliff edge, John's life was changed forever. The date was May 22, 1994.

As John described it, "One minute we were building a cairn, joking around, enjoying the peak, and then in a few minutes the young man who had kept us laughing during the whole traverse was gone."

John and four friends—Randy Stoltmann, Jessica Shintani, Bryan Evans and Dave Lammers—were three weeks into a ski traverse of the remote snowy ridges of the Kitimat Ranges high above the Kitlope Valley, about 340 miles (550 kilometres) northwest of Vancouver. They were a few days away from their exit at the Gardner Canal, some twenty-five miles (forty kilometres) from Kitimat, where a boat was to pick them up.

At thirty-two, Randy Stoltmann was seventeen years younger than John Clarke, but he had already devoted more than a decade of his life to conserving the wild places of British Columbia. An unusually talented and visionary young man, he had grown up on

Vancouver's North Shore, where the mountains were as familiar to him as his next door neighbours. While still in his teens, he had begun exploring the valleys and mountains of southwestern BC with his brother Greg, and this had led him to seek out the giants of the forest—the most venerable trees—and start a Registry of Big Trees, listing eighteen trees from thirteen species. The largest western red cedar in that registry measured 62 feet (18.9 metres) in circumference, and the tallest Sitka spruce was 314 feet (5.7 metres) high. Today these records are held by BC's Ministry of Forests and Range and include the vital statistics for 190 trees of 37 species.

Randy quickly became an accomplished mountaineer and backcountry skier, and although a draftsman by profession, he was also a sensitive and passionate writer. He was widely known as a powerful voice for wilderness protection through his three books: *Hiking Guide to the Big Trees of Southwestern British Columbia, Written by the Wind* and *Hiking the Ancient Forests of British Columbia and Washington.* Those were the years of diatribe and emotional outpourings between those who sought to protect BC's wilderness and those who sought to diminish it through resource extraction, but Randy's reasoned, calm and good-humoured approach earned him respect from conservationists and industry alike. He played a pivotal role in preserving the

Happy times in the Kitimat Ranges. *Left to right*: On the summit are Dave Lammers, Bryan Evans, Jessica Shintani and Randy Stoltmann, 1994. PHOTO BY JOHN CLARKE, COURTESY OF ANNETTE CLARKE

Carmanah Valley on the west coast of Vancouver Island, which sub-sequently led to the creation of the Carmanah Walbran Provincial Park in the 1990s.

A month before his tragic death Randy had submitted a formal proposal to the BC government's Protected Areas Strategy Steering Committee to preserve a 640,000-acre (260,000-hectare) roadless landscape straddling the divide between the Toba and Elaho Rivers. At the time this wilderness was one of only three untouched land-scapes in excess of a 250,000 acres (100,000 hectares) in southwestern BC Garibaldi Provincial Park, the Stein/Mehatl/Upper Nahatlatch wilderness and the Clendenning/Elaho/Upper Lillooet wilderness. These diverse ecosystems, ranging from valley bottom to mountain-top, are vital habitat for the maintenance of a wide variety of plant and animal life, but only the first of them had been classified as a park at that time. More worrying still was that of the six remaining pristine valleys within these areas, four were part of the Ministry of Forests' Five-Year Plan and scheduled to be logged.

Randy had named the area he proposed to preserve the Stanley Smith Wilderness in memory of the rugged explorer Stanley Smith, who had traversed this wild landscape exactly a century earlier in search of two missing surveyors. In 1993 Randy and several friends had retraced part of Smith's epic route, backpacking from Meager Creek to Princess Louisa Inlet. En route he had documented in words and on film the rich diversity of the land and its value to the 2.1 mil-lion people of the city of Vancouver, which was less than a day's travel away.

On that fateful day in May 1994 he had cruised happily along the ridges high above the Kitlope Valley with not a logging road any-where to desecrate the view. In fact, until the tragedy it had been a marvellous trip. As John wrote:

> While tent-bound for five days early in the traverse, we joked about the fact that we were seven days from Mussel Inlet [the start of the trip] and had only moved nine kilometres. Randy was always ahead of the rest of us. We would ski up to a rocky perch to find Randy doing his favorite thing—gazing down onto the sandbars, forests and waterfalls

of a pristine coastal valley, so overwhelmed by the wonder of it all that he himself appeared to be part of the magic of the place.

Randy's own journal reflected his deep connection to the land: "Great views of Kowesas River Valley and mountains all around! Distant roar of rivers, two ravens soaring, playing on the air currents." And later from the summit of Mount Marmor, he wrote:

> Sandbar over a vertical mile below, and the great roar of falling water rising out of the depths of the rainforest, 70 km to the west, range follows range, snow peaks fading to soft dark ridges and the final golden glimmer of the open Pacific Ocean. Mountains on the edge of the continent, nurtured by the sea; four very happy days!

John and Randy were sharing a tent on this trip and soon developed a close friendship and mutual respect. They swapped stories of adventures and talked about big trees, conservation and future trips together. What impressed John about Randy was his dedication to conservation and the fact that, though an alpinist, he'd given up so much "prime time" in the mountains to do this. To John this was a huge commitment: "Mountaineers are greedy—they never want to give up any time." For Randy, the regenerative and spiritual value of the wilderness was an elemental part of its appeal; he saw it as a sanctuary for people and a place for renewal in an increasingly crowded, hectic environment. It was, he said, a repository of "existence values."

John was shattered by Randy's death. He wrote to Catherine Stafford: "Everything is crazy—I don't think I'll get over it." Mountaineering in the Coast Mountains was supposed to be fun. This wasn't the Himalayas; people shouldn't die here. He talked to his friends about the ordeal—how he'd stood on the summit with Randy only moments before the tragedy. How Randy had set out first to ski down from the summit, and how John and the other three had watched helplessly as an avalanche carried him over the edge of the 1,000-foot cliff. He spoke about how he and his friends, unable to reach Randy, had used their emergency locater to call in a rescue team. But by that time it was dusk and it wasn't until the next day that they were able to recover Randy's body. John kept vigil on a rock that night and thought about his young friend.

Although a conservationist at heart, John's addiction to the Coast Mountains seemed incurable and he would push aside anything that looked as if it might compromise his climbing season

But ten weeks after Randy's death John's tribute to Randy, published in the *Canadian Alpine Journal*, hinted of a change:

> Everything Randy said, did and wrote all pointed to one thing—his powerful affection for wild landscapes. It saturated his writing, guided his actions and was the main reason for the effectiveness of his environmental work. His biggest impact was communicating this affection for wilderness with his research and his books. Through his example he showed us the way and the best tribute we can pay him now is to maintain his vision of preserving wild places as a celebration of his life.

Randy had striven to share his experiences, insights, understanding and love of wilderness with others in order to promote a greater understanding of its unquantifiable value and to ensure that this heritage endures. As he wrote in his book *Written by the Wind*:

> The realization that so much of society has lost its affinity with the land brings frightening visions of what the future might hold. But in wilderness is the opportunity to re-kindle a love and respect for the earth and for each other ... Stop. Think. Listen. Hear the roaring vastness of a great valley, or the sigh of wind in the treetops, or the eternal thunder of breakers on the shore. Then go back and speak to the world from your heart.

15

Speak to the World
From Your Heart

*The big value of wilderness travel is we're dipping our toes into
that landscape from which we evolved, back to a time when
our lives and even our spirituality were guided by the weather,
the animals, the plants, the seasons and the tides.*

—John Clarke

After Randy's death John Clarke went through a period of gestation. He had a serious talk with himself, and he would speak of "rats in his head"—things that were chattering inside his mind, things that he needed to deal with.

John's friendship with Bryan Evans and Jessica Shintani grew after the tragedy on the Kitlope traverse, and whenever he visited their cosy little house with its picture-book backyard just off trendy Main Street, he would imagine fleetingly how his life could have been different. Bryan, whose work involves community-based land use planning and natural resource management, had been Randy's good friend through their mutual interest in conservation and mountaineering.

John was always keen to hear about what I was doing ... you could see his eyes open wide ... and he was clearly incredibly supportive of my [conservation] work, but I don't think at that point in his life he saw himself involved in that work. It was Randy's death that was the catalyst for John. He clearly said, "I need to do something for conservation. I need to take over Randy's legacy ... "

John's chance to have an impact came in 1995 after the NDP government of BC appointed a Regional Public Advisory Committee (RPAC) that was dedicated to completing the park system in southwestern BC. This RPAC's specific task was to ensure that 13 percent of the land base was set aside as parks in accordance with the mandate of the Rio Convention on Biological Diversity, which had been held in June 1992. The government had already established the important concept of ecosystem representation as the fundamental premise in the identification and selection of new protected areas. However, the RPAC process was not open to the public. Instead, it involved negotiations between representatives from industry, trade unions, outdoor recreation programs and conservation groups. Even the Squamish Nation was not invited to join the process, although much of the land under consideration for park status was within their traditional territory. In response to this closed-door policy, an ad hoc coalition of conservation and outdoor recreation organizations formed the Southwest Wildlands Alliance. Its goals were to educate the public about the best possible selection of the remaining wilderness areas to be set aside as parks and to provide the public with the information and tools to get involved and flex their democratic muscles.

John became a pivotal player in the Southwest Wildlands Alliance strategy, picking up the conservation torch where Randy had left off. Although he eventually returned to the Coast Mountains, he never did another full six-month season of mountaineering. He put away his ice axe and his climbing boots and took the wilderness to the people of British Columbia. He toured throughout the Lower Mainland giving slide shows and talks, his classic brown leather briefcase—recycled from the dump—manacled to his wrist, his projector and oversized 12-by-12-foot (3.5-by-3.5-metre) screen at the ready. His attention to detail was just as apparent on these speaking tours as it was in the mountains. He would carefully record his monthly agenda on the calendar he had designed to fit exactly within his briefcase. This, along with endless to-do lists, ran his daily life: "If you do something that you hadn't written down," John would say, "jot it down so that you can cross it off."

As one who was used to gaps—gaps between and within mountains, gaps in his resumé—John was the first to point out the glaring omission from the discussions between government, industry, environmentalists and conservationists. It was the general public, the people of British Columbia, who had been left out of the equation of how to divvy up the remaining wilderness. But the people of BC were completely uneducated when it came to understanding the Protected Areas Strategy and what was at stake, and he saw it as his job to fill this gap. Through his multimedia presentations he educated thousands of people about the remaining intact valleys of southwestern BC, what was unique about each one and why they might merit conservation status.

No venue was too small or too large for his presentations—from cramped church halls to the roomy Robson Media Centre in downtown Vancouver. With his images of remote wilderness, his encyclopedic knowledge, his energetic speaking style and his unique brand of humour, he captivated the hearts and minds of his audience. Bryan Evans recalled that:

> John was very different, and I appreciated that because he was too emotionally intelligent to be pedantic and holier than thou. He never bashed people over the head with an environmental message. His style was humour and personal experience and wonder and wisdom. He would go and talk to people and he wouldn't start with this depressing message. He'd start with "Isn't this an incredible place we live in? Aren't we extraordinarily lucky to be here? Look at these places! Isn't this fantastic? By the way, there's a way for you to get involved and help keep Nature beautiful." It was an empowering message, not a debilitating message.

I attended many of John's slide shows and observed how he synthesized complex facts and information into an enjoyable, easily digestible presentation. He taught by example, presented the evidence and let people make up their own minds and draw their own conclusions. His was an effective and powerful approach. Even the skeptics were won over in a time when environmentalists were often considered to be the bad guys—tree huggers who jeopardized forestry jobs in their attempts to preserve the ancient forests.

John would set the scene by projecting a series of archival photographs while he described the history of logging in British Columbia. "The industry started in the 1800s with very low-scale logging with oxen," he would say, showing an image of oxen yoked together to haul a single giant red cedar log. Then, using photographs, maps and satellite images, he would take his audience on a journey up the coast, from inlet to inlet, valley by valley, showing the incursions of the timber industry as they clear-cut valley after valley, rendering the ancient giants of the forest into two-by-fours. He told his audiences:

John Baldwin poses by a Steam Donkey abandoned on the banks of the Fyler River, upstream from Toba Inlet, 1986. PHOTO BY JOHN CLARKE, COURTESY OF ANNETTE CLARKE

> One of the problems with the industry is that it has the same appetite that it had when there was an enormous supply, and now that the supply is very small, it is creating an accelerating effect on the harvesting so that the last few stands of old growth are being liquidated at a terrific rate ... I used to think they would stop one day, but then I realized they never would because they always took the best of what was left. They high-graded the ancient forests. One of the most profound things that's ever happened to me in that regard is camping in a grove of Douglas fir in Toba Inlet and then coming back to the same spot after the logging and actually finding the place where the tent had stood in the stumps. I never forgot that profound change. It didn't even look like the same planet.

John's conversion to conservation was a breath of fresh air for many in the environmental movement. His approach was unconventional, personal and enjoyable, and he relished the whole process of keeping up-to-date. He scanned the daily papers for information; chatted with the local conservation organizations such as the Sierra Club, the David Suzuki Foundation and Sierra Legal Defence Fund (now Ecojustice); attended meetings; and knew every detail of the forest industry's five-year plan for timber harvesting. Like Randy, he was liked and respected by everyone regardless of which side they were on. His first visit to the office of Joe Foy, national campaign director for the Wilderness Committee, was memorable. Joe, an avid outdoors person, had read of John's many first ascents:

> [W]hen John dropped by our office, I was fairly awestruck. He came in on a particular mission. He had a picture in his pocket, which he hauled out and handed me. It was a picture of the pictograph in the Douglas Creek valley [which he and Dave Lammers had discovered on their trip to Mount Mason in 1990]. He explained how important it was that the Douglas Creek valley be protected as part of the overall strategy ... One of John's techniques was to go down to the Forest Service office and ask to see maps. He would photocopy them and ... then would go over [them] and he'd see where the biggest trees were in the areas that were likely to be cut. Then he and his friends would cut a little trail into those areas [and they] would become the basis of some of John's educational trips.
>
> John came into the movement at a very difficult time, and he was hugely effective. He had a wealth of knowledge, a great deal of courage, a *huge* sense of humour and the gift of the gab. And he was able to step back from those angry times and make a really big difference in the area of education ... He helped to open up another entranceway for people to come into the issue, which by that point in the late '90s had really become controversial.

John ran his new life on all cylinders. By 1995 he was not only working with the Southwest Wildlands Alliance but he was busy creating a network of trails in the Upper Lillooet Valley, which was under imminent threat of logging. A handful of his conservationist friends joined him on those early weekend forays, and together they started a campaign to preserve the Upper Lillooet as part of what Randy

Stoltmann had called the Stanley Smith Wilderness but his friends now called the "Stoltmann Wilderness."

On one of these forays John met photographer and artist Nancy Bleck, who had worked with Randy in the Carmanah Valley on the west coast of Vancouver Island. She had spent her days there high above the ground photographing the canopy of the giant Sitka spruce. On this occasion Joe Foy, the organizer for the Save the Stoltmann Wilderness campaign, had invited John to speak to the hundred or so people who had gathered on the banks of the Elaho River for the weekend. John put on a slide show in the amphitheatre of the valley with the starlit sky above,

John Clarke, conservationist, admires an ancient Douglas fir in the Elaho Valley, 1997. PHOTO BY NANCY BLECK

the clear-cut as a backdrop on one side of the screen and the ancient forests on the other. His projector had quietly hummed, hooked to its life-support generator. Next day, as the rain pelted down in traditional West Coast style, John and Nancy became acquainted. "We met around the campfire," John said. "And of course great things happen around campfires." Nancy agrees that there was an immediate spark between them as they brainstormed new ways to engage the public's awareness of wilderness. "I had the amazing fortune to have known Randy and to have known John because they are the best of the best," she recalled as we spoke about those times.

"Okay! What do we do now? We can't just go home," Nancy told John as she took out a pen and soggy paper. Combining their talents, they then devised a strategy to engage the public. They would organize camping weekends for city folk in the Upper Lillooet Valley to introduce them to the threatened wilderness. "There's no substitute for people swatting bugs, getting rained on and reconnecting to the landscape," John said. "They are then in a position to judge for themselves what is being reported in the media [about ecology, logging and land use issues]." Through this increased public awareness and the consequent media attention, they hoped to influence the outcome of the Regional Public Advisory Committee (RPAC). It was the intensity of the experience and the sense of urgency during those long, hot summer days of 1995 that cemented Nancy and John's friendship. Each weekend they made the six-hour return journey from Vancouver to the Lillooet Valley. They knew its fate would be decided in the next few months.

About this time Randy's legacy was also changing my life in a way that would connect me with John Clarke and Nancy Bleck. Ever since reading Randy's vivid description of his alpine traverse between Princess Louisa Inlet and Meager Hot Springs—now named the Stoltmann Traverse after Randy—I had resolved to explore that wilderness area and stand on the summit of Mount Tinniswood, a prominent peak at the head of Sims Creek. To prepare for the journey, I phoned John Clarke, although I hardly knew him at the time, but he was *the* guy to chat to about planning a long traverse. I had no inkling how enthusiastic and helpful he could be when talking about his favourite subject—the Coast Mountains. "No problem," he said as he brought me up to speed on the art of mountain travel.

In July my husband Peter and I teamed up with two mountaineering friends and started our trek across the high country. Three days later we were camped on flat rocky slabs high on the approach ridge of 9,016-foot (2,748-metre) Mount Tinniswood. Below us, in the fading light, we could see clouds swirling and scudding across the ghostly glaciers. Next morning mists clung to the rocky ridge, parting once to reveal a tantalizing glimpse of the steep route ahead. Nearing a massive cornice, I caught a glimpse of the spectacular peak and bolted for the summit. Soon I stood in a pool of sunshine—its rays piercing a cerulean blue hole in the overcast sky.

A substantial rock cairn crowns the summit and stashed within it was a weatherproof canister containing a logbook. As I browsed through it, I found an entry dated August 17, 1993: "Traversing from Meager Creek via Elaho Mountain, Racoon Pass, Clendenning Glacier. Day 18, heading for Princess Louisa Inlet ... Climbed

Tinniswood via east ridge—a classic! May this land remain wild forever." It was signed by Randy Stoltmann. Inspired, I scribbled my commitment to help keep these wild lands wild.

On my return from the wilderness I became involved in the RPAC process and for several months attended the roundtable meetings as an alternate representative for the BC Mountaineering Club. I was also involved in the Southwest Wildlands Alliance campaign and started to get to know John. Just before Christmas 1995 there was a stunning turn of events in the campaign to save the Stoltmann Wilderness. On December 23 I received a phone call from Bryan Evans. "I've got bad news," he said. "A friend of mine just returned from hiking in the back end of the Squamish Valley and noticed the construction of a bridge across the Elaho River."

"No way! That can't be true. Isn't there a moratorium on any development in the proposed areas?"

"There sure is."

"We've got to stop them!"

"Them" in this case was International Forest Products (Interfor), which was obviously preparing to log the west bank of the river, even though there was a moratorium on timber extraction until the RPAC process had been completed and the new park boundaries drawn. I phoned John and we made a plan. By the next day we'd received permission from Mountain Equipment Co-op to set up a couple of tables behind the phalanx of cash registers. On Boxing Day we started an educational and letter-writing campaign—one handwritten letter is ten times more effective than a form letter—enlisting the help of the public and putting democracy to work. Over the next three months, with help from Bryan and many friends, we informed people about the illicit bridge building by Interfor, whose representative sat at the RPAC table. By March 1996 over 3,500 letters had reached the government in Victoria. The bridge was never completed and the supports remain today as an unofficial gateway to what is now known as Clendinning Provincial Park.

By May of 1996 a compromise solution was finally reached by the members of the RPAC. The new park boundaries were drawn on the map and 134,000 hectares (331,000 acres) were preserved, including almost 30,000 hectares (74,000 acres) of the Clendenning Valley. This was part of Interfor's Tree Farm License (TFL) 38, which is within the traditional territory of the Squamish Nation. Unfortunately, it was a far cry from the Stoltmann Wilderness Provincial Park proposal of 260,000 hectares of mountains, glaciers and ancient rain-forested valleys.

Although the official announcement would not be made for several months, John and I celebrated the gains that had been achieved by making an alpine traverse from Princess Louisa Inlet across to Sims Creek, a tributary of the Elaho River. I had never fully realized the depth of John's passion for the coastal mountains until the moment when we burst into the alpine meadows above Princess Louisa Inlet. They lay spread before us in their full glory, glimmering in the evening sunlight. John stopped, stunned. "Ah, my Coast Ranges," he whispered as one united with a lover. It was John's third year of foregoing his climbing season after the death of Randy Stoltmann. As we made our way to the high ridges, Mount Tinniswood beckoning across the dividing valley, both of us were thinking about Randy's legacy and how much more needed to be done to keep this wild land wild forever.

The new parks were officially announced on October 28, 1996. In the minds of both industry and government, the preservation needs in southwestern BC had been met by the negotiated process and a

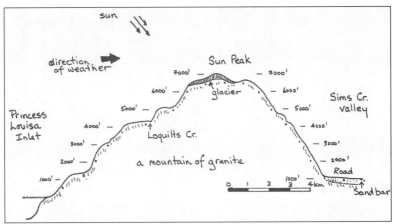

John Clarke's 1997 sketch of the elevation profile of the route from Princess Louisa Inlet to Sims Creek. COURTESY OF ANNETTE CLARKE

balance had been achieved. For several environmental groups, however, the decision was unacceptable. A huge publicity campaign began in an attempt to preserve the entire "Stoltmann Wilderness," and this was the start of what was dubbed "the war in the woods," loggers and environmentalists lining up to do battle over the future of the last vestiges of wilderness in southwestern BC.

John knew that, like all battles, victories are seldom won by violence but by dialogue, mitigation and compromise, and being willing to see the other party's point of view: "We all live on the same planet and we're in this together" was his attitude. The peace and education he advocated were in direct contrast to the weapons of confrontation and rhetoric used by many environmentalists at that time. Reflecting on those days, John later acknowledged:

> There are a lot of skills out there in the conservation movement, but the hole that needed to be filled was somebody who had been to all these places, was familiar with them, familiar with the politics, and someone who had photographs of it. It was so easy just to slide into [that hole] that I'm thinking now I should have done it years ago.

John's commitment to conservation was equally as powerful as his commitment to exploring the Coast Mountains. Although he may have felt at the time that he'd turned his back on the mountains, in fact there was no dividing line between conservation and exploration. His love of the Coast Mountains permeated his whole being and dictated the course of his life. And Randy Stoltmann had shown him the way, as is clear from a note in John's diary at the time: "11AM—meet with BC Wild. *What would Randy do?*"

16

Witness/Ut'sam

Being called to witness in the Coast Salish tradition is a sacred honour.

—Chief Bill Williams

In the spring of 1996, soon after the Regional Public Advisory Committee (RPAC) process came to a close but before the official parks announcements had been made, John's work with the Southwest Wildlands Alliance came to an end, as did my own involvement with the RPAC. It was also that spring, after learning that the Upper Lillooet Valley would become one of the new parks, that John switched his conservation focus to the then little-known Sims Creek valley, a tributary of the Elaho River in the most northern part of the Squamish Nation's territory, fifty-two miles (eighty-four kilometres) northwest of the town of Squamish. He realized that, with the creation of the new parks and the lifting of the moratorium on timber harvesting, the lucrative old growth in the Sims Creek valley, which had not been included in the protected areas, would be logged the very next year—1997.

To the provincial government and the logging industry the Sims Creek valley is known simply as Tree Farm License (TFL) 38. For the Squamish Nation, the valley is part of their traditional and cultural heritage. They call it home. However, logging in TFL 38 had begun in the 1950s, and was managed by a number of different companies without any consultation with the Squamish Nation. In 1960 the BC government had awarded TFL 38 to Weldwood Canada; in

John Clarke guides a group of Witness participants through the ancient forests of Sims Creek, 1997. PHOTO BY NANCY BLECK

1995 International Forest Products (Interfor) took over Weldwood's tenure.

John's commitment to the preservation of the Sims Creek valley was formidable. Every weekend from April to October in 1996 he headed off to the valley accompanied by a group of city folk. With help from volunteers—Nancy Bleck, Heather Kirk and Doug Brown—they set up camp on the pristine sandbar at the confluence of Sims Creek and the Elaho River, and John would guide them on tours of the ancient forests. In the long summer evenings they would gather around a campfire and share their experiences of the wilderness. Long, lazy mornings on the sandbar were restorative and relaxing and the urbanites returned to the city with a new awareness. One participant commented that the area was "beautiful, tranquil, peaceful, informative, educational, fun, secluded, untouched," and then added, "I got John Clarked."

In time the steady stream of city people making the pilgrimage back and forth to the Sims Creek valley captured the attention of Chief Bill Williams, hereditary chief of the Squamish Nation and watchman for the northern part of their territory. An astute man, reserved by nature, he goes quietly but firmly about his business, and on September 28 he decided to investigate. It happened to be the last weekend of the gatherings at the Sims sandbar for the year, and more than sixty-five people had assembled there. Many had attended several of these camping weekends already, myself included, and we considered ourselves part of the Sims Creek family. Nancy Bleck had brought gifts for all the volunteers, but just as the gift giving was about to start she noticed Chief Bill standing off to one side. She introduced herself and he handed her his card. She was stunned when she saw who he was. Although aware of First Nations protocol, she realized that the Sims group had never asked the Squamish Nation's permission to be on their territory. She invited the chief to address the group and introduced him by his Squamish name, *telàsemkin-si-yam* (pronounced *Ta-lall-SAHM-cane.*) Then she gave him an eagle feather, which in the Squamish Nation's culture is an acknowledgement that people honour and value you.

Chief Bill spoke to the group and explained that, because the logging road had been constructed without approval or consultation with the Squamish Nation, protocol had been breached and therefore he could not give the campers a formal welcome. However, he told them he would be prepared to help with their long-term vision to protect the valley as long as they embraced the First Nation's traditional ceremonies and their perspective on the land.

"Witness," or *Ut'sam*, was the name chosen for the new alliance between the explorer, the artist and the Squamish First Nation chief because it is the name of the traditional Coast Salish ceremony that is used to record important "work" or events in their oral culture. Witnesses hold a stake in the community's future, and if there are doubts or questions concerning a past event, it is up to the witnesses to verify what happened. They are the eyes and ears of the land. The Witness Project became the flagship program of the newly opened Roundhouse Community Centre in downtown Vancouver, which is also on traditional Squamish First Nation territory.

The program's launch in the early summer of 1997 coincided with an escalation of the war in the woods as environmentalists and Interfor, now aggressively logging the Elaho and Sims valleys, clashed. To prevent the entry of environmentalists into TFL 38, the loggers had set up a blockade on the Squamish logging road. It quickly became evident that Interfor suspected John Clarke, always conspicuous because of his crazy white hair and ebullient personality, was a key leader in the war in the woods and they were on the lookout for him.

Chief Bill Williams, hereditary chief of the Squamish First Nation, wears a traditional button blanket, 1998. PHOTO BY NANCY BLECK

Chief Bill had contacted those in charge of the blockade and informed them that he would be leading a large group into the Sims Creek valley to conduct a ceremony on Saturday, July 12. The blockaders insisted that everyone who entered the TFL had to sign a waiver to indicate they were entering for recreational purposes only. To simplify the process, Chief Bill's group of ninety signed waivers ahead of time. After passing through the town of Squamish, the Witness cavalcade snaked its way along the dusty logging road, the Squamish Nation Peacekeepers in the lead in their big trucks, Chief Bill right behind them. John Clarke was suspiciously absent. Suspecting the loggers might be watching for him, he had enlisted the help of Chief Ian Campbell, a young man with a well-honed sense of humour. Before the cavalcade reached the blockade, Chief Ian stashed John under a pile of ceremonial blankets in the back of his Dodge Ram crew cab.

At Mile 21 on the logging road, where a large crowd had gathered around the blockade, Chief Bill handed over the sheaf of signed waiver forms and drove on through. The loggers knew they couldn't refuse the chief entry. They also knew that, if push came to shove, the Squamish Nation had the ultimate authority to close down the road. As the Witness convoy headed off, it was clear to Chief Bill, who had his radio on, that the loggers had failed to check through the wad of signatures until the party was three miles down the road and had noticed too late several unwanted signatures. The conversation over the radio went something like:

"What the hell are we going to do?"

"How are we going to stop them?"

When the Witness cavalcade arrived at the bridge crossing the Squamish River, a truck straddled the bridge blocking their way.

"What's going on?" Chief Bill asked the man standing in the middle of the bridge beside his truck.

"My truck broke down. I can't move it."

"No problem," said the chief. "Just put it in neutral and we'll push you out of the way."

So they pushed the truck off to the side while Chief Bill waved on the first five vehicles in the cavalcade. Chief Ian and John were in the second truck that barrelled past. When the rest of the Witness cavalcade pulled up at the sandbar on Sims Creek, John was there to greet them, an even wider grin on his face than usual. There were no further attempts to stop his access to TFL 38.

At the core of Witness were Chief Bill Williams, Nancy Bleck and John Clarke. Chief Bill represented the Squamish Nation and conducted the sacred Witness ceremony and informed the participants about Coast Salish culture, traditions and rights. Nancy raised funds, brought in speakers and artists to conduct a wide variety of workshops, coordinated the media, designed the brochure and documented the weekends through her photography. She became the first artist-in-residence at the Roundhouse Community Centre.

John connected urban people with the wilderness, introduced them to the art of camping and hiking, and informed them about current land-use issues. He crafted a network of trails through the old-growth forest, including a vertiginous trail to Bug Lake in the al-

Photographer Nancy Bleck at work in the Sims Creek valley, 2006. PHOTO BY BETH CARRUTHERS

pine some 3,000 feet above Sims Creek. The irony wasn't lost on him that he'd spent all his life in the wilderness and now he was making endless trails—since they were frequently destroyed by the next wave of clear-cut logging. "The same spot where only a decade ago it had taken me two weeks to walk I can now drive in two hours." His guided trips through the old growth were memorable, and not only because of the juxtaposition of the 800-year-old trees with the gaping clear-cuts. Surrounded by a horde of adoring kids, he could often be seen leaping across the fallen logs to go into the untouched forest. If it hadn't been for the difference in size and John's white hair, he would have been indistinguishable from the youngsters.

For many Witness participants this was their first camping experience. They had never set up a tent, drunk water straight from a creek, experienced the awe of an ancient forest or seen the devastation of clear-cut logging. The rich diversity of people engendered lively and interesting discussions around the campfire far into the night. This was the stuff of magic.

Drew Leathem, a volunteer with the Witness Project who had been in his early twenties when he signed up for a Witness orientation weekend, admitted he'd had no idea what to expect. John had immediately taken centre stage as they travelled in Scott Mason's luxurious Land Sea Tour bus along the rutted logging road to the sandbar. Clad in his all-white mountain attire, he had kept up a running commentary. "He's looking kind of youthful and kind of like a mental patient at the same time," Drew recalled, laughing. "Every time he got out of the bus, it was like watching a kid on Christmas day—hands in the air, too excited to quite stand still, and running around like he was discovering presents from Santa." But as the weekend progressed, Drew started to grasp the depth of John's knowledge. "It was

Life on the run! John Clarke bounds across Sims Creek, 1997. PHOTO BY NANCY BLECK

like trying to get the sense of how big an iceberg is from sitting on its peak. You start to realize that this thing must go down a ways."

Drew remained associated with Witness for the next ten years. "John was the reason that everybody volunteered," he said, and continued:

> He was the catalyst in the most faithful scientific sense. He was the ingredient without which the job would not have gotten done. In all of the years of Witness there were a very, very small handful of accidents and health and safety concerns. It was all because we were all so attentive and worried and put so much intentionality into taking care of everybody—because John did.
>
> John kept [Witness] pure. He kept it innocent. He kept it light. He kept it as much about loving the outdoors as it was about controlling land use. But he wasn't shy about analyzing forest cover, he wasn't shy about talking land use planning, he wasn't shy about talking exact boundaries, jurisdictions and forest development planning. But he brought a level of gaiety and levity to it, really made it possible. It would have been awkward without John.

The Witness ceremony, the focal point of each weekend, was conducted by Chief Bill or another member of the Squamish Nation. People gathered in a wide circle on the sandbar and four witnesses were invited to express what they had observed, and they were paid a ceremonial fifty cents for their "work." They would then take

The Witness ceremony takes place on the Sims Creek sandbar, 1997. PHOTO BY NANCY BLECK

what they had learned back to their families, friends, neighbours and communities, thereby re-creating the ancient aboriginal oral tradition. "People would speak from their hearts," Nancy recalled, "and explain why they felt that this area was important to them. It became a form of democracy unlike anything I have ever known." Everyone took away something from those weekends, including members of the Squamish First Nation community. One of them wrote:

> As a First Nations person raised in foster homes and away from the land, it was an eye opener and it felt like going home again. I feel that this is the beginning of the path back to my heritage.

John and Chief Bill developed a deep respect for one another through their work and connection to the land, and one day in the late summer of 1997 the chief asked John to take him across his own territory. For five days the mountaineer guided the Squamish Nation chief from Princess Louisa Inlet across the high country to Sims Creek—a land that he'd never seen. On the last Witness weekend that summer a small ceremony took place on the sandbar. Chief Bill wrapped John in a ceremonial blanket, designated him as Speaker on behalf of their

Bob Baker of the Squamish First Nation drums during a Witness ceremony held on the sandbar of Sims Creek, 2006. PHOTO BY NANCY BLECK

Wrap-up weekend at Sims Creek, Sept 28, 1996. John Clarke, amidst a flurry of kids, unwraps gifts. PHOTO BY BRYAN EVANS

land and placed in his hand a traditional talking stick carved like a miniature totem pole. Then Chief Bill spoke of Nancy's pivotal role in engaging the Roundhouse Community Centre and gave her an eagle feather.

The year culminated in an art show at the Roundhouse with all Witness participants invited to take part. The exhibition was exceptional in its richness, depth and variety, and a testimony to the powerful effect of reconnecting urban people to their wilderness heritage. At the closing ceremonies of the art exhibition on January 18, 1998, the Squamish Nation adopted John as one of their own in a sacred naming ceremony. By now Chief Bill and members of the First Nation had seen him in action and recognized that his attitude toward the land was almost identical to that of a traditional Squamish person. "John did not try to take anything away from the land," Chief Bill said. "He always tried to leave the land as pristine as possible and at the same time just experience what is there as a human being. And that is what we have always done." They named him *Xwexwselken* (pronounced "hoksolken"), or "Mountain Goat," a thoroughly appropriate choice for a man who was as much goat as man, with his white hair and beard and his trademark climbing uniform of white long johns and a white cotton shirt. Like the goats, he loved to ramble among the remote peaks, but he was also, like them, obliged to descend in winter for shelter and nourishment.

Meanwhile, Interfor continued logging the old-growth forests in the Elaho and Sims valleys, advancing a mile or two (two to three kilometres) each year. By early 1998 they were approaching Sims Creek canyon, which would require the construction of a bridge across the raging torrent to access the valley on the other side. In an effort to reach even more people with his message about the unabated logging in the few remaining watersheds and the urgent need to protect them, John gave more and more public presentations. On a raw February evening in 1998 he spoke to a packed audience at the HR MacMillan Planetarium. Many people were turned away at the door so a second show was arranged for the following week.

For once John had almost lost his sense of humour as, grim-faced, he came out fists raised in defense of wilderness. The title of his presentation, "Captured Territory," referred to the remaining pristine valleys within the Squamish Nation's traditional lands, now locked between the jaws of government and industry. His photographs revealed the devastating changes wrought on the BC landscape over the last few decades. His final words remain a wake-up call to all:

> In fifty years it won't be the place with the most malls and golf courses that will have the edge for tourism but the place with the most grizzlies and wild salmon. One thing we humans have a hard time with is to accept that we are not needed to *manage* nature. The forests of the Stoltmann were *not* waiting for us to get here to manage them. If there's a basic shift that needs to take place, it's for us humans to approach landscape with a little humility and a reverence for what is already there.
>
> We've seen the richness that once was these valleys, the speed at which it was lost, how little is left and how fast we plan to consume the rest. These trees are our own Taj Mahal. Nature *bats last*! This means we may be in the lead now. The natural world may seem the underdog, but when we've finished our act and hit the grand slam, Nature has an extra inning coming all to herself—unopposed and unending. No one will be

keeping score any more ... Are we to go down in history as a generation that stood by? God only knows how we are going to be perceived by future generations. Nobody fifty years from now is going to say, "Well, that *shouldn't* have been saved."

Witness continued to grow in influence and scope. In 1999 Drew Leathem spearheaded a program for the youth of the Squamish Nation, a program that became known as the Aboriginal Youth Ambassador Program, designed to involve them in the Witness Project, to reconnect them to their own territory and strengthen their level of engagement within the Squamish Nation community. (Today Native youth go to the Squamish Lil'wat Cultural Centre in Whistler to be instructed not only in the lore of the land but also in the skills needed to work in tourism.) Drew recalled:

> Every year the first thing that we did with these young people when we arrived at the Sims sandbar was give them to John ... It wasn't that John would ever preach. It was just his presence and the example by which he led. He connected to those young people, even if he didn't know them for very long. They'd joke together, bad-mouth each other and have fun. It was surreal ... but he did the most for race relations in the shortest amount of time that I think I've ever seen anybody do.

Witness continued every summer and gradually an awareness grew within Native and non-Native communities regarding land use issues and the Squamish Nation's traditional culture. But when early in 2001 the Squamish Nation approached Interfor about conserving what was left of the upper Sims Creek valley for traditional uses, an Interfor employee questioned whether there was enough public interest in the area to warrant its protection. Astonishingly, it seemed the company was oblivious to the growing public interest in and significant turnout at the Witness weekends over the previous four years; by that time some 5,000 people had participated in the Witness Project in the Sims valley and of those some 1,500 had stepped forward as witnesses.

The Witness team immediately called a meeting with head

forester Rick Slaco in his Squamish office. "We looked like a crazy motley crew," Nancy Bleck remembered, laughing, and she continued:

> We looked like characters in a strange movie: Bill looking very political, Gregory looking very Greenpeace, Aaron looking very cultural, and John with his briefcase and white hair looking like a character out of a cartoon, and there's me. I think I arrived in a miniskirt with a leather jacket. We looked like the most unlikely group you've ever seen. And Slaco is saying: "I want to cut this area. What do you think of that?"

The area under threat was identified simply as Block 72-4 on Interfor's detailed logging plan, but for John and Witness participants, that block of forest had become an integral part of their lives. And while the delegation to Slaco's office may have looked bizarre, they were all smart and fast thinkers. With the backing of the Squamish Nation they devised a strategy based on an 8,000-year-old Coast Salish ceremony called *Texwaya7ni7m* (pronounced "tach way natum") and on words written in the Squamish Nation's Assertion of Aboriginal Title concerning the duties of witnesses: "If, in the future or at any time in their life, there is a concern over what took place they, as witnesses, have to recall what they have heard and seen with regard to that event." Now Chief Bill Williams sent out letters to all the witnesses who had come to know the Sims Creek valley so intimately over the past four years. The letters read in part:

> Only the most urgent need for your assistance motivates this request. The time has come when you can make good on the commitment you made as witnesses for the wilderness lands of the Sims Valley.

It was an impressive sight on April 28, 2001, when over 300 people gathered on the logging road at Sims Creek in response to Chief Bill's urgent request. Never before had both Native and non-Native speakers gathered to take part in this traditional Coast Salish ceremony. Speakers and witnesses encircled the blazing ceremonial fire, brilliant against the stark backdrop of the denuded mountainside, while onlookers perched on massive piles of discarded timber. After members of the Squamish Nation had spoken, witnesses, including Nancy

Squamish Nation drummers at the Texwaya7ni7m [pronounced tach way natum] ceremony, Sims Creek valley, 2001. PHOTO BY NANCY BLECK

and John, told their stories. At the invitation of Chief Bill, Rick Slaco spoke on behalf of Interfor. This was a politically astute move on the chief's part: by acknowledging the validity of this 8,000-year-old traditional ceremony, Interfor forfeited the right to harvest cut Block 74-2. And Slaco was aware of this fact when he accepted Chief Bill's invitation to speak.

As a consequence of this democratic process, Interfor had no further legal hold on Block 72-4. Today you may drive to the end of the logging road in the Sims Creek valley, walk up the John Clarke Trail to Bug Lake and see for yourself the remaining magnificent trees— the link between land, water and sky.

This historic event on the logging road and the discovery of ancient ceremonial sites in the upper Elaho and Sims valleys served to further empower and awaken the Squamish Nation's desire to take control of developments within their own territory. They were also empowered by the decision of the Supreme Court of Canada in the Delgamuukw case in 1997, which confirmed that aboriginal title does exist in British Columbia and that this title is a right to the land itself and is based on the First Nations' relationship with the land. From then on government has had to consult with, and possibly compensate, those First Nations whose rights are affected.

Another process that would affect the Squamish Nation's land claims was unfolding at this time. In 2000 the province started a process intended to ensure the "long-term sustainability of cultural and ecological values, and provide greater certainty for local economic development." This was known as the Sea-to-Sky Land and Resource Management Plan (LRMP). However, at that time the government would only allow input from the Squamish Nation after the plan was finished. This propelled the Squamish Nation to make their own plan, and Chief Bill asked John Clarke to recommend a person to hire to draw it up. He chose Bryan Evans, who had just completed another land use plan and was familiar with the terminology and format required by the provincial government. The resulting Squamish Nation Land Use Plan, called *Xay Temixw*, or "Sacred Land," designated the Sims valley, the Upper Elaho and several other areas in Squamish Nation territory as "Wild Spirit Places." Official recognition from the BC government for this plan was finally granted in 2005, but the First Nation was then informed that they would have to compensate the holder of the tree farm license for the loss of the harvestable timber in the Wild Spirit Places. Unbeknownst to the government, however, the Squamish Nation was already negotiating with Interfor to buy the TFL, and in 2006 they purchased the 540,000 acres (218,000 hectares) for $6.5 million. "Of course, the province now has to compensate the Squamish Nation for the loss of the very valuable timber that can no longer be extracted from the Wild Spirit Places," said Chief Bill, a twinkle in his eye.

Witness volunteers, *left to right*: Jeremy Williams, Drew Leathem, Gregory Byrne, Shel Neufeld. PHOTO BY JEREMY WILLIAMS

Chief Bill looked back on Witness as a unique journey:

It went on for ten years and unfortunately John passed away during that time period, but at the very end the objectives of John, myself and Nancy were complete ... The agreement that we signed ... between the Squamish Nation and the provincial government set aside all the areas that we identified for cultural purposes so that the work that we had started as a group of three was, in fact, completed.

Many of those who came to Sims Creek during those ten years became volunteers, drawn by John's energy, inseparable from the wild lands around him. Among them was Shel Neufeld, who came to his first Witness weekend in 1997, freshly arrived from Ontario. "I'd never seen such colossal trees in my life," he said. "I remember sitting in the 'magic cedar' grove, incredulous that anybody would want to harvest these trees." The next thing he saw was this white-haired man wandering among the vast cedars with his tripod and camera, a cluster of people buzzing around him. "I could hear the passion in his voice, and feel the connection he had with the forest. He obviously had so much knowledge that I wanted to listen closer to hear what he was saying." The following year Shel signed up as a volunteer for Witness. "John valued people's contributions, no matter how insignificant they might feel they were," said Shel. "He would remind us: 'No matter what's left [of Sims Creek valley] after this is over, it wouldn't have been here had we not done something about it.'"

In 1999 John invited Shel to join him to climb the peaks in the Upper Pitt River area of Garibaldi Park. Shel was nervous because he had never done a mountaineering trip. "I remember John pulling out these pound slabs of butter ... 'I don't think I'm going to eat all that,' I told him. But I didn't realize how hard it would be carrying my huge pack." For two days they bushwhacked up the wild Pitt River Valley, where the salmon were spawning and bear trails revealed deep indentations where they'd been placing their paws in the exact same spot for hundreds of years.

After a while I was almost wishing I had more butter! But the greatest thing about that trip was the direct and indirect advice John gave me about photography, mountaineering and appreciation of the wilderness ... A highlight for John was reaching the summit of Katzie Mountain and seeing a cairn up there. "Yeah!" he said, "I was up here in '71." He pulls out this old style film canister—his hands were almost shaking. "Wow! Here's my original cairn." The canister disintegrated in his hands and he was left with his note from 1971. No one else had added their name since.

Today Shel Neufeld's business, Wild Art Photography, combines his passions for photography, music and mountaineering.

Jeremy Williams volunteered for ten years with the Witness Project. A photographer, videographer, environmentalist and mountaineer, Jeremy lives in Powell River, BC. Recalling his years with Witness, he said:

> Witness was such a departure from other forms of environmental activism—it was about building a vision for the future, going out on the land to effect change in a peaceful, multi-faceted way ... I started following in [John's] footsteps by giving slide shows. I learned a lot in terms of my presentation skills from him and was also inspired to move into doing documentaries to reach broader audiences ... I think his real magic, in terms of his effectiveness, was that he didn't just sing to the choir, he didn't preach to the converted, he had the ability to reach people in a way a stereotypical environmentalist would not be able to speak to.

John's enduring lessons about life made many youngsters want to emulate him. Drew Leathem said, "I was going to be a lawyer before I met John." Instead, he got his MBA and specializes in providing business development and public relations services for aboriginal and non-aboriginal community and economic development projects. He said:

> The reason that I'm doing what I'm doing today, my whole career path—working with First Nations, developing communities, working on cause-based projects—is because John showed me how to do it, how to work on a cause-based project in a way that could fire you up, could make you really energetic, could bring you closer to a community of people and enable you to have a fulfilling life and have fun ... [Now] I actively work to *not* try and drive but to be an active participant, open

John Clarke guides Witness volunteers and participants on a 1998 traverse of the high country above Sims Creek valley to the summit of what is now Mount John Clarke. *Left to right, back:* Jeremy Williams, Greg Maurer, Scott Mason, Drew Leathem, Nancy Bleck, John Clarke and Mac. *Front:* Shel Neufeld and Gregory Byrne. PHOTO BY JEREMY WILLIAMS

to where things might go, to *not* label and to *not* judge too much ... And one of the things that I do sometimes when I'm in a tough situation, I think, *What would John do?*

Before joining Witness as a volunteer, Gregory Byrne had worked in environmental groups and movements for over a decade and had often found it a negative, depressing experience. "When I met John," Gregory said, "I was immediately drawn to him, I wanted to work with him." As with the other volunteers John was an exceptional mentor for Gregory and taught him how to train future volunteers. "I had a broad awareness regarding what was happening with logging and industry and environmentalism in BC, but John really gave me the specific facts and figures. In the first few years of Witness I listened hard to everything he said." By Gregory's third year he was taking on a lot of John's educational responsibilities and went on to become the main educator for new volunteers.

John changed my life by being a living example of what genuine devotion and passion towards our planet exemplifies ... He gave me confidence in exploring the back country and wilderness of the Coast Ranges, which I will continue to do for the rest of my life. He went with me to buy my ice axe for my first trip, [and now] it's battered and scarred and smashed through all my trips. But I bring John Clarke with me wherever I go in the mountains with my ice axe.

Janey Chang, a volunteer with Witness for two years, stated that "Without having been exposed to John's fire, I truly believe that I would be on a different and much less satisfying path than I am today. Likely still in the corporate world because that's what I was always told I was good at doing." When she signed up with Witness in 1999, Janey was freshly transplanted back in Vancouver after a thirteen-year stint in Toronto. She was struck by John's incredible energy: "He seemed almost tornado-like, zipping from one place to another, never really sitting still." But when he did stop for a moment, Janey says his lifestyle and his stories really changed her life. She found a new career working with youngsters in the outdoors. She volunteered for the Northwest Passage Outdoor School for youth at risk and went on to acquire a diploma in adventure tourism. Today she is the manager of the Outdoor Education Department at Mount Seymour. She says:

> I'm eternally grateful to John for exposing me to a career that has integrity, one that I am truly passionate about. For modelling his leadership style—humorous, humble and heart-felt. For his genuine zest for life.

In 2009 Janey joined the Ride to Conquer Cancer. When she cycled the 163 miles (262 kilometres) to Seattle, the sticker on her bicycle read: **I ♥ JOHN CLARKE.**

17

The Wilderness Education Program

We've been taking from this land for so long that it's time we put something back, and that something is ourselves because, if we are familiar with the earth, we are less likely to abuse it.
—John Clarke

At the same time John began working to save the Sims Creek valley from logging in the spring of 1996, I began to think about his future. I'd seen him in action throughout that year and was blown away by his natural ability to teach, his message of advocacy and education, his captivating speaking style and his powerful images of the Coast Mountains. His talents were very different from those of other conservationists so there had to be a special career niche for him, and since his commitment to conservation issues had become so profound, I had no doubt that mountaineering would now be taking second place in his life.

"What are you going to do now that the Regional Public Advisory Committee has wound up?" I asked one day as we crowded around my kitchen table for supper.

"Well, I think I might work for one of the conservation organizations campaigning on the central and north coast."

He had spoken to me about his colleague and friend Ian McAllister and his wife Karen, who were undertaking a systematic inventory of the coastal rivers, forests and estuaries extending from Knight Inlet in the south to the Portland Canal on the BC–Alaska border. Before their inventory not a scrap of biological and ecological information was to be found about this 25,000-square-mile (64,000-square-kilometre) area—more than twice the size of Vancouver Island, and the largest tract of coastal, temperate rain forest left on the planet. The McAllisters had founded the Rainforest Conservation Society and named this region the Great Bear Rainforest. (Later they also founded Pacific Wild, a non-profit conservation organization dedicated to protecting Canada's Pacific Coast.)

John had already contributed valuable information to the initial conservation proposals and plans that the members of the Rainforest Conservation Society were compiling. As he journeyed from the river valleys to the high country and peered down from the clouds into the inlets and valleys, he had been able to amass information and make observations on country that was inaccessible to Ian, who was exploring the river mouths and estuaries. At the end of their respective seasons—mountain high and ocean low—the two would meet to share information. John could tell him about the type of wetlands and lakes he had seen in the back of the watersheds and where he had found signs of grizzly bear or moose habitat, or huge swaths of Sitka spruce, or alluvial-type forest or steep, rocky, avalanche-prone slopes. Ian explained:

> To really rely on detailed information about what these places looked like up in the backs of these river systems was ideal because we were spending so much of our time in the estuaries and the mouths of the rivers—that's where the main spawning reach was and a lot of the ecologically important habitat for a lot of wildlife species that we found. So being able to connect the dots in terms of what was further up the rivers and in the back country—places we couldn't get to—was incredibly important information.

However, in the spring of 1996, instead of encouraging John to work with conservation groups on the central or north coast, I told him that we should be taking the wilderness into the schools. "We need to get youngsters excited about nature, get them outdoors. These are our future leaders and decision makers. How about it, John? You will be the wilderness educator and I will look after the organizational side of things."

When he agreed, I wondered exactly what I had committed myself to. At the time I didn't know him all that well. I didn't know if he'd turn up on time in the schools. I didn't know if he'd show up in his uniform of long white cotton underwear and white shirt. I didn't know how he would interact with the kids, the teachers and the principals. But I also had no idea that he had been giving slide presentations all his life, adored kids and was at heart an entertainer and educator. In fact, John had the ideal pedigree for teaching wilderness education.

We named our new organization the Wilderness Education Program (WildED), and in order to strengthen our fundraising leverage and our reach, we became a program under the fiscal sponsorship of the Federation of Mountain Clubs of BC, which includes mountain and outdoor recreation clubs from most regions of the province. During that first year we put together a broad program that was available for all ages of young people, from kindergarten to post-secondary students. WildED offered four components: classroom-based lectures and slide presentations, follow-up field trips to a local park, workshops for teachers and extended backpacking trips to wilderness areas.

At this time John's home was in his parents' basement at the far end of No. 7 Road in Richmond where, fortunately, the rent was free. In any case, he practically lived in our house in Kitsilano, camping out in the upstairs bedroom recently vacated by our two boys—the "dorm," as John called it. He'd bound out of bed in the morning, run down the stairs and swing around into the kitchen—in a way that only John could—bubbling with enthusiasm. "Morning all!" And I wondered where he got that irrepressible good humour at that time of day. Then he'd grab his projector and gear from our basement and we'd help load up his old Volvo. Lastly, we would shove his oversized screen into the lurid green poly pipe that was secured to the roof of his car. The "Scud," as this rooftop appendage was affectionately called, made John's car instantly recognizable on his tours around Lower Mainland schools. He was always punctual, showing up at each school with plenty of time to assemble his array of equipment and props.

John had a gift for delivering his information at exactly the right level, no matter the age of the children. His message was clear and he never talked down to his audience. The most essential ingredient was *fun*! His goal for the very young was to simply introduce them to the wilderness and the plants and animals that he'd encountered on his journeys through the Coast Mountains. For the older students he would skillfully weave a conservation message into stories from his lifetime of adventures. Often the teachers would request him to emphasize some particular aspect, such as the geography of the Coast Mountains or resource extraction or wilderness skills that tied into what they were dealing with in the curriculum.

The best entertainment you could ever have was to watch him in action with a seething roomful of youngsters sitting cross-legged right in front of the giant screen. They would be beside themselves with excitement and enthusiasm, a bit like John himself, who always felt like a hero as the first slide filled the screen and the entire class exploded into wows, gasps, wriggling, pointing and flailing arms. He loved it, especially when the kids were out of control and the teachers were trying in vain to get them to calm down. "This is my absolute favourite thing in the whole world," he would say, beaming, "being with students—talking about mountains." And he would chuckle to himself as he watched these kids, their eyes like fried eggs, captivated as much by his stories as the images leaping from the screen. After his slide show he would haul out "treasures" from his red backpack—the tuna can that the hungry grizzly bear had popped into its mouth, a slice of an ancient cedar tree salvaged from a clear-cut, a fistful of mountain goat wool. The kids would crawl into his tent, try on his backpack and his headlight, check out his tiny stove and observe how little he needed to survive for weeks in the wilderness.

After he left, the kids would draw and describe what they had seen. Often he would receive letters from them thanking him and begging him to come again:

Dear John Clarke,

I liked all your slides, but my favourite ones were the ones of the animals and the can the bear crushed. I can't believe that bear crushed that can. I wouldn't want to meet that bear! I also liked the music you set the slides to. I wouldn't want to do some of the things you did, like staying in a tent covered with snow or eating some of the food you talked about. I also wouldn't want to pack so much and then have to walk for long distances to get to a food supply and find it gone because an animal got it. I also wouldn't want to get so dirty and then come back to civilization looking weird. I probably wouldn't want to go on a trip like that, but I admire people who do.

Kerry (grade 7)

Dear John Clarke

We really enjoied your slide show. Espially the one with all the Bald Eagles … Those Crampons were really cool. We also liked the slide with your fluffy hair and beard! We really like your tent. Tammy really likes the part with the grizzly bear and baby goat. Please write back.

Tammy and Marika(Grade 4)

And John would reply to their letters.

He was also a big hit with the teenagers and it took but a few seconds for them to realize "this guy is *cool*." He loved the attention, the clapping and jostling and their incessant questions. "I mustn't let this go to my head," he would say, laughing. He would first set the stage then weave the appropriate historical and political context into his presentations for them. "If we were to single out one thing that is most marvellous about our planet, it would have to be its diversity

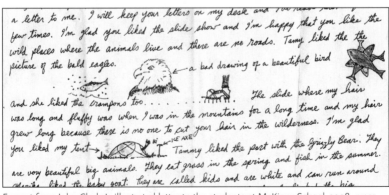

Excerpt from John Clarke's illustrated letter to the students at McKinny School, 1998. IMAGE COURTESY OF WILDED ARCHIVES

Elementary students loved to draw what they liked best about John Clarke's slide shows. Here Samantha has captured the thrill of Steve Sheffield's attempt to reach the far side of Jump Across Creek. As another student remarked, "I wonder if he made it?" He did, but John forgot to tell the class. IMAGE COURTESY OF WILDED ARCHIVES

of life," he would explain while showing an image of our blue planet floating in the black of outer space. "But what really makes our part of the world special—our west coast of British Columbia—is the close juxtaposition of three widely different types of geography: the ocean, the forests and the glaciers—these blinding white glaciers where the ice age never went away." The teens' attention was gripped as, slide by slide and story by story, he took them on a journey from urban to wild. "Wilderness is a place where not only are there no towns, no roads, not even any trails ... It's as if Columbus never came."

His stories and images were so vivid that when he spoke of standing on the summit of some snow-capped peak and looking out to the horizon, the young people felt as if they were right there beside him. "This is about as good as it gets in the Coast Range, you guys. You're up on top of this fantastic ice cream cone sticking up above the valleys and you can see the sun glinting on the open Pacific. It's just pure saltwater all the way to Japan. You really feel like you're on top of the world." When appropriate, he would introduce the topic of resource extraction in BC, touching on the history of logging and the resultant changes in the diverse community of plants and animals. These presentations imparted important lessons about life and created a lasting impression among many of the teenagers and educators:

> If there is something in a person's life they really would like to do, all they have to do is put their mind to doing it—no matter what.
> —Amar, Grade 11

> He was so enthusiastic with the way he talked that he made me want to be at that certain place right at that time.
> —Pei, Grade 9

John was also a unique role model for students who had found traditional schooling less than appealing. As one teacher wrote:

> I cannot give a higher endorsement than that of one of my students. High school was not an engaging event in this young man's life. However, he made the comment that the best thing that happened to him at high school was seeing John's slide presentation.
> —Evelyn Feller, Counsellor, Semiahmoo Secondary School, Surrey

As well as giving presentations at schools, John often provided workshops for teachers—he was the keynote speaker at the annual science teachers' conference many times—and presented at the University of BC as well as local colleges. These educators were as appreciative as the young people, as demonstrated by some of their comments:

> Students in our [school] system need to hear and learn about the wild places of British Columbia ... John creates a sense of wonder about our own province. Through his slides, narrative and accompanying music, John is able to capture the imagination of his audience and take them on a journey that few will ever experience first hand ... British Columbia students will indeed be fortunate to hear this mountaineer extraordinaire.
> —Steve Cardwell,
> then-president of the BC Science Teachers'
> Association, later superintendent of schools and
> CEO for Vancouver School District

[John's] presentations have been unanimously considered by both students and faculty to be one of the highlights and greatest inspirations of the course [Natural Resources Conservation]. . . His knowledge of BC's coastal environments and issues associated with them is unsurpassed. [He is] an extremely effective communicator who commands our students' full respect.

—Dr. Michael Feller, Department of Forest Sciences, UBC

Ironically, in his new career as an educator, John felt that forty years of wilderness living had left a few gaps in his own education, and he resolved to remedy that. After failed attempts at Typing Tutor and Starting Your Own Business, he decided to try something more artistic. He signed up for a course entitled: "Finding Your Voice: Getting a Grip on Existence Through the Art of Writing, Poetry and Performance." Thankfully, computer literacy was not required, and he could stick to writing by hand.

John showed up punctually at the packed, hot, stuffy room for the first session. Always the dutiful student, he read over the helpful advice supposed to get him started on the creative writing process:

Keep your hand moving.

Lose control.

Don't think.

Go for the jugular.

Be who you are.

With these instructions ringing in his head, he proceeded to the "Words of Wisdom," offered by none other than Franz Kafka:

You need not leave your room.

Remain sitting at your table and listen; simply wait. (John had a hard time sitting still at the best of times.)

You need not even wait; just learn to become quiet and still and solitary. (John was certainly used to being solitary.)

The word will freely offer itself to you to be unmasked. It has no choice; it will roll in ecstasy at your feet.

In a near panic he finally began writing:

Wow! I'm in trouble here. The scariest thing in the world is a blank sheet of paper. Don't stop—keep writing and see what happens. I'm going to keep on writing drivel until something comes and if nothing comes I'll just keep on writing drivel. I think my expectation of getting great thoughts to write down is actually limiting my ability to make that happen. If I could just calm down. Now I'm even out of drivel! What to do? I'll just keep going with NO expectations and then something will happen. (Damn there I go again with the high expectations putting pressure on myself). I wanted to come up with something profound for the shallow reason of impressing everybody. Why do I always *do* that? The earth, the children of the earth. Don't think—just write. I hope I'm not blowing this by never getting to the POINT! BE OUTSIDE. If in doubt go outside. Buildings have walls and beds—boring in there. Go outside for the air, the magic and the poetry. You don't go for a walk in the mountains—the mountains take you for a walk. We spent 2 million years out under the stars living with the weather, the seasons and the tides. GOING outside is coming home. LISTEN!

This was John's first and only completed assignment for the course. He came to the conclusion that he really did do better outdoors and his interest in taking courses faded into the background.

A key aspect of WildED was to connect kids with wild places, and whenever possible John would take them on a nature hike to a local park, forest or wetland. The Seymour Demonstration Forest was one of his favourite places. He would lope down the trail and dive off into the bush, kids following on his tail—the smallest of them hidden by the towering sword ferns. "Will we see bears?" they wanted to know. "Not a chance with all that chattering," he would tell them. They scrambled over fallen trees, ducked through the blueberry bushes, stared in disbelief at the primeval broad green leaves and pungent yellow flowers of skunk cabbages. Pointing up to the towering cedars, he would say, "This is what your front lawn would look like if you let it grow for a thousand years." Then he'd pause by a huge boulder and trace a finger along the grooves etched by a passing glacier millennia ago. When they burst out of the bush, the kids were never quite prepared for the might of the Seymour River.

WildED in action: John Clarke poses with a group of students on an outing in the Seymour Valley, 1999. PHOTO COURTESY OF WILDED ARCHIVES

No trace of city life here—no hum of traffic, no smell of exhaust; no roads, no trails.

At the end of a full day they would return to their bus, feet muddy, hair damp, cheeks pink. A teenage girl once proudly announced, "I went in a girl and came out a man." And John himself commented in an interview:

> The irony is [that] it was only after we started doing presentations in schools that I discovered the necessity of introducing kids to nature and the outdoors because of the number of things in their lives these days that plug into the wall and conspire to keep them indoors. The first few times I took students out on hikes I realized there was a high proportion of every class that had never been in the forest before. That really brought it home for me that perhaps I might be doing this for a long time.

John's influence extended to parents as well. In conjunction with the schools he'd take families on weekend camping trips to wilderness areas such as Sims Creek. There was a striking contrast between the ancient forests and pristine sandbars and the ravages of recent clear-cut logging sites. Barry Hodgins, who was the principal of Richmond District Incentive School at that time, attended several of John's camping weekends and noted their impact:

> To actually be there in a wilderness area with somebody like John was a huge, huge influence … John's way of looking at the world was something that I think was a new way of looking at anything for many of these parents.

In preparation for WildED's extended wilderness trips, John and I had made a reconnaissance of the high, glaciated ridges between Princess Louisa Inlet (located near the head of Jervis Inlet on the Sunshine Coast) and Sims Creek at the headwaters of the Squamish River. This short traverse is a microcosm of the Coast Mountains, and although it stretches only seven miles (eleven kilometres) as the eagle flies, it has all the features of a full-scale traverse. The following summer, at the invitation of Tim Turner, founder of the Sea to Sky Outdoor School, John guided six adults and six youth across this rugged terrain.

Meghan Smith, one of the six young people on the traverse, recalled that life-changing week:

> Princess Louisa has got to be one of the most amazing spots. It's right out of a fantasy movie or a Maxfield Parrish painting. You go through those rapids at Malibu, which are crazy enough, and then you go all through that narrow inlet; it's just cliffs and waterfalls. At the end there's Chatterbox Falls, and all these red jelly fish. It's magical.

The group left the tidal flats with John in the lead and over the next two days worked their way up to the high country in pouring rain. Once there, the rain turned to sleet and snow. "You couldn't see anything," John reported. "Everything was white—up, down, left, right. It was like you were suspended in a void of white." No one questioned his leadership. "He was never bossy," Meghan recalled, "or telling you what to do or making you feel lesser. He was someone you wanted to imitate and follow and do what he did and listen to what he was saying." The storm raged for two days while everyone hunkered down in their tents. Meghan joined her younger brother Colin in his sleeping bag for warmth. "John disappeared into his little slug-shaped tent and we didn't hear from him for a long time ... I just assumed, Okay, he's looking at maps or he's doing what he needs to do." Eventually John emerged from his tent with his decision made: they would keep going.

Tim Turner, reflecting on that moment of decision, said:

> John was this wonderful mix of carefree, happy-go-lucky, joie de vivre, passion-on-his-sleeve, hilariously funny, but a real undercurrent of focus and deliberateness and attention to detail. You just knew that the guy was ultra-observant, and he was paying attention to the details that perhaps some of the rest of us were oblivious to, but that were informing his decision making. I really appreciated that mix within his personality.

One unimaginable day the sky brightened and John pointed to a braided strip of blue-grey snaking its way through the valley far below. "The Elaho River and the land of Interfor," he announced. They worked their way down the snow-covered rocky ridge to Bug Lake, 4,000 feet (1,200 metres) below, to set up their final campsite before heading farther down through the ancient forests to the Sims Creek valley. On

John Clarke and members of the "Stoltmann Wilderness School" ready to head out to Jervis Inlet, 1997. PHOTO BY CONNIE SMITH

arrival at Bug Lake, warmed by their exertions and a hint of sun, the six young people flung off their clothes and plunged into the narrow crescent of ice-free water. "Oh my god! Ohhhhh!" echoed up into the mountains.

The world changed to every shade of green as they left the snowy glare of the alpine and descended into the cathedral-like forest cascading down the mountainside to Sims Creek, 3,000 feet (900 metres) below. Only a year earlier John had built this trail connecting Bug Lake to the banks of Sims Creek and many of the trees along the way were old friends. "I'll show you just about the biggest yellow cedar that I've seen in a long time," he said, raising his voice above the scream of a woodpecker. "It's probably a thousand years old." Then, as they neared their exit from the forest, John spoke about his work to conserve Sims Creek valley and described the short-term goals of the timber industry.

We're looking down into a classic coastal valley where the second growth forests never will be any match for the tight-grained beautiful wood from the old growth. We're making two by fours out of this stuff!

WildED in action: John Clarke guides students from St. George's School through the alpine area above Sims Creek, 2000. PHOTO BY NEIL PILLER

It's like making sandpaper out of diamonds. It's using beautiful antique wood with close grain for a very utilitarian purpose. The main thing about this is that it is very profitable for a few people at everyone else's expense. The wealth that's here—the best thing would be to capture this wealth incrementally over a long period of time and direct it at the communities that are close by. What's happening is, it's being captured really quickly and being directed at [Interfor's] shareholders. So those are the two things that have to change. The wealth has to be captured from the landscape slower and it has to be directed at the local communities. That's not happening.

But John was powerless to prepare them for the shock as they stepped out of the trees into the open clear-cut where 1,000-year-old trees lay felled. The complexity and beauty of the forest was unrecognizable: the towering trees, carpets of moss, bird sounds, earthy fragrance, all denoting life, had been transformed into a minefield of slick mud, bare rocks, broken limbs, amputated stumps and charred remains.

The twelve "students" who had set off from Princess Louisa Inlet were not the same people who stepped out onto the brand new logging road eight days later. Each one came away with a different experience and it affected their lives in different ways. They didn't rush out and become conservationists or mountaineers. The changes went deeper, were more widespread and influenced their day-to-day lives. "I remember coming out feeling energized and just loving to laugh and having fun," Meghan said, "but also thinking and respecting."

Her brother Colin, who is now a geologist, was equally influenced by his trip with John Clarke:

I was thirteen years old at the time and completely unaware of the profound impact this man would have on my life ... There was just as much to learn from John about the world within us as the world around us ... He defined humility, and this made him truly great ... [but he never took] himself too seriously ... [he] could crack a smile out of stone ... his legacy will live on forever.

Some weeks after the traverse was complete, Meghan gave John a gift from all who had been on the trip in appreciation of their life-changing experience. She had drawn a pencil sketch of him and entitled it "Here comes Johnny." Below she wrote, "Thank you for the best week of our lives."

This was only the first of John's many extended trips with young people. Whenever possible, he would guide them on a journey of discovery where the wilderness was their teacher. Invariably they would return with a new appreciation for nature and a deeper understanding of themselves. Meanwhile, Tim Turner of the Sea to Sky Outdoor School and John had become close friends. Tim had many opportunities to observe his friend in action through WildED and

Sketch of John Clarke "Here comes Johnny" by Meghan Smith. A gift to John after completion of the 1997 traverse from Princess Louisa Inlet to Sims Creek. In the lower left corner Meghan inscribed: "Thank you for the best week of our lives."

during John's assignments with the Sea to Sky Outdoor School, in both the indoor and outdoor wilderness classrooms:

> John was a gifted educator, [and] "languaging" was one of his greatest assets. He would articulate in ways that caused people to suddenly get it or laugh out loud or appreciate something they had not appreciated before. It was because of how he chose his words. John has made me a better educator because of what he was able to show me ... He used his sense of humour. He didn't hide his passions, he didn't hide his convictions. He just laid it all out there. He made himself very vulnerable but very real at the same time. WildED's greatest contribution to the world was letting that amazing human being get circulated—his energy and vision and power and magic.

Each year thousands of young people and hundreds of teachers participated in WildED, and it seemed that John's career as a wilderness educator and conservationist was set for life. He relished the flexibility,

John Clarke and friend and fellow conservationist Will Koop enjoy a Guiness, 1997. PHOTO BY WILL KOOP

the unaccustomed financial security and the opportunity to return to the Coast Mountains each summer. In the space of just six years he received four awards for excellence in environmental education, including the prestigious British Columbia Minister's Environmental Award in 1999. WildED attracted media attention and John was profiled on national radio and TV shows such as CBC Radio's morning show and *The World This Weekend* and CBC TV's *Gabereau Live!* Articles appeared in the *Vancouver Sun*, the *Richmond News* and the BC teachers' monthly journal, *Teacher*. The Wilderness Education Program continues today, and is one of John's more visible and influential legacies.

Even in the midst of his involvement with WildED and the Witness Project, however, John was busy squeezing in other commitments. One of the reasons that Vancouver has some of the finest drinking water today is thanks to his efforts in conjunction with the Society Promoting Environmental Conservation (SPEC), which worked to raise the public's awareness of the logging that had infiltrated the Capilano, Seymour and Coquitlam watersheds. Through John's public presentations and the efforts of other advocacy groups, logging in the watersheds was finally halted.

Will Koop, SPEC's campaign organizer at the time, commented:

> John definitely helped me to see the world in a different way through his own interpretation of the world, his ability to communicate that to others, mixed in with his unique spirit and character. That's what set him aside: his deep respect, not only for the natural world, but for the people around him.

18

The Last Traverse

John
the night we met
you were carrying
rocks brought
from Sims Creek
to Robson and Seymour
to honor Randy Stoltmann
one rock at a time
carrying the weight
setting them down
so others could
honor him
And now we
will take the weight
and multiply you
　　　　　—Sandra Semeluk, January 11, 2003

The new millennium heralded change in John's life—sweeping in like a gale, accelerating and compressing his life. The unimaginable happened. Unresisting, John fell in love with Annette Lehnacker, an attractive, vivacious young woman from Germany. They had met the previous summer at Sims Creek; Annette had become involved in the environmental movement and the Witness Project while she was studying wildlife trees as a marker of the old-growth forests in British Columbia. (In Annette's study, wildlife trees were those that indicated the presence of other creatures: grizzly bear claw marks, woodpecker holes, remains of cones and fungi under the tree, birds nests or bear dens.)

My husband Peter and I watched the love affair blossom as parents might when their kids fall in love for the first time. Early on in their relationship John introduced Annette to the North Shore mountains, and of course there was the mandatory trip to Mount Brunswick that all his potential girlfriends were required to undergo. She proved to be

Annette Lehnacker and John Clarke at the author's log house on Pender Island, 2001.
PHOTO BY LISA BAILE

a keeper. I remember John sitting at our kitchen table, shaking his head in disbelief and singing softly to himself or anyone who cared to listen, "She loves me—I can't believe she loves me"—a snatch of a song that echoed his feelings.

That fall friends gathered for the wedding that they had believed would never happen. John and Annette were married in Lighthouse Park, the ocean at their feet and the mountains above, surrounded by friends and family. Early in 2002 Nicholas was born and John's life seemed complete. He now balanced his life as a dad with his work with the Wilderness Education Program, though it was clear at times that late nights and fatherly

Newlyweds: John and Annette Clarke on their wedding day in Lighthouse Park, West Vancouver, 2001. PHOTO BY NANCY BLECK

duties were tough on John, who
did not enjoy multitasking.

Early in March John left
Annette and his six-week-old
son to do a round of all the
schools in Victoria. Then one
day I got a call from the principal of one of the schools: "Where
is John Clarke? He hasn't shown
up." I had no answer. John had

John Clarke holds newborn son Nicholas in
his arms, January 2002. PHOTO BY LISA BAILE

never been late, let alone missed a school commitment. And because John and I didn't use cellphones, I had no way of contacting
him. When I finally spoke with him and asked why he hadn't turned
up, he said simply, "I couldn't find the school." I puzzled over this. It
didn't make sense that explorer John Clarke had lost his way. It just
wasn't possible.

But it was. Just days later I got another call. John was in hospital
and had been diagnosed with a malignant brain tumour.

Awaiting the verdict, John and I sat rigid in a cramped alcove
in Vancouver General Hospital. The surgeon, Dr. Honey, was blunt
(there must have been some mistake in his name): "If we do nothing,
you have about three months. Surgery will give you more time." John
opted for surgery. Outwardly he was calm, but I could only imagine
how he felt.

When I visited him on the ward a few days after his surgery, he
was propped up on pillows, his head swathed in bandages. A nurse
came in to check on him. "Thank you, Ellen," he said as she walked
out. I was flabbergasted—he hadn't missed a beat. He always had a
way of remembering everyone's name. But I never saw that face-splitting smile of his again.

John returned home to the apartment he and Annette had rented
on the first floor of an old mansion on the corner or Seventh Avenue
and Balsam Street, to begin his last precious days with his wife and
little Nicholas, the family he had never quite believed he would have.
Whenever possible they'd go to the beach or walk the trails, and on
a couple of occasions they camped out on the Sims Creek sandbar,
hanging out with friends and chatting around the campfire. John

would walk along the familiar sandbar with Nicholas in his arms, his tiny fingers grasping his dad's big hand.

On another excursion their family visited us at our log house on Pender Island, where they soon settled into rural island life. John wrote in our journal:

QUIET HERE THIS MORNING. Just the sounds of Annette making fruit salad and Nicholas on the floor. Now Nicholas is swinging silently in the hammock. Sometimes his look is "unsure" when he's swinging. He'll get used to it. He's just stuffed down a whole mushy ripe peach. It's all over his face and he's heading for the bathroom to get wiped down. He's back with his new shiny face to show off to the world. Makes no difference to him, though. Sometimes blackberries cover his face from his eyes to his chin—a real comedian.

And then: "We're just heading up to Iona Farm to get some goat cheese and vegetables." And some days later: "A quiet Pender morning; leaves are falling—slowly at first ... Nicholas had a splashy bath on the deck. He wailed at first as we had the water a bit too hot. Then everything calmed down."

In the late summer John received the Order of Canada for his

John Clarke introduces baby Nicholas Clarke to Sims Creek, July 2002. PHOTO BY ANNETTE CLARKE

John Clarke receives the Order of Canada from Governor General Adrienne Clarkeson, Vancouver 2002. PHOTO COURTESY OF ANNETTE CLARKE

lifetime of exploratory mountaineering in the Coast Mountains and his recent achievements as wilderness educator and conservationist. Ironically, he was just in the process of becoming a Canadian citizen, and he was granted his citizenship *after* he'd been awarded the Order of Canada. John chuckled as he recalled the judge asking him the required skill-testing questions about his adopted country. "What is the name of BC's highest mountain?" asked the kindly judge.

As the days shortened and John's health deteriorated, Peter and I decided it was time to reunite John with the Coast Mountains. We chose Racoon Pass—one of the spots he treasured most. He was delighted. "It should be perfect in September. The bugs will behave themselves [with the colder nights]." And then, always the optimist, he added:

We may try to climb Blackfin Peak [8,200 feet/2,500 metres] or Breaker and Comber peaks at the head of the Wave Glacier with their views into Lunar Creek Valley. Once you climb up out of the greenery of Racoon Pass you are in an arctic wilderness. Ice everywhere, pouring down off the high peaks. The land of white. Then back down for supper in the

John Clarke (left) and Lisa Baile enjoy views of the Wave Glacier from Racoon Pass, 2002.
PHOTO BY PETER PARÉ

relative green of Racoon Pass with its lakes and gardens and creeks and stunted trees.

"Wow," he breathed when a few days later the helicopter set us down in Racoon Pass. For John it was a homecoming. His first visit to this magical spot had been in the late summer of 1977, and afterwards he had written:

> I knew there were some lakes there (Racoon Lakes), but I wasn't ready for the incredible beauty of the place. The broad pass is composed of very erosion-resistant rock, which was heavily scrubbed by ice age glaciers, leaving waves of polished whale-back ridges interspersed with royal blue lakes, heather and clumps of stunted trees.

Content, John slowly hauled out his well-worn gear, set up his tent and soaked in the familiar views. The next morning we set out at a leisurely pace down the valley to the head of the Toba River. From our lunch spot among the fading summer flowers we peered into the impossibly steep valley and the infinite blue of Toba Inlet. In the afternoon we meandered back past the many lakes and swirling creeks. Although tired, John appreciated every moment. Next day thunderclouds gathered as the helicopter whisked us back to another world.

He often talked wistfully of getting back into the schools. We had put so much effort into making WildED a success that neither of us wanted to give it up, but we needed new educators and more help than the Federation of Mountain Clubs could provide. I searched for a new home and found one with Ric Careless, founder and director of BC Spaces for Nature. He agreed to take on WildED as one of the BC Spaces programs and help assemble a new team of educators.

Then, despite his deteriorating health, John became determined to give a presentation at Kitsilano Secondary School, and with timely help from WildED's new team, his wish was realized. When some two hundred students poured into the auditorium, his face lit up. Of his many jobs, wilderness educator was his absolute favourite. "I'm in this for life," he had often said.

Two weeks later John was admitted to the palliative care unit (PCU) at Vancouver General Hospital. Throughout the previous year friends had been supporting John, Annette and Nicholas in every way they knew how, and now they gathered to give John their undivided attention. For the next seven weeks his family and friends stayed by his side day and night. Friends would enter their names in a roster to keep track of who would be at his bedside and when. They said that it was a privilege to be with him. During the time he was hospitalized, at least 90 percent of the visitors to the PCU were there to see John—high school friends, climbing friends, friends from his communal days, First Nations friends, conservationists, teachers, students and even people who'd only met him recently. He had touched them all.

"So many people loved John," said his mother, Brigid. "That kind of love has nothing to do with marriage or sex or male or female—it's just a universal love that needs no further explanation. People just loved him unconditionally." And Theresa Lammers, who had remained close friends with John after they'd split up in the early 1970s, recalled the time, years earlier, when she had told him, "You know, John, when you're dead and long gone, people aren't going to remember you for what mountain you climbed. They're going to remember you for your love, that you were a wonderful lover." And for once he had been speechless.

After he was admitted to the PCU, Theresa would drop by to visit whenever she made the journey to Vancouver from her home in Kamloops. She recorded one of their conversations:

"I'd give you the moon if I could."

"I'll take it all," says John ... "It's like a kid—when you give them everything, pretty soon you end up with the moon in your backyard ... and maybe the Burrard Street Bridge."

At that moment the nurse pops her head around the door.

"I'll be back with your meds."

"I'll be right here," says John. "I'm not going anywhere."

When Theresa visited John around Christmastime, she was accompanied by Harry Lidster, who wanted to marry her, but she couldn't decide because he was twenty-five years her senior. She slipped out of the room, leaving the men to talk. "When I came back in,"

Theresa told me some years later, "Harry left and John whispered, 'Theresa, he's a really good man—I really like him.' So that really helped me to make that decision." Theresa and Harry married in the spring of 2003, shortly after John's death. "Harry's just the most wonderful person," she told me. "He and John would have been the best of buddies."

Children are accepting, but for independent adults, accepting the loss of independence is often difficult to achieve. John, always the big kid, had no such problems and accepted care and help and love with ease and grace, good humour and appreciation. He relished the food that friends and family brought in—Carol's "good old porridge," a fresh papaya or a slab of Sylvia's homemade Christmas cake. He never lost his sense of humour, perhaps because it was hard-wired into him. His one-liners were irrepressible. His favourite breakfast was a fresh brown egg laid by one of his dad's Rhode Island Red hens, and he would light up when he saw a dozen of these eggs arrive. One morning his sister Cathaleen, feeding him breakfast, spilled some yolk down his chin and it dribbled onto his hospital gown. Later that day his elbow strayed over the gate on the side of the bed, and when Cathaleen lowered the gate, his arm got stuck in it. And when a third "bad thing" happened that day, Cathaleen said, "Oh John! I'm *sorry*. When am I going to stop hurting you?" And he replied, "Well, now would be a good time." Cathaleen, recalling that day, said, "And here he is in palliative care!"

Even in the midst of his pain and suffering he was acutely aware of the people around him. I remember the day Will Koop dropped by with a CD of birdsongs he'd made for John—"Voices from the Wilderness" he called it. Will hadn't seen John for several months, and when he entered the room he stopped short, seeing him so changed and helpless. John glanced up. "Cat got your tongue?" he asked. Will's jaw dropped further.

I had soon discovered the waiting lounge of the PCU was *the* place to meet John's friends, and over those weeks I caught a glimpse of the extent and depth of their friendships. But I quickly realized that not all of these friends would actually get to see him, so I provided a folder and labelled it "Messages for John." Here friends and family poured out their hearts and shared memories, jokes, climbs and adventures. Often they were embellished with drawings and memorable photographs:

John, we are all like waves in the ocean of shared experience. Each wave affects the whole ocean and thereby all other waves. John, your "wave" is one that has guided so many through the momentum and energy that you express in the way you live. You are an explorer and true leader. Reading your articles and then doing trips with you has defined my life more than you probably know. Thank you.

—Dave Sarkany

Every memory is important and fun and special—but do you remember … Making me instant coffee and KLIM with your cook stove the first day I met you at 4th and E.13th? Gawd! Remember 4th and E.13th? Making granola in the baby bath? How exasperated you were with me the first time I looked at your mountain pictures when I said they looked like postcards and the water was too blue? How many of our meals were macaroni and tomato sauce—did anybody keep track? Ick! Keep on trucking, Mona. Love you lots,

—Carole [Kerekes]

One of my clearest memories of you is one day in the early '70s, I met you on the street somewhere around Burrard St. You were striding off on long treks in the city with the mission of taking photos of all these buildings which are being torn down. I walked with you for a while as we talked about the disappearing architecture of Vancouver. Whatever happened to those photos and that project?

—Paul Starr

John: Long before I met you, I would spend hours poring over old *Canadian Alpine Journals* reading your stories. I would always wonder, "Who the hell is this guy and how can I meet him?" I figured anyone who could spend weeks at a time alone in the Coast Mountains had to be very introverted and somewhat anti-social and a bit nuts. I was correct about the last part. Phoning you up to invite myself on an expedition with you was like phoning Wayne Gretzky to ask him to join your hockey team. When I recounted details of your Coast Mountain trips from you *CAJ* accounts, you were amazed: "You mean somebody actually reads this stuff?!" Recognizing that I shared your obsessions with the Coast Mountains, you consented to having me as a partner on your 1987 trip up Elliott Creek ... I look back on our Coast Range trips as some of the most magnificent and happy times of my life. I could never have gone there without you. Thank you for everything. With much love,

—Jeff [Eppler]

John, you probably don't realize what an impact you have on young people. Even those students that only have the fortune to spend a few days with you always talk about their experiences. You are quite a legend around St. George's! I think what strikes them the most is how modest you are about your incredible experiences ... It is your ability to touch the hearts and minds of young people that will always be remembered ... I know none of them will ever forget the time they spent with you in the wilds of the Coast Mountains. We love you, John, and your spirit of the mountains and all places wild will live on in the hearts of all of us.

—Neil Piller

John, I feel extremely lucky to have spent as much time as I have with you. All those years together of building the "group with no name," then Witness, was an honour for me to be part of. I especially enjoyed all those long conversations we had in the car in those early years driving back from the Elaho, Upper Lillooet and Sims Creek, inspired by our time in the rainforests, and how that fuelled our passion and determination to make things better. Thank you for teaching me about the land. That experience itself has helped to make me a healthier and stronger person. Thank you for your magic, laughter, insight and friendship. Love,

—Nancy Slanay Sp'ak'wus [Bleck]

Dear John, dear 'Wind': You did come back, again and again and again, and each time, oh, did you ever speak from the heart ... You, Mr. Wind, remain a beacon for me. Your humour, your child-like wonder, your eye for beauty, your advocacy for the Wild, your contagious spirit, your pika imitations. I always feel so alive, so connected in your company, which is what I will miss most of all. I love you, and you know that. Unbridled joy is a rare thing and you delivered it effortlessly. Your energy, example and legacy will be huge if each of us whom you touched find their way of speaking out on behalf of a wild British Columbia. As your living is an inspiration for all of us, so too is your dying. Thank you, John, for your joie de vivre that cuts through the glaze of a hospital room in the heart of Vancouver so that grace, dignity and meaning might find its way into all the lives that come to your bedside to celebrate their friend. I will so miss you.

—Tim [Turner]

John Baldwin, determined to be one of John's caregivers despite his deep-seated phobia of hospitals, signed up to do a night shift at his bedside. For Baldwin, the word "friend" was an inadequate way to describe their bond. "What is it called when you climb mountain after mountain together, walk until you both can't walk any more, spend hundreds of nights together in a small tent, share the rain and the snowstorms, see the sunrise and the sunset, and bask in the silence and magic of an entire range of mountains together?" But Baldwin's time with John was cut short when he collapsed, overwhelmed by the sight of his friend in his failing body. Baldwin then relayed a last letter to him. It read in part:

Dear John: Sorry to "drop out" on you like that! It caught me totally by surprise when I fainted and was whisked off to emergency. (I guess I'm not cut out for hospitals even though I was born in one and will probably die in one.) The truth is I think it broke my heart to see you so weak. I don't imagine it's very easy for you either. Life sure has some curveballs! Thank you for all our trips together! I'd do it all over again in a flash!! If we both come back as goats some day, I'll meet you at the big split rock in Whitemantle Creek, and maybe we can go do some cairn maintenance! Love

—John

John invited everyone to be part of his journey—it wasn't an explicit invitation but a complete acceptance of whatever physical or spiritual offering people had to give or share. He enjoyed the massages that Motte Tilden gave him almost as much as Motte enjoyed giving them. Motte told him: "You're one of the best massage receivers I've met, which I know comes from being such a good giver ... I always leave feeling a great sense of peace and presence."

And Cathaleen described a day of giving and receiving when:

> Sylvi and her Mom brought in some Christmas cake ... Later Chief Bill Williams of the Squamish First Nation came in. John was sleeping and Chief Bill said some prayers. Annette's birthday is today ... Gene [Eugene Harry], the Native spiritual healer who married John and Annette, was here with his wife. He did a beautiful ceremony and painted John's face with colours made from the earth. Nicholas was there, of course, and received a very special prayer and blessing. Also Annette was there and Klaus [Lehnacker, Annette's father from Neus, Germany] and me and Nancy ... there were twelve of us for this beautiful ceremony, which is normally reserved for tribal elders who have gained a place of particular honour. John said Annette tells him all the time that she loves him and he said he tells Annette he loves her. This he has told me three or four times this past week. This makes John very happy.

John gave Annette a special gift for her birthday, an exquisite silver medallion crafted by their friend Aaron Nelson Moody. On one side was *Xwexwselken*, the mountain goat; on the other the iconic Mount Tinniswood.

John yearned for the mountains, the outdoors, the fresh air, but his room was often hot and stuffy and his view was reduced to a glimpse of the North Shore mountains. When Cathaleen offered to open the window to get some fresh air, he quipped, "Yeah—fine place to get fresh air—Broadway and Heather!" To try to compensate for the absence of anything natural in his room, friends and family festooned the walls with photographs of his favourite peaks, camping weekends at Sims Creek, Racoon Pass and ancient forests.

When John was still able to sit in a wheelchair, we would take him down to Jericho Park and stroll along the beach, where he could feel the wind on his cheeks and see the North Shore mountains. But now it was different. He wanted to return to the mountains, and visit snow-clad Mount Seymour almost 5,000 feet (1,500 metres) above where he lay inert in his hospital bed. Two days after Christmas, Bryan Evans and I prised John from his bed. Bryan recalled:

> It was a big deal because John had to be lifted out of his bed and wrapped in a sleeping bag. I used my big down Gortex bag and wrapped him up in it [then we] lifted him up with a crane. We had to get a special taxi. I rented a taxi for the whole day ... But in the end it was a horrible day. It was raining—a horrendous day. I said to John, "You can't see in front of your nose outside. Do you still want to do this?" And he said, "Oh yes." We went and visited Annette and baby Nicholas. We were out on the sidewalk, walking down the sidewalk in the rain with John on the stretcher, and me trying to hold the umbrella over him. We couldn't get the umbrella up and the rain was hitting him on the face, and I said, "I'm really sorry, John," and I just remember him saying, "I wouldn't want anything more than this rain falling on my face."

Witness volunteer Gregory Byrne drove John to Mount Seymour. "I wanted him to feel the cold, pure wind, the voices of the spirits and see the mountains he worked so hard to protect," Gregory said. "To let the whisper of all the things that he had worked for in the natural realm fill his pores, and for him to know and sense the surrounding that he was truly at home in." High above the city, with the covers pulled back, John lay exposed to the elements—the sleet, the snow and the wind. A final blessing.

Thinking back on his friendship with John, Bryan Evans said:

> It's not even really John's accomplishments that I admired. It doesn't really matter to me—probably any more than it mattered to John— whether he climbed 400 peaks or 600 peaks. It was more his way of being in the world. How to be totally alive and enjoy life and doing it in a way that is respectful of the environment ... You always felt that, when you were with John, you were on the cusp of doing something exciting because he was *always* doing something exciting. And if you could free up the time in your life, you could go and do something exciting with him too. It always amazed me that he could travel around in a society and a place where everybody was so much wealthier than he was

materially, and yet he seemed to have the best life ... You'd look at John and think, that guy is doing precisely what he wants to do and having a heck of a time doing it.

John gave us a last gift: he showed us how to die. It's not often, if ever, that you receive a lesson on how to die. Very few people experience a trial run, and John gave us that. If he was afraid, he didn't show his fear. If he was in pain, he didn't complain. If he felt resentment because life wasn't fair, he never said so. It was as if he had the ability to ignore certain things in order to let us be closer to him, to not scare us away. He allowed us to be part of his journey. Like the young people on the Stoltmann Traverse, he didn't want us to be "freaking out and ruin our time." He faced death as he faced unexpected obstacles in the mountains, as part of the journey, and he resolved the dilemma with humour and equanimity and, above all, acceptance of what was.

John Clarke died on January 23, 2003. He would have been fifty-eight years old on February 25.

> *May your journeys over mountain ridges,*
> *down bending rivers and out to sea,*
> *be safe with spirit and light.*
> *Feel it all, listen to their wild voices.*
> *Taste the skim of sweat falling off your brow.*
> *Hear rustling leaves in an unfelt breeze,*
> *in your soft passing.*
>
> —Greg Maurer, 2003

Epilogue

The celebration for the naming of a mountain in John's honour took place on the banks of Sims Creek on Squamish Nation land on August 28, 2010. Chief Bill Williams hosted the event and Aaron Nelson Moody conducted the sacred ceremony. Many of John's family and friends stepped forward as witnesses to honour him and share what they felt in their hearts. After the ceremony a number of John's extended family members left the circle and prepared for the first official ascent of Mount John Clarke.

As befits a pilgrimage, our climb up the near-vertical trail through the old-growth forests was measured, slowed by the weight of our packs and the late-afternoon heat. Some pilgrims surged ahead, others lagged behind, but the persistent attention of insects discouraged any thoughts of stopping for a rest. In any case, there was no time to dawdle as we had 5,000 feet (1,500 metres) to climb to the ridge where we would camp. By sundown, as temperatures plunged and the last rays of sunshine gleamed pink on the snow-covered slopes, three camps occupied the ridge.

Next day the pilgrims converged to ascend the glaciated ridge leading to the rocky summit of Mount John Clarke. Amid brief bursts of sunshine and thickening clouds we climbed single file to reach John's peak, and as we gathered rocks to complete his cairn, we thought about what he had brought to each of our lives. Within the heart of the cairn we placed a canister to hold messages to John from his family and friends, a reflection of our love and him being an undiminished source of inspiration.

Mount John Clarke is a modest peak, but it commands

breathtaking views of the surrounding landscape. The land falls away in every direction to provide unobstructed views of the peaks and valleys that were his constant companions on his alpine journeys. Across the valley at the headwaters of Sims Creek is Mount Tinniswood, where Randy Stoltmann left his message to the world.

The mountain named in John Clarke's honour lies at the apex of his classroom. It was on the sandbars of Sims Creek and the forests and ridges above that creek that he initiated the Witness Project. It was there, through the Wilderness Education Program, that he introduced many eager youngsters to their first and unforgettable taste of wilderness. It was there that he shared with Chief Bill Williams the beauty and grandeur of the Squamish Nation territory on their high traverse from Princess Louisa Inlet to Sims Creek. And it is on the shores of Sims Creek and in the ancient forests he helped to preserve that his ashes lie.

John's spirit lives on and is embodied in Mount John Clarke. His light has brightened our lives and shown us the way. Let us shine his light upon the world.

Lisa Baile and Brigit McLarty (a former WildED educator) celebrate the first official climb of Mount John Clarke, August 29, 2010. PHOTO BY PETER PARÉ

JOHN CLARKE'S PUBLICATIONS

1. John Clarke's publications in *Canadian Alpine Journal*

The *Canadian Alpine Journal* is published annually by the Alpine Club of Canada.

Vol. 51, 1968, p. 171, "Manatee Ski Expedition"

Vol. 53, 1970, p. 63, "First Ascent of Lillooet Mountain"

Vol. 54, 1971, p. 66, "First Ascent of Mount Crerar"

Vol. 55, 1972, pp. 36–37, "Whitemantle Ski Expedition"

Vol. 55, 1972, pp. 70–72, "First Ascents in Garibaldi Park"

Vol. 56, 1973, pp. 38–39, "Niut Range"

Vol. 56, 1973, pp. 59–62, "Climbing Reports: Coast Range"

Vol. 57, 1974, pp. 4–8, "Klinaklini Clouds"

Vol. 57, 1974, pp. 63–64, "Klattasine"

Vol. 58, 1975, pp. 2–4, "Coast Mountains 1974"

Vol. 59, 1976, pp. 3–5, "Pointer Peak 1975"

Vol. 60, 1977, pp. 4–10, "Coast Mountains 1976"

Vol. 66, 1983, pp. 21–23, "North of Jervis Inlet"

Vol. 66, 1983, pp. 29–33, "Satsalla Glacier"

Vol. 66, 1983, pp. 43–47, "Montrose Glacier"

Vol. 66, 1983, p. 48, "Toba Glacier Area"

Vol. 67, 1984, pp. 12–17, "Mount Willoughby"

Vol. 67, 1984, pp. 24–26, "The Coast Mountains"

Vol. 68, 1985, pp. 4–7, "Machmell Ski Horseshoe"

Vol. 68, 1985, pp. 28–31, "Toba Wanderings"

Vol. 69, 1986, pp. 7–10, "Beyond Kingcome Inlet"

Vol. 69, 1986, pp. 31–32, "Portal Peak Revisited"

Vol. 69, 1986, pp. 56–58, "Autumn in the Coast Range"

Vol. 70, 1987, pp. 35–42, "Exploring the Coast Mountains:
Mountains near the Tahumming River, Klinaklini Country,
Klattasine Area, Knight-Bute Country"

Vol. 73, 1990, pp. 49–50, "Bentinck Arm to Rivers Inlet"

Vol. 73, 1990, p. 58, "Two Trips in the Coast Mountains"

Vol. 74, 1991, pp. 75–79, "On the Coast Again"

Vol. 75, 1992, pp. 46–48, "Coast Range 1991"

Vol. 76, 1993, p. 75, "A Coastal Pair"

Vol. 77, 1994, p. 78, "Coast Range 1993"

Vol. 78, 1995, pp. 36–37, "Treasured Days With Randy Stoltmann"

Vol. 78, 1995, p. 72, "Jump Across Creek"

Vol. 78, 1995, p. 73, "The Ski Traverse"

Vol. 82, 1999, pp. 97–99, "Gitnadoix – Gilttoyees"

Vol. 83, 2000, pp. 109–12, "Around the Wahu in 47 Days"

2. John Clarke's publications in the BC Mountaineering Club's biannual journal, *The BC Mountaineer*, and in the monthly newsletter of the BCMC (called *The Mountaineer*)

Vol. 45 (11), 1967, p. 2, "Manatee Ski Expedition: Manatee Peak"

Vol. 45 (12), 1967, p. 2, "Manatee Ski Expedition: Wahoo Tower and
Mermaid Peak"

Vol. 49 (12), 1971, p. 3, "Whitemantle Ski Expedition: Comrade
Peaks"

Vol. 50 (1), 1972, p. 2, "Whitemantle Ski Expedition: Unnamed Peak
(9700 ft)"

Vol. 62, 1994, pp. 85–91, "Coast Range 1993: the Oat Route"

Vol. 65, 2000, pp. 54–60, "Mt Pitt, South Ridge, Sept 1999"

SELECTED SOURCES

Alpine Club of Canada. *Canadian Alpine Journal.* Canmore, AB, 1968–2000.

BC Mountaineering Club. *The BC Mountaineer.* Biannual journal. Vancouver, 1967–2000.

Bivouac Mountaineering Directory. Located at www.bivouac.com.

Dale, Mark. "Brush and Bush Rating System." Located on the Alpenglow Gallery website at: www.alpenglow.org/themes/subalpine/brush-ratings.html. Accessed August 7, 2012.

Dowling, Phil. *The Mountaineers: Famous Climbers in Canada.* Edmonton: Hurtig Publishers, 1979.

Gabriel, Alex. "The Zen of Exploration," an interview with John Clarke. *Climbing* 117 (December 1989–January 1990): 50–55.

Johnston, Elaine. Excerpt from her script about John Clarke, 2008.

Mason, Roy. *Ice Runway.* Vancouver: Douglas & McIntyre, 1984.

Maurer, Greg, taped interview with John Clarke, 1998. Transcribed by Lisa Baile. Not published.

The Mountaineers. *Mountaineering: Freedom of the Hills.* 8th edition, edited by Ronald C. Eng. Seattle: Mountaineers Books, 2010.

Muckle, Robert J. *The First Nations of British Columbia.* Vancouver: UBC Press, 2006.

Noble, Bill. *Child of the Wind.* Video documentary and outtakes, 1995.

Rossiter, Sean. *The Immortal Beaver: The World's Greatest Bush Plane.* Vancouver: Douglas & McIntyre, 1996.

Sarkany, Dave. "Recreating in the Hills." Unpublished manuscript on the history of the Coast Mountains. 1995.

Shipton, Eric. *Blank on the Map*. In *The Six Mountain-Travel Books*, Seattle: Mountaineers Books, 1985.

Scott, Chic. Notes from an interview with John Clarke. Vancouver, January 1997.

Scott, Chic. *Pushing the Limits: The Story of Canadian Mountaineering*. Calgary: Rocky Mountain Books, 2000.

Selters, Andy. *Ways to the Sky: a historical guide to North American Mountaineering*. Golden, CO: American Alpine Club Press, 2004.

Serl, Don. *The Waddington Guide: Alpine Climbs in One of the World's Great Ranges*. Squamish, BC: Canada Elaho Publishing Corporation, 2003.

Stoltmann, Randy. *Hiking Guide to the Big Trees of Southwestern British Columbia*. Vancouver: Western Canada Wilderness Committee, 1987.

Stoltmann, Randy. *Hiking the Ancient Forests of British Columbia and Washington*. Vancouver: Lone Pine Publishing, 1996.

Stoltmann, Randy. *Written by the Wind*. Victoria: Orca Books Publishers, 1993.

Tsui, Hali. *Stoltmann Wilderness School*. Video documentary, 1997.

Various contributors. *Messages for John*. A compilation of messages written for John Clarke in the last seven weeks of his life, December 2002–January 2003.

Vaughn, Floyd. Excerpts from a typescript/memoir written for his grandchildren, 2006.

Williams, Chief Bill. Letter to Witness Project participants, 2001.

Williams, Jeremy. *Celebration of the Naming of Mount John Clarke*. Video documentary, 2010.

Woodsworth, Glenn. Biographical sketch of Neal Carter when he was made honorary member of the Alpine Club of Canada, 1974.

ACKNOWLEDGEMENTS

My thanks go to Annette Clarke, to whom I am indebted for her permission to use material from John's writings, images and topographical maps.

I thank John's parents, Brigid and Kevin Clarke, for their support, and especially for sharing their memories. To Cathaleen Clarke, John's sister, thank you for your friendship, laughter and tears as you shared stories, letters and your tatty photo albums, and for introducing me to many of John's friends. My thanks to Kevin Clarke Jr. for his memories of his much missed brother, and to Margaret O' Reilly who regaled me with tales of the Clarke family and their life in Ireland.

Without the help, enthusiasm and encouragement of all John's many friends and colleagues from every aspect of his life this biography would not have been possible. I appreciate every moment you spent sharing your memories with me. My heartfelt thanks goes to: Paul Adams, John Baldwin, Barbara Bernhardt, Nancy Bleck, David Boyd, Sandy Briggs, Gregory Byrne, Janey Chang-Mar, Peter Croft, Lona Croisant, Fin Donnelly, Bryan Evans, Joe Foy, Dwayne Himmelsbach, Barry Hodgins, Elaine Johnston, Esther and Martin Kafer, Carole and Garry Kerekes, Tami Knight, Will Koop, Fran Lacey, David Lammers, Drew Leathem, Cheryl Leskiw, Diane Lavoie, Theresa Lidster, Ian McAllister, Roy Mason, John and Tsippy McAuliffe, Shel Neufeld, Bill Noble, Tom Perry, Father Placidus, Dick Rogers, Mark Ruelle, Dave Sarkany, Chic Scott, Don Serl, Steve Sheffield, Meghan, Colin and Connie Smith, Jamie and Gwyn Sproule, Will, Cyrus and Catherine Stafford, Claora Styron, Tim Turner, Phil

Van Gils, Floyd Vaughn, Chief Bill Williams, Jeremy Williams, Flora Wood and Glenn Woodsworth.

I am grateful to all who have contributed photographs, slides and images: Annette Clarke, Cathaleen Clarke, Brigid and Kevin Clarke, John Baldwin, Nancy Bleck, Sandy Briggs, Rick Brine, Beth Carruthers, Janey Chang-Mar, Bryan Evans, Dwayne Himmelsbach, Elaine Johnston, Carole and Garry Kerekes, Will Koop, Theresa Lidster, Greg Maurer, Ian McAllister, John McAuliffe, Peter Paré, Neil Piller, Dick Rogers, Mark Ruelle, Nick Schwabe, Steve Sheffield, Megan and Connie Smith, Gwen Sproule, Catherine Stafford, Jeremy Williams, Flora Wood and Glenn Woodsworth

Thanks go to Alison Azer and Norma Charles who provided the impetus to get me started on the task of writing. I am grateful to Greg Maurer for permission to use excerpts from his recorded interview with John Clarke, and to Chic Scott for permission to use material from notes of his interview with John Clarke. I am indebted to videographer Bill Noble for generously allowing me to use excerpts from his award-winning documentary, *Child of the Wind*. I thank and acknowledge the Alpine Club of Canada for their permission to use excerpts from John Clarke's publications in the *Canadian Alpine Journal* and from the video documentary *Child of the Wind*. Thanks goes to the BC Mountaineering Club for permission to use excerpts from John Clarke's articles published in *The BC Mountaineer*.

I am grateful to John Atkin and Michael Kluckner for sharing their knowledge of John Clarke's interest in and his contribution to the history of Vancouver's heritage buildings. I am indebted to Chief Bill Williams and the Squamish Nation for hosting the naming ceremony for Mount John Clarke, and to Aaron Nelson Moody for conducting the ceremony.

I thank Chic Scott, Anthony Paré and Glenn Woodsworth for their critical perusal of my first, fat draft of the book. Thanks to John Baldwin and Glenn Woodsworth for answering all queries to do with the Coast Mountains, and more thanks to John Baldwin for helping me track down and compile John Clarke's first recorded ascents in the Coast Mountains. Special thanks goes to Peter T. Paré—my computer guru. Without his expertise, help and unlimited patience life would have been hell! Huge thanks goes to Tim Wilson for his invaluable expertise and crucial help in producing many of the maps, and for creating the map of John Clarke's first ascents.

I thank Betty Keller for her skilful and careful editing, Pam Robertson for her keen eye and insightful copy editing and the publisher and team at Harbour Publishing—it has been fun and a wonderful learning experience to work with all of you. If I have overlooked anybody I hope you will forgive me.

Thanks is not enough for the encouragement, love and support that I received every step of the way from my partner-in-life, Peter D. Paré. He has a marvellous ability to see the big picture and, as my first-in-line editor, would extricate me as I disappeared under the mound of details. If it weren't for Peter, I might still be tracing the footsteps of John Clarke through the wilds of British Columbia.

INDEX

Photographs indicated in **bold**